Human Rights in Translation

Human Rights in Translation

Intercultural Pathways

Edited by
Michal Jan Rozbicki

LEXINGTON BOOKS
Lanham • Boulder • New York • London

Published by Lexington Books
An imprint of The Rowman & Littlefield Publishing Group, Inc.
4501 Forbes Boulevard, Suite 200, Lanham, Maryland 20706
www.rowman.com

6 Tinworth Street, London SE11 5AL, United Kingdom

British Library Cataloguing in Publication Information Available

Library of Congress Cataloging-in-Publication Data Available

ISBN 978-1-4985-8141-7 (cloth : alk. paper)
ISBN 978-1-4985-8142-4 (electronic)

♾™ The paper used in this publication meets the minimum requirements of American National Standard for Information Sciences—Permanence of Paper for Printed Library Materials, ANSI/NISO Z39.48-1992.

Printed in the United States of America

Contents

Preface

The goal of this volume is to explore, from a variety of angles, a specific question: what happens when the concept of universal human rights crosses the cultural borders between different communities of knowledge. The advantage of looking at human rights in terms of their transcultural implementation is that it expands our gaze beyond nation states, and allows us to consider instead how these rights interact with diverse cultural, political, and legal institutions. This larger query raises several further issues. What is the historical and cultural ontology of such rights, and how does it affect the endeavors to implement them in diverse contexts? What should promoters keep in mind when attempting to further this goal? How should they "translate" the general principles of human rights from the abstract universality of the 1948 United Nations Universal Declaration of Human Rights, or the 1789 French *Declaration of the Rights of Man and Citizen*, into indigenous worlds of meaning? Are they translatable at all?

Ever since Immanuel Kant popularized the notion of an essential, common nature of humanity shared across the globe, this premise has been a central ingredient of most definitions of human rights. Yet, it is rooted in an eighteenth-century Enlightenment concept that universalizes a set of specifically Western ideals of the time by extending them to all societies of the globe, and proclaiming them to be a fundamentally normative model. When confronted with the practical reality of diverse cultures of the world, these noble abstractions are frequently found to be incommensurable with the particular, historically shaped norms and values guiding each of the communities involved. This crucial, but relatively recent, realization largely undermines the belief in a homogeneous, unified theory of universal human rights that can be realistically applied globally in political and legal practices, and instead suggests that the path and prerequisite to a successful, worldwide implementation of such rights is a deep understanding of the process of intercultural dialogue, and specifically the cultural "grammar" involved in relationships of otherness.

The inherent contradiction residing in the concept of a unified and global set of human rights—between their international universality and the atomized localisms of the world's innumerable cultures—is a perennial source of tensions. It is not a problem that will go away. Difference is not just an impediment to the spread of human rights; being different is a fundamental attribute of being human. Particular identity of a group that had evolved through collective historical experiences of its members is not just a perception of who one is, but—more crucially—also a distinct epistemic tool that enables humans to recognize and interpret reality. Often overlooked by intellectuals, the very universalism they promote can, in certain circumstances, pose a threat to universal human rights. Claims to full equality and universality can and historically have provoked a backlash in the form of identity ideologies, sometimes violent, that reassert ethnic, racial, or cultural difference, whether it is India's caste system, nationalism in 1930s Germany, or recent anti-immigration movements within the European Union. At the same time, legal and institutional players find it imperative to maintain that human rights are universal, if only to create a fixed and stable starting point for global dialogue, and counter the often chaotic diversity of cultures.[1]

There is no easy solution to this dilemma. The emerging consensus among scholars seems to be that the best way forward is to practice "cultural translation," where each concrete application is tailored to a specific knowledge environment. It is a convenient metaphor that anthropologists have used since the 1950s, but we should be aware that translating culture is a great deal more complex than translating a book, an act that itself presents major challenges.[2] It requires cultural brokers rather than translators. It requires accepting flexible solutions, even in legal approaches (some have called for "legal pluralism").[3] Others have proposed "ecumenism" in human rights studies, envisaged as a spectrum where UDHR-like universals are at one end, and local meanings on the other. The argument is that that such an approach is necessitated by the fact that human rights "have become de-centered" and we are now forced to sail in a pluralistic sea of differing normativities.[4] It would seem, however, that it was not human rights as such that underwent such change, but the Western, universal concept of these rights that became decentered by the realization that its presumably global "centrality" was illusory, while the worlds countless cultures have always been solidly diverse. Either way, this is an overall positive development that reverses the earlier tendency of scholars to dismiss "culture" as an outdated concept, clearly a view from the ivory tower. Both sides will probably never sing from the same hymnal, but the dialogue has become more intimate and productive.

There is another issue that impedes such a dialogue. It is the top-down view of cultural translation, often surfacing among authors writing from a legal perspective, as a belief that the universal rights template needs to be "remade into vernacular." Sally Engle Merry, one of the top specialists in the area of law and human rights, rightly notes that mere repackaging of rights in more understandable language will not do. What is needed is accessing and engaging the cultures of local communities. A real dialogue requires that *both* the outside activists and the locals to give up some of their taken-for-granted norms in the name of something that both agree is a greater good. But even Merry's interpretation is not entirely free of Western, taken-for-granted givens; she writes of the role of international rights activists as "interpreting the cultural world of transnational modernity for local claimants."[5] This book suggests instead that the process of worldwide expansion of human rights should be primarily viewed not as "transnational" but as intercultural, and that it can be achieved not so much by enlightening the provincials and bringing them out of their localism to presumably global and Western modernity, but through a dialogue between one knowledge community with another. Success in this endeavor will depend more on the promoters' deep understanding of the epistemic stance of the group they are working with, than on their own visions of rearranging relations among indigenous people. It would be wise here to follow the advice of a leading Muslim activist for human rights, Abdullahi An-Na'im: place less faith in laws as vehicles for implementing rights, and foster intercultural dialogue that gives an active role to indigenous activists who can access "the hearts and minds" of local communities because they understand "the underlying values of culture and religion that people live by."[6]

The essays in this book, instead of using the template of universal rights as a yardstick to assess how different groups *comply* with them, look at a variety of ways in which human rights can be translated between diverse communities and spaces of knowledge. Some of the contributing scholars take a more theoretical approach, while others examine actual applications, contemporary and historical, and case studies from across the world. Overall, the book offers a spectrum of reflections on how to think about human rights interculturally at philosophical, legal, and policy levels.

Part I of the volume contains reflections on the conceptual frameworks that could be useful for a variety of cultural brokers that undertake the challenging but indispensable task of translating human rights into local spaces of knowledge. Michal Rozbicki's essay contemplates the "grammar" or rules and ingredients that make up the intercultural process involved in indigenizing human rights. It sorts out some of the conceptual quandaries faced by translators, from axiological justifications for universal rights, through the conflict between universalist assumptions and the localism of cultures, the changing understandings of multiculturalism, the ways that particular cultures constitute reality, and the gap between anthropologists' dismissal of the concept of culture and the power of actual cultural identities among the peoples of the world, to the proposition of redefining culture in a more adequate way as a place or community of knowledge.

Mario Ricca's chapter is concerned with applying proper anthropological approaches to human rights law in a way that includes adequate acknowledgment of people's daily life experiences, and the imaginaries through which they interpret it. He stresses the importance of historical awareness to any attempts at cultural translation of human rights, something crucial in interpreting the language of the Universal Declaration of Human Rights in a way that is inclusive for people of all cultures. He ingeniously explains the mechanism of achieving such an interpretation by comparing it to the processes of connotative decomposition and intercultural recomposition employed by four modern painters: Paul Gauguin, Juan Gris, Paul Klee, and Alberto Savinio.

Part II focuses on the inherently complicated relationship between religious traditions and the implementation of modern human rights. Jeffrey A. Redding raises some fundamental questions about the origins, meanings, and implications of contemporary transgender rights movements around the world by focusing on the case of Pakistan. He looks comparatively at three time periods and locations: the post-9/11 context of an embattled Pakistani state under General Pervez Musharraf's rule, when the first inklings of a contemporary transgender rights discourse emerge in the country; the origins and meanings of Pakistan's transgender rights movement is the colonial period; and finally, the historical links of current transgender activism in Pakistan with precolonial Islamic past.

Melisa Vazquez examines the Western European secularism project, viewed through the lens of human and universal rights. She suggests that the incompleteness of this project may be playing a role in inflaming violent conflicts. After the November 2015 terrorist attacks on Paris, leaders condemned the attacks as an affront against all of humanity and "universal values," but separated religion from acts of terrorism, while the terrorists claimed they were attacking European "Crusaders." Vazquez points out that the Western invocations against the barbarism of a self-declared religious enemy may, in fact, be practicing religiously infused, unaware secularism, especially that not a single state leader has responded to the overtly religious accusations of the attackers with a defense of secularism or even laicité, a key French state policy. The larger question she poses is whether the unfinished project of secularism has naturalized Christian values to such an extent that they are no longer seen or nameable, even as they directly inform critical political responses.

The persistent conflict between the Universal Declaration of Human Rights (UDHR) norms and Islamic is scrutinized by Shazia Ahmad by looking at the case of colonial India. She argues that support for religious freedom by Indian Muslim political elite (and future administration of Pakistan) had strong material implications for mostly "lower-caste" Muslims because of how "personal law" determined an individual's civil and property rights by the religious or caste community into which he or she was born. Using "migration" as a metaphor to conceptualize religious conversion as the movement of individuals across jurisdictional boundaries under "personal law," she reviews a series of civil suits in which colonial courts restricted freedom of conscience and belief in order to maintain jurisdictional boundaries under personal law (conceiving of Hindus and Muslims as being governed by separate systems of law). These cases show that the strongest resistance to an interpretation of Islamic law that accorded with the right to freedom of belief came from upper-caste Hindus, upper-caste Muslims (Muslims of foreign descent), and the colonial administration. Thus, the right to religious freedom, as it developed into a human right, compromised jurisdictional boundaries that maintained an unequal distribution of rights.

Part III explores interactions between the legal and the cultural spheres that emerge in relationships between immigrants and host societies. Hisako Matsuo and Rachel Santon survey the cultural ambiguities in the commitment to human rights among Americans. Although the popular view is that the United States is a melting pot of cultural diversity, research on prejudice has found that attitudes toward immigrants are best described as ambivalent, as they reflect a tension between two strong, yet conflicting, sociocultural values. Whereas Americans hold egalitarianism in high regard, their firm faith in the Protestant Work Ethic, which stresses individual hard work and merit, fosters the belief that immigrants are deserving of their low status. On the one hand, many believe that Americans have responsibilities toward refugees from the perspective of human rights; on the other hand, some argue that certain groups of refugees are not welcomed (recent international developments regarding Syrian refugees may serve as an example). The authors survey this ephemeral nature of people's commitment to human rights from utilitarian and intercultural perspectives.

Tomasso Sbriccoli draws on his experience with South Asian asylum seekers in Italy as a legal consultant as well as a linguistic and cultural mediator in presenting select case studies of Bangladeshi applicants for asylum. As these cases make clear, in Bangladeshi asylum seekers' narratives themes like religion, politics, risk, persecution, debt, and dependence overlap in ways that challenge Italian asylum law's precise categorial divisions, often making it difficult to match the logic informing the applicants' stories with that required by the human rights' discourse in asylum cases. Such apparent incommensurability often disqualifies asylum seekers' applications, as Commissions and Courts fail to identify continuities and translatability that exist at a deeper level between the narratives they are presented with and the norms and principles they are supposed to apply. The author shows how an anthropological and semiotic approach can bring such continuities to surface by opening up cognitive spaces, and expanding our interpretation of the universality of human rights.

The role played by human rights frameworks in integrating refugees is taken up by Rachel Santon. The prevalent tendency of governments, nongovernmental organizations (NGOs), aid agencies, and policymakers to conceptualize refugees through security and victimization frameworks not only prevents refugees from making valuable economic and social contributions, but also restricts their agency. With this in view, the author investigates common policies regarding the legal, economic, and social integration of refugees into their host societies, and their impact on refugee lives in their new environments. She shows that a conceptual shift in the refugee aid industry is needed—from a victim paradigm to one of empowerment and acknowledgment of refugee capacity. Also, a better cooperation between governments, the UNHCR, NGOs, and businesses is necessary in order to foster conditions that enable refugees to make economic and social contributions.

The different and often strikingly unique manifestations of human rights principles in diverse historical and institutional contexts are at the core of the essays in Part IV. Elizabeth Blake uncovers circles of transnational and intercultural brotherhood and solidarity in supporting human rights among nineteenth-century Russian, Polish, and Lithuanian political prisoners who found themselves persecuted by tsarist Russia. The author demonstrates how the experience of shared suffering in Siberian penal camps and prisons by writers and intellectuals—who initially held very different views about the nature of universal human rights and the ability of their articulations to transcend national and cultural borders as well as local conflicts—generated a much expanded understanding of injustice, liberty, and rights. Individuals who were previously deeply rooted in their own nationalisms as well as different, often conflicting political interests, came to recognize a common ground in the transnational interdependency of freedom, as expressed by a slogan embroidered on banners by Polish fighters against the Russian occupation of their country: "For your freedom and ours."

Marcella Ferri takes an international and legal perspective and considers the Declaration on Human Rights, adopted in 2012 by states belonging to the Association of South-East Asian Nations (ASEAN), as a case of human rights translation, demonstrating that a universal recognition of human rights does not imply that they have to be implemented in a uniform and homogeneous manner. On the contrary, putting them into practice has to take into account the cultural features of each context. The concept of "cultural adequacy" is, in fact, frequently invoked by the United Nations Committee on Economic, Social and Cultural Rights, and specifically refers to "the realization of a specific human right in a way that is pertinent and suitable to a given cultural modality or context, that is, respectful of the culture and cultural rights of individuals and communities." This is a crucial framework, although harmonizing universal human rights standards and cultural diversity remains a major challenge. The most significant criticisms of the universalist approach to human rights have come from Asian countries. Ferri identifies the ASEAN claims on human rights and its reservations with regard to other human rights treaties. She then compares the ASEAN Human Rights Declaration with the Universal Declaration on Human Rights, concluding that despite their differences, the former should be viewed as a positive example of translating human rights in a way that adapts them to the cultural claims of ASEAN countries.

Finally, Anders Walker examines the thought of African American intellectual and writer Richard Wright. Long celebrated for writing *Native Son*, a strongly critical portrait of race relations in America, Wright represents an interesting and unorthodox view of human rights in the context of American race relations in the mid-twentieth century. Deeply disheartened with his experiences in Chicago, he resettled in France, where he encountered dilemmas related to European colonialism, and consequently reassessed his view of human rights. Perhaps surprisingly, he came to advance a strong case for certain Western values that should be seen as the intellectual foundation for the progress of human rights. He praised secularism, rights-based legal reasoning, and scientific inquiry as positive traits capable of countering postcolonial racial and religious conflicts and framing an appropriate role that the United States could play in Africa, Asia, and the Middle East.

The essays that follow were originally presented at an international conference "Human Rights in Translation: Intercultural Pathways," sponsored by the Center for Intercultural Studies at Saint Louis University in 2016.

M.J.R.

NOTES

1. Mary Ann Glendon, *A World Made New, Eleanor Roosevelt and the Universal Declaration of Human Rights* (New York: Random House, 2001), 223.

2. Peter Burke, *Cultural Hybridity* (Cambridge UK: Polity Press, 2009), 55–56.

3. René Provost and Colleen Shepherd, eds., *Dialogues on Human Rights and Legal Pluralism* (Dordrecht: Springer, 2013).

4. Mark Goodale, "Introduction. Locating Rights, Envisioning Law between the Global and the Local," in *The Practice of Human Rights: Tracking Law between the Global and the Local*, ed. Mark Goodale and Sally Engle Merry (Cambridge: Cambridge University Press, 2017), 5, 3.

5. Sally Engle Merry, *Human Rights and Gender Violence: Translating International Law into Local Justice* (Chicago: University of Chicago Press, 2006), 1, 5.

6. Abdullahi Ahmed An-Na'im, "Banning Sharia Is a "Red Herring": The Way Forward for All Americans," *Saint Louis University Law Journal* 57, no. 2 (Winter 2013): 288.

Part I

CONCEPTUAL FRAMEWORKS

Chapter 1

Human Rights and the Grammar of Interculturality

Michal Jan Rozbicki

CONCEPTUAL QUANDARIES

Contemporary human rights talk routinely invokes certain beliefs—deemed to be axiologically fundamental and universal—on which such rights are based: dignity equally inherent to every person, common human nature, and the natural state of liberty. However, any international practitioner or activist in this field instantly finds that the norms and values of diverse cultures are often incommensurable, even incompatible, with such assumptions of global homogeneity. This inherent tension within the imaginary of rights creates quite a bit of conceptual confusion in thinking about them. It especially obscures the basic fact that the only truly common attribute that inherently links all the diverse human communities across the world is difference. Peoples' attitudes toward life divide humanity, and unless one is an ardent utopian or is attracted to grand abstractions, reconciling them does not look like a plausible or even desirable option. Rather than search for the ontological foundations of human rights, it is intellectually more fertile to look at these rights as emerging from discursive exchanges within particular communities of knowledge that lead to a certain consensus. These rights do not exist in and of themselves until a specific cultural group agrees to create or adopt them in some form; one can neither "possess" them nor "put them in practice" before that is accomplished.[1]

Those who assume the organic wholeness of humanity often tend to call for a convergence of world cultures around the universal idea of human rights, understood as shared by diverse peoples at a "deeper" level. The problems with this view are the same ones that Claude Levi-Strauss once faced: that the existence of such "deep" structures is unprovable, and that the very quest for the homogeneity of humanity not only contradicts the respect for the vast diversity of cultures, but also casts doubt on the right to uphold each group's distinct culture.[2] A similar but modified position has been to acknowledge the cultural differences in interpreting human rights, but treat them as mere variations of a presumably existing fundamental, and thus universal, set of standards. This approach, however, calls for drawing some sort of a line beyond which the universal would be invalidated by the local, a problematic undertaking at best. Furthermore, both outlooks suffer from ahistoricism.

Even more conceptual perplexity related to human rights is generated by the venerable fiction of "human nature," which is probably the most frequent point of departure when arguing for a unified theory of rights. Being human is by this definition assumed to imply both the presence and the ownership of human rights. This is doubly misleading because it passes over the highly dissimilar ways humans across the globe think and act, and because it suggests that human nature consists of timeless and fixed characteristics. The only way such a claim could be made valid is to see it as a reference to a *transcendent* human nature, either divinely created or a metaphysical form of sorts, that somehow guides the actions of human beings. Such abstractions may be rhetorically useful but are not very helpful in analyzing what human rights are. Jack Donnelly—one of the top authorities in this field—argues that one has rights "simply because one is a human being," and that as their universality derives from the fact that one cannot stop being a human being, they are inalienable. In fairness, he also points out that human rights are not "timeless, unchanging, or absolute" but "historically specific and contingent." And yet, he argues somewhat ecumenically that "the particularity of human rights is compatible with a conception of human rights as universal rights" because they derive from human dignity and our moral nature.[3]

Because "human nature" is an abstraction unrooted in any group's particular history, it is endlessly flexible in applications and defies precise definition, a fuzziness that carries over to any attempts at reaching a broader consensus on what precisely human rights are. What has emerged instead is a polarization of opinions. At one end, there are those whose focus is mainly political and legal—especially human rights activists and politicians, neither of whom are theoreticians of culture. They tend to think of rights as largely universal, even if they acknowledge that flexibility in their implementation among indigenous cultures is needed. At the other end, there are those who are skeptical about introducing a single general model of rights into different cultures—considering the dramatic differences in the meanings of justice— and who instead stress taking indigenous systems of justice as a point of departure, and only then seek commonalities across cultures.

Some scholars have valiantly attempted to bridge this gap and maintain the universalist perspective while acknowledging deep-seated cultural differences. For instance, Brooke Ackerly constructs the edifice of universality using the building blocks of difference.[4] She rightly notes that hopes for achieving a "global public reason" are not a realistic foundation for achieving worldwide human rights, and that there are deep disparities of views between activists and theoreticians on what human rights are. However, she then concludes that as the two groups—despite their diverging views—pursue the same larger goals, universal human rights should be viewed as immanent, rather than as transcendent abstractions. This turns the problem into a solution: the tensions between the two views could bring about an agreement on a unified meaning of rights. This approach seems to be based more on hope than anything else but, more importantly, it skirts the problem that universalism—whether from the bottom up or top-down—does not align with the deep diversity of world's cultures, a reality that must be at the foreground of any attempt to indigenize the concept of rights.

Another factor that has contributed to the conceptual turmoil around human rights is the outdated but still lingering, whether implicitly or not, Western idea of teleological progress that would inevitably lead all countries to achieve some of the key norms that Western culture considered axiomatic, and therefore universal. This view was most recently well expressed in the idea of "modernization," an analytical category applied to societies to measure their "progress" in achieving "modernity."[5] What this perspective quietly assumed was that distinct societies and groups have inevitably been evolving along the same historical trajectory, with some having to catch up with the more modern others. This assumption conveniently bestowed moral power on advocates of international human rights, but it also created a barrier to achieving this goal. It made the existence of indigenous cultures—with their own ideas of justice—an *obstacle* to the spread of such rights, directing attention away from native values and norms and toward overcoming them. René Cassin, one of the framers of the Universal Declaration of Human Rights, captured the modernization standpoint well when he wrote that "men, cultures and nations must first mature inwardly before there can be effective international machinery to adjudicate in complaints about the violation of human rights."[6]

A related analytical weak spot among Western proponents of human rights is that they often fail to realize that ushering in external—and so, by definition, initially disruptive—concepts of rights into a group's existing cultural matrix is not cost free to the recipients. A recent illustration may be found in the tense ideological debates within Colombian society over the peace accords between leftist guerillas and the government.[7] In Western democracies an analogous, if less dramatic, process takes place everyday; differing factions in parliaments must participate in a dialogue with those who do not share their assumptions and worldviews, so any conclusive results must involve compromise, and therefore certain costs to both sides. In societies without long historical traditions of *institutionalizing difference*, the costs of change or compromise are much more unsettling.

In recent decades, another sociopolitical process that has been taking place in the West, especially in the United States—identity politics—has contributed to the fragmentation in thinking about human rights. Decades of multiculturalist policies and the abandoning of the "melting pot" theory as excessively assimilationist and leading to a denial of the right of groups (especially minority ones) have led to an outlook that emphasizes and celebrates difference by upholding and protecting *particular* group identities. This shift has combined with an increasingly widespread utilization of group identities for political ends, with the result that much of the rights talk now amplifies *separateness*, and disapproves of integration and assimilation, a trend that points public attention away from cooperation and shared civic responsibilities among groups.

The unanticipated outcome of this turn is that public discourse has been fostering an often essentialist and rigid view of particular group identities as homogeneous and fixed—in contradiction to the original calls of multiculturalism for intergroup openness and inclusiveness.[8] Western theorists, especially anthropologists, who have been widely questioning the very existence of culture on the grounds that the concept was too imagined, rigid, and essentialist to be useful as an analytical category,[9] are now facing assertions within their own societies from various newly politicized groups claiming to possess strict and impermeable defining attributes, as well as from non-Western societies and groups that are strongly defensive of their distinct cultural identities. Any debate over the nature of rights must now take this state of affairs into account.

Finally, some of the conceptual obstacles to theoretical reflection on this topic lay in the fact that although thinking about individual human rights has a long history going back to Enlightenment philosophers and revolutionaries,[10] a global perspective on such rights (and on related foreign policy and international law issues) is a relatively recent, post–World War II phenomenon, so there has not been much time to develop a coherent model for action. The rise of the global approach has engendered at least two major consequences. On the institutional side, international organizations were established, with limited cross-country jurisdiction, that serve as vehicles for promoting, if not enforcing, certain rights. On the theoretical side, the taken-for-granted global universalism of Western concepts of rights has been disrupted by postcolonial scholarship, which in turn led to the current search for new interpretations. At this point, there is at least a general agreement among scholars and activists that human rights as defined in the 1948 Universal Declaration of Human Rights are predominantly a product of Western political and cultural heritage, and that in order to become more truly universal they need to be brought much closer to the values and norms of indigenous cultures.[11] What is just as important is the growing awareness that it would have to be a two-way, dynamic process between different spaces of knowledge. Yet, all these realizations are still quite far from being converted into a sound and coherent blueprint for thought and action.

INTERCULTURAL TRANSLATION OF HUMAN RIGHTS

An approach that carries considerable promise in this regard involves a focus on the intercultural translation of human rights. Instead of using such rights as yardsticks to measure diverse cultures on compliance with them, a much more useful perspective is to shed light on the different cognitive contexts that produce a variety of meanings of rights, to identify spaces of intercultural crossings where differences can coexist, and to come up with usable narratives and metaphors that could mediate between distinct knowledge communities. Such a quest would in effect be a case of identifying and interpreting the differences between cultures through the prism of human rights. To pursue this angle, human rights should not be viewed as an integral and fixed goal, but as a dynamic process of constructing them. Intercultural mediation of this kind would be a multifaceted endeavor to find common ground within and outside of differences between communities, by both respecting continuity and introducing change, and by both valuing existing diverse identities and promoting certain obligations and responsibilities that could extend over several—otherwise particular—cultural spaces.[12] Such a dual and flexible approach has the potential of bringing about an understanding among the communities involved that strongly held cultural predispositions (in the sense of prejudgments) are not fixed but relational, and that reality is not determined but constantly constructed by people—especially so when they find themselves dealing with otherness.[13] The advantage of the interculturalist approach is that it harnesses difference as positive cultural capital, and makes it a tool of mediation, unification, dialogue, and civic participation.

To be competent, if not sure footed, when crossing the borderlands of alterity, mastering the grammar of the intercultural process is indispensable. We need to be familiar with the mechanisms that are in operation when we undertake an attempt to translate the world of values, beliefs, customs, and behaviors that constitute a way of life of one group into those of another. Even if we put aside the polarizing political forces that are always at play, each community encompasses a peculiar, historically acquired, shared knowledge that enables it to attach particular meanings to their experiences, and thus to make sense of them. Put differently, their historical, collective experiences supply the tools, with which they interpret and *constitute* reality.

What this means is that there can be no one-size-fits-all textbook on how to practice intercultural mediation in the area of human rights. It has to be written for each particular relationship, and it needs to be solidly rooted in the cultural contexts—both horizontal (contemporary) and vertical (historical)—of the two knowledge groups involved in the conversation.

This is a daunting task. Indigenizing human rights calls for a wholly different set of skills than those associated with political or legal activism. Those who pursue the latter two fields often tend to think about implementing such rights in international and global terms. Unfortunately, such a viewpoint can become a major barrier to a successful employment of intercultural methods to expand rights across the world. Globalists are naturally inclined to take a bird's eye view of humanity, and often find searching for "global systems" and large-scale generalizations seductive because macro-scale perspectives imply attaining world unity and harmony. For the same reason, they are inclined to assume that there exist large and substantial commonalities among the world's peoples—despite their dramatically different long-term experiences—that could be summoned to help unify societies around common conceptions of rights. There are two reasons why this is not the best way to proceed. First, it is the *incompatibilities* among cultures that pose the biggest threat to achieving such goals, and thus require the most attention. Second, a transnational ethos of rights is not a good point of departure in thinking about them, because specific rights can only *become* transnational if and when they are locally indigenized by more than one group.

At the political and legal level, many human rights proponents also tend to focus on *supranational* institutions, not infrequently imagining that at this stage of history the nation states are inevitably waning, and will ultimately be replaced by some sort of world government that—not hindered by the resistance of particular traditions and local beliefs—will be able to put into effect a uniform canon of rights for all. This perspective, whether one calls it utopian or not, is tempting because it offers a vision of an integrated world and a more harmonious humanity. Yet, while economic and informational globalization does bring about certain uniformities, when we shift our gaze back to actual, local cultures and societies, this process appears far less significant than its promoters would have it. The existing supranational institutions have relatively very little power over nation states, and the present tendency among the latter—even within the Western world—is to reassert their democratic sovereignty by resisting outside decisions that are perceived as infringing on local cultures. The recent fractures in the European Union—a huge transnational institution—may serve as examples of this process. Nation states firmly remain as the mainstays of the international system.[14]

A macro-scale, transnational outlook is also conducive to totalizing presumptions about taking certain favored ideals to be worldwide norms, a position that makes local departures from such norms mere "idiosyncrasies."[15] Some globalist scholars point to "deep patterns of human history" that may be recovered by looking at past millennia," suggesting that such timeless concepts could acquire scientific legitimacy.[16] But a dismissal of localism is not helpful in gaining a deeper understanding of any given knowledge community's concepts of justice, a condition of an effective dialogue about rights. Such concepts can and do change, but outside transfers are usually adopted when such transfers are domesticated into the indigenous cultural matrix. That process can only take place locally.

To sum up, perhaps the most prominent conceptual obstacle to intercultural translation and worldwide promotion of rights has been the belief in their inherent universality. At the philosophical level, its advocates have imagined that such universality requires not so much a translation across cultures as the *enlightenment* of members of these cultures. The premise here is that when fuller knowledge is achieved, it will ultimately overcome the "barriers" of localism that stand in the way of a global expansion of a unified canon of rights.

The United Nations 1948 Universal Declaration of Human Rights largely promoted and—through its authority as a transnational, world body—legitimized this view of rights. But its articulation of rights was in reality local too, not global, in the sense that it was a product of specific, regional traditions. Those who framed the Declaration represented and shared a particular, not universal, kind of knowledge—modern Western constitutional and political traditions, going back to the American Declaration of Independence of 1776 and the Constitution of 1787—that provided them with the conceptual tools to formulate and structure their message in a certain way. These tools were at the time not available to most of the world's societies, whose spheres of knowledge derived from their own histories, and their own ways of categorizing and interpreting social and political experiences.

It should therefore not come as a surprise that for over seven decades the most common complaint about the Declaration has been that its implementation among the countries of the world has not only been far from universal, but that it was beset by a myriad "violations" of its standards. But one cannot "violate" principles that one does not hold. Some societies and groups simply do not share the presuppositions behind such rights. For instance, the right to religion, speech, and assembly are not only absent in the legal systems of many countries, but they are not even supported by the public. From today's perspective, the Declaration's unanticipated weakness seems to be the premise that these rights have an existence of their own, beyond the specific historical and cultural context from which they emerged, and that they pertain equally to all mankind. In other words, the language used to define their *raison d'être* clearly suggests—especially in Articles 1 and 2—that their core meaning is supranational and supra-cultural. Although the framers of the Declaration privately admitted that particular implementations of these rights may differ due to varying local contexts, its very text emphasizes throughout that their essence is constant.[17]

WHAT IS "CULTURE" IN "INTERCULTURAL"?

The above observations indicate that the central issue in making a success-ful turn to intercultural translation of human rights as a vehicle of expanding them across the world is a deeper understanding of the role of culture in this context. Two generalized concepts of culture—paradoxically, often mutually exclusive—are currently circulating in the public sphere. At one end, there is a de-essentialized, postmodern, and relativistic view—found mostly among academics, especially anthropologists—that culture, if it can be said to even exist as such, is not rigid, timeless, and bounded, as it was understood in the past, but a fluid assortment of individual communicative acts, with as many meanings of "texts" being communicated as there are recipients. In short, ascribing any durability or homogeneity to it has no scientific grounds. At the other end, there is the popular view, readily identifiable among the world's peoples at local level, that culture is a fairly coherent system that guides people's thinking and behavior, defines and perpetuates ethnic identi-ties, and integrates societies by reproducing itself over long periods of time. By current academic standards—or, better, when viewed from the ivory tower—this is an essentialist and reductionist definition. Viewed through the prism of grassroots practices of groups and peoples around the world it is as real as daily life, and far from being passé. On the contrary, it has a robust life in everyday usage, and is widely utilized as a crucial presumption in formulating major arguments in social and political interactions between groups. But above all, it is not just a popular, in the sense of unrefined, view. It is supported by objective analysis, even if anthropology and political science do not currently seem to have a good hold of this issue. People's actions look forward, but they are interpreted backward, through the cognitive lens and filters construed by past experiences. Groups with distinctly different histories cannot be interpreting their lives—and by extension, rights—in the same way.

We should note that both definitions are right to a certain extent. The popu-lar model is rhetorically and politically powerful, but some academic claims about its essentialism are true; it does not fully take into account that culture is a man-made entity, and that people are active agents, continuously making changes—through migration, trade, and information exchanges—that disrupt its presumed homogeneity. On the other hand, such awareness is not a condi-tion for it to function effectively on the ground. The academic model, in turn, is logically consistent with postmodern epistemology, but it is an abstract construct of little relevance for peoples' everyday life. The huge gap between these two definitions is mostly artificial, caused by incompatible premises, but it becomes a real barrier to interpreting people's life-worlds.

For our purposes, it is important to note that while in the *practice* of everyday life people may not need academic arguments or scientific sanction, they very much do need the explanatory and unifying functions of the popular view of culture. Consider the following example. The idea of American exceptionalism that has long been a highly influential popular narrative describing the United States as a country whose democratic way of life and constitutional system made its history separate and different from any other. In the past several decades, historians have spent much time and ink rebuffing it on rational grounds that there can be no such thing as one country being specifically exempt from the usual course of history. But this otherwise obvious, "scientific" interpretation misses two important *local* aspects of the phenomenon that—as a real, genuine, and widely shared belief—actually did shape the country's history. Exceptionalism in America was connected with faith in the divine, and so viewed as a *transcendent* destiny for the country ever since the Puritans' creed of the "City upon a Hill" in the 1620s. Furthermore, it was primarily a subjective belief, a shared metaphor, a serviceable fiction serving to consolidate the identity of a young country.[18] It could be all this by fulfilling the need of people to make sense of their experiences.

It was possible because culture, as a fiction of sorts, can serve the people and construct their group identities *only* by being subjective and essentialist (something that escapes so many academics). It supplies the building blocks of shared and legitimized knowledge about the makeup of their existence, and provides a meaningful order for their lives—in a particular time and place, not immutably and not universally. It is not a transcendent entity that directs people to act in a certain way, but a set of man-made assumptions that have been embedded in a group's collective consciousness by their shared historical experiences. These "commonsensical" assumptions, once entrenched, are mostly pre-reflexive and constitute the body of taken-for-granted knowledge that enables people to identify and account for the reality around them. Such apperceptions form much of a group's shared epistemic system. One way to describe this system is to recall Martin Heidegger's observation that all humans happen to find themselves immersed, right at birth, in a *particular* cultural (but also social and political) environment from which they absorb specific ways of recognizing the world and making sense of reality. Most of these ways are frameworks of apperceptions, or prejudgments, through which people interpret the world around them. In other words, people function mostly on autopilot, until disrupted by something, such as an encounter with difference or a revolutionary situation that makes them aware of this habitual mechanism. He points out that even scientists who claim to be studying their object in a "dis-worlded" manner (objectively) have a framework, previously produced by the scientific community, of how to think about that object.[19]

A productive path to utilize this important perspective analytically has been suggested by French historian Christian Jacob, who uses the term "lieux de savoir," or places of knowledge, as both a spatial metaphor and a heuristic tool for linking all kinds of knowledge among members of a group or several groups within a society who share their "reality" through conventionalized ways of relating to objects, people, time, space, and nature. The advantage of this concept is not just that it replaces "culture," which today has too much semantic baggage, but that it embraces all types of knowledge within a distinct group—pre-reflexive givens as well as conscious acts, and even mystical beliefs—without the usual atomization of categories prompted by academic disciplines. Consequently, it allows us to avoid inadvertent distortions caused by conflicting disciplinary methods or *en vogue* approaches. Equally valuable is the fact that it also encourages a focus on practice. People's actions are guided by a combination of cultural structures *and* the need to respond to contingencies (where the response is also shaped by the cultural structures).[20] It is through studying practices that scholars can best witness the social construction of knowledge. A performative approach means that the process, rather than theory, gets priority, something that is absolutely crucial to understanding culture where all aspects of human existence operate together.[21] A similar approach to knowledge is taken by Stanley Fish, who uses the term "interpretive communities" to emphasize the culture-delimited, shared epistemic stance of a distinct group with a common historical experience and a common system of internalized apperceptions that enable members to recognize and interpret reality. Fish goes even further than others in stressing that no one can perceive the world in terms that extend beyond the cognitive tools that one's culture allows.[22] Whatever the nuances of these approaches, the overall conclusion must be that, when what used to be called "culture" is defined and understood this way, it very much does exist.

IS INTERCULTURAL TRANSLATION ACHIEVABLE?

With all this in mind, let us imagine a stranger arriving in a space populated by a group with a distinct epistemic stance. He is carrying new knowledge in his backpack—proposals to implement human rights that are unfamiliar to the group. Invoking the venerable argument of "common humanity" or an appeal to cosmopolitanism are not likely to be of much help in getting attention, but gaining a deep understanding of what members of the host society know, how they know what they know, and how they apply their knowledge in practice would be a good start. Once this is accomplished, he is ready to unpack and illuminate his project by "translating" it into something recognizable within the interpretive context of the local community. In the process, he must overcome two inherent ethnocentrisms—that of his own and that of the hosts. He must rise above his instinctive inclination to universalize and normalize his own group's assumptions, and he must, as it were, enter the heads of his hosts to employ their metalanguage and their commonsensical thinking. But is such translation possible at all?

To answer this question, it is useful to consider the nature of linguistic translation as an analogy. Literary translators know well that there can never be a perfect, definitive translation from one language to another. This is because there are no *invariants* in the source text that are supposedly available to the translator to render whole and undamaged in a different language. Their existence has been a popular assumption ever since Italians, disappointed with the early French translations of Dante's *Divine Comedy*, coined a phrase "traduttore-traditore" to lament that the translators were traitors who "betrayed" the original. But the nature of translation is such that every text being translated first has to be decontextualized, that is lifted out of the original cultural and historical context that supplied it with meanings, and recontextualized into another context that would now deliver its meanings. As a result, any translated version, as Lawrence Venuti has persuasively shown, always injects—must inject—new and different elements that were not in the original source text.[23] This is why translation is best viewed as an act of interpretation. Translating a text is an act of intercultural mediation, and as such it involves not just language but also culture. Language is only the visible tip of the iceberg of culture. One can only convey the meanings of the original culture to the extent that the new language and its culture can approximate them. And conversely, the translator will inevitably, if unintentionally, inject certain assumptions and meanings from his own cultural matrix. Put differently, no one can fully acknowledge the otherness of the Other.[24]

Indigenizing human rights is also a case of intercultural mediation, and cannot be viewed as a finite act ending in an exact translation of some presumably universal invariants. It should instead be viewed as a process, a long-term, dialogic effort. There can be no set of standard interpretive tools that can be applied to all interacting cultures. Instead, an awareness that people do not live in the world but in their local knowledge communities would go a long way in helping to clear the path for various disciplines to devise new ways of gaining true access to the mechanisms of meaning and coherence that are the glue holding such communities together—instead of waving the flag of universalism as an incentive for their members to march toward global sameness. "Culture" in this local sense inherently seeks to *preserve* its beliefs and behaviors because they unite people by offering them membership and belonging, as well as a sense of stability. It does so by constructing universals that *serve* as "invariants" that stabilize it in a changing and often chaotic world. It instinctively reacts to external influences that might undermine that self-evident sense of enduring order and confident identity. It *will* change and accept outside influence if that novelty is offered in a translation that allows the group's epistemic categories to recognize it as something that can potentially be usefully incorporated into their own way of life.

Good examples of how knowledge communities inherently resist external structures imposed on them by political means may be found in postcolonial Africa. A number of otherwise authoritarian regimes that evolved in that period have nominally democratic constitutional systems—based on European models, and introduced by European-educated leaders. But at the local level traditional political and cultural practices with a long collective history have continued unabated, resulting in the parallel presence of two different institutional systems. The effect of this duality has been that the political elites have often moved back and forth between ostensibly supporting the Western state structures and—when politically expedient—identifying with the more informal, local traditions of governance. Predictably, human rights have suffered in the process as they are by definition a form of restricting the powers of rulers.[25]

However, once culturally validated, human rights can exist in different versions among different knowledge groups, and in time these versions can spread and evolve to become broader in their social reach. The American Declaration of Independence of 1776 defined a series of human rights and framed them in universal terms as equally applicable to all people. It took a very long time—until mid-twentieth century—to implement them literally across all groups in society. But the original text gained national legitimacy early on, and as a result could serve as a yardstick for various groups that had been excluded *in practice* from the listed rights to frame their calls for inclusion. One of the early, modern examples of such use was a 1786 anti-tax rebellion of backcountry farmers in Massachusetts headed by Daniel Shays. To present their grievances to the republican government (then run by former Revolutionary leaders), the rebels used the very same language of protest that these leaders created and widely popularized a few years earlier when fighting against the violations of the colonists' rights by the British imperial government.[26]

An approach that insists on a full and prompt implementation of the Universal Declaration's definitions of rights already contains the seeds of failure. The goal should be to fuse rights concepts into indigenous knowledge and practices, so they are gradually internalized and ultimately transition into broader legal and political reality. This is what was done in Botswana where the traditional authority of local chieftains has been recognized by incorporating it into the constitutional system (House of Chiefs), and assigning them considerable political and judicial powers; and in South Africa where practices of local cultural, religious and language communities have been institutionalized by allowing them to apply customary laws to certain areas like adjudicating disputes and advising the legislature of the province on indigenous, traditional principles.[27]

To succeed in *intercultural* translations, we need to find a new language that avoids incompatible vocabularies, and to take special care that it is *not defined by past experiences of one group*. To convey the message of rights, we need metaphors with which all groups can connect. We need to keep in mind that the metaphor itself does not contain the message that persuades; only the meaning that a given cultural group attaches to it does. Academic abstractions will not work; only a vocabulary rooted in the epistemic stance of the targeted cultural group will.

Furthermore, we need a language that not only salutes alterity, but also helps to graft the intercultural standpoint into the various group identities. This can be done by promoting inclusive, cross-cultural spaces of knowledge that all groups can enter without fear that their self-understanding and hierarchy of values will be disrupted. A language that remembers that indigenous identity and values emerged slowly, *historically*, through local practice until they became taken-for-granted knowledge, while the modern concepts of human rights arrived from outside as intellectual abstracts. Consequently, indigenous identity is incomparably stronger and more resilient. It cannot be understood in current time; the outsider first encounters it in contemporary time, but understanding them requires tools taken from a long stretch of time.

In other words, this new idiom should not be centered on achieving unity in the world as a stepping stool to attaining universal human rights for all. Instead, *difference* should be constitutive of this new language, just as it is constitutive of all society. Only in a utopia can distinct epistemological stances produced in deep time by particular group's experiences be summarily merged together by an act of political will or legal action. Engagement with the Other, not abolishing divisions, should be the goal, and the new vocabulary should offer people conceptual tools to advance it. The typically dismal demise of recent totalitarian systems taught us that at their root was a denial of inherent differences and pluralism among people, as well as attempts to homogenize them by political means.[28]

There can be little doubt that successful intercultural mediation is far from simple or straightforward. It requires substantial theoretical knowledge that is not usually available to activists and politicians. Two basic models of such mediation can be usefully distinguished. One is a spontaneous, grassroots-level "translation" of otherness. It occurs when two different groups happen to encounter each other, and a practical need arises to negotiate their differences. The main point to note is that when these two parties are initially gazing at each other, it is not an intercultural act as such. Their relationship does not involve knowledge about the other side, or self-reflection about one's own ways of knowing. There is instead a naturally ethnocentric reading of the Other—in terms of one's group interpretive yardsticks. It is not a case of "misreading" otherness, because there exists no alternative possibility of "reading" it properly, as people simply do not have the knowledge to do so. All such readings are to some degree misreadings because no one is able to fully see the Other objectively, outside of one's own knowledge, and no one possesses global epistemological capability. This kind of process has been taking place continuously over the ages, producing conflict as well as—over time—adaptations.[29] The other model of intercultural mediation is primarily reflexive rather than spontaneous, and it occurs when a "translation" involves significant familiarity with the cultural matrix of the other side, self-reflection on one's own interpretive presuppositions, and substantial awareness of the 'grammar" of intercultural relationships. Only such a comprehensive and painstaking translation can produce a suitable mediating idiom capable of encouraging local adaptations of outside patterns of knowledge.

REALISTS AND ESSENTIALISTS

In the debates over how to implement human rights, the two most common positions that divide the theoreticians and practitioners alike can be labeled as essentialist and realist. The essentialists are inclined to assume that the notion of human rights is universal and resides deep in human nature, so all people are inherently predisposed to seeking them, even if some have not yet *progressed* enough to be fully aware of their benefits. In this view, such rights are part of the constitution of humanity as such, a highly romanticized claim if we consider the astonishing variety of the world's knowledge communities. The realists, in turn, believe that only legal and political means can provide a viable path to putting rights into practice because such measures alone are capable of introducing as well as enforcing them in any given society. They acknowledge the diversity of peoples and their "cultures" but tend to see it as an impediment to achieving the universality of rights. Both of these positions are flawed, even if we accept that using certain idealized concepts of rights can make a lot of practical sense, and that the enforcement of rights through the application of political power and the rule of law is ultimately necessary.

Consider a Cold War episode involving human rights—the so-called Helsinki Accords. It was an agreement signed in 1975 in Finland by thirty-five nations, including United States, the Soviet Union, Canada, and most European countries taking part in the Conference on Security and Cooperation in

Europe. The agreement declared that "participating States will respect human rights and fundamental freedoms, including the freedom of thought, conscience, religion or belief . . . . They will promote and encourage the effective exercise of civil, political, economic, social, cultural and other rights and freedoms, all of which derive from the inherent dignity of the human person and are essential for his free and full development." To the "realists" this statement was purely nominal, with no more chance to be put into practice within the Soviet sphere of influence than any other idealistic fiction. US Secretary of State Henry Kissinger was among the greatest skeptics because it was not backed by political power to enforce it.[30]

What followed showed otherwise. The Soviet Union signed the agreement, driven by a belief that, ironically, might also be called "realist" as it was solidly based on recent history—that a few idealistic phrases in the Accords might help the relations with the West, but would in no way oblige Moscow to implement its provisions or affect its domination of Eastern Europe. The premise backfired in an unexpected way. The declaration was taken up by opposition movements in Eastern Europe—buoyed by supportive rhetoric from the Western press and political leaders—and became a *cause célèbre* of dissident activity, a powerful metaphor expressing the glaring moral contradiction between the noble tenets publicly pledged by the Kremlin before the whole world, and the repressive domestic policies it enforced. The abstract principles of "human rights" in the document were thus "translated" by freedom activists, and later the public, into a language of resistance, a fighting tool, a universally applicable set of norms that were being violated by Communist governments. The episode contributed significantly to the political climate that in a relatively short time led to the end of the Soviet domination of Eastern Europe.

The larger lesson of this episode is that broad cultural fictions and ideal models do not have a prior, transcendent life of their own, but they can facilitate adopting concrete concepts of rights by a given knowledge community—once the ideal types are internalized into their vernacular and become a source of metaphors that its members can use to make sense of the world. Their "fictionality" does not matter because it is representations that *constitute* the group's distinctive knowledge, usually more so than presumably "objective" facts and "scientific" viewpoints. Even at a reflexive level, people invoke ideal models to deal with reality; for instance, whenever they plan a rational course of action, they employ a utopia of sorts by imagining a perfect result to be achieved. Incidentally, these ideal types have another socially useful quality—if formulated in the conceptual categories of a given knowledge community, they can steer people toward common goals, such as human rights. As noted above, the American Declaration of Independence, like the Helsinki Accords, was also a nonbinding document, but as an ideal model it had an enormous influence on the trajectory of rights in American history.[31]

If ideal models can thus be useful for expanding human rights, the new language that would facilitate this process should look for utilizable fictions and representations that can further this goal. It needs a targeted vocabulary through which community members will think about rights and construct indigenous models of rights. Ideally, such serviceable imaginaries would take the form of narratives and metaphors that could resonate in more than one knowledge community (for example, among political elites and ordinary people, among minorities and the majorities, or among neighboring ethnic groups), so they could be absorbed into their distinct worlds of meaning and their peculiar ways of interpreting reality.

The new language should contain both unifying, agreed upon, broad core principles that are capable of crossing cultural borders ("human dignity" would be a good candidate), as well as locally specific variants that are compatible with these core principles *and* already well rooted among the group's members.[32] In other words, the new lexicon must be able to fuse rights into the indigenous knowledge of the community. One might note here that the language of the Universal Declaration of Human Rights already offers idealistic fictions of equal and inalienable rights; the difference is that it applies it uniformly to the entire world, without attempts at intercultural mediation.

Ideal models are especially useful in political discourse. Democracies make use of such collective fictions as "society," "the people," or "the nation" because such metaphors are vital for governing and for a unified rule of law.[33] Such constructed fictions are not autonomous; they are intimately connected with the objective reality of social and political life. In fact, the entities they are representations of would not exist or function as such without these symbolic depictions, because they enable groups to attach meanings to various aspects of their identity as groups, and to their relations to others. At the same time, they also carry an important subversive potential that is far from fictitious—they enable marginalized groups to unite in publicly demanding full inclusion in the space of rights and liberties.

And yet, as in game theory, the means may often be more important than the ideal. When advocating human rights among differing cultures, the outcomes are the ultimate goal, but the choice of strategies for the initial dialogue between different actors, and especially their relevance to the distinct spheres of knowledge of the groups involved, will be more important to achieving that goal than if the primary attention is centered on the goal itself. However, whether it is the means or the outcomes, the crucial condition of a fruitful dialogue about them is the freedom of discussion that enables the public to examine the claims for human rights. As Amartya Sen has rightly pointed out, in some cases such public scrutiny will not necessarily produce an acceptance and justification of rights or approval for a wide spectrum of such rights, but without an unobstructed public discussion, the plausibility—and therefore success—of rights claims will remain in doubt.[34]

LAW AND RIGHTS

What role can law play in indigenizing human rights? One thing is clear; it cannot be effective if it is the only tool, just as it cannot be effective if it is seen as an external imposition. Nor can it be the first tool; cultural indigenization of rights must take place first. Then, in close synchronization with local culture, law can play its indispensable role in *institutionalizing* and enforcing them. Law, by its very nature and "majesty," tends to consider itself universal, even timeless (it cannot function if seen in relativistic terms), but in this case it needs to be flexible in adjusting to local customs and concepts of justice.

But doesn't the very concept of human rights presuppose the rule of law? This is true but there are at least three prerequisites for this model of thinking to be valid: there first has to exist a culturally acceptable law that could "rule;" second, the rulers who enforce the law must defer to it; and third, the people who are to be ruled by the law must share a strong and collective belief that the law should rule, and that this rule is indispensable as a guarantor of their rights and liberties. Otherwise the rulers will not enforce it because it inevitably restricts them, and the citizens will not honor it because it is not a part of their legitimate cultural apparatus (this is especially true in cases of ethnic nationalism, such as, for instance, is found among certain Hindu groups in India). Cultural legitimacy must necessarily come before the law, or the law will have no hope of enduring success. Law ultimately grows out of culture, not the other way around. In a given community, certain principles must first be publicly raised to become thinkable, questions about their applications must be made askable, and their violations must become unacceptable, before law can truly validate them. This is the main reason why uniform, international law on human rights simply cannot be effectively enforced globally, and why nation states are still, and will be for long, indispensable to their implementation.

Finally, in any attempt at translation, it is crucial to keep in mind the particular place and time of the cultural origins of the belief in the rule of law. This belief, so central to the Universal Declaration of Human Rights (UDHR), is a result of long, Western historical experience, articulated especially in the eighteenth century European and American debates about "natural rights" and the "rights of man."[35] It was the rule of law that made the rise of modern democratic systems possible. Over centuries, the belief in the rule of law became a cultural axiom and a means of achieving the ideals of liberty and rights shared by countries within this knowledge group. Other societies that have not had the same historical experiences cannot be expected—as globalists often imagine—to spontaneously recognize and accept these same axioms—precisely because they too have their own axioms—historically shaped ideals and structuring patterns of culture that supply meaning and construe reality for their people. Just as in the West, many of these patterns are cross-cultural and international in scope. For example, unlike in societies with long traditions of separating religion and state, many Islamic countries share the belief that the absolutes of faith and the absolutes of law are inherently tied together. This makes Islam one of the most successful and durable transcultural institutions in history. It ties peoples' loyalties to their localities as well as to a larger, transnational league of believers, with similar worldviews and moral rules, despite their otherwise different historical experiences and identities. They too believe in "the rule of law," not Western law but the long-established Sharia law. All this is why in societies where the political is not separate from the religious, promoting human rights faces a formidable difficulty, as it is problematical to argue that secular human rights law—an explicit *constraint* on the powers of the state, as defined in the Declaration—should rule supreme over religious and metaphysical givens.

Such and other similar concerns arising from historically rooted distinctions among various knowledge communities are and will inevitably remain an inseparable part of the pursuit of human rights. And yet, such a pursuit cannot and should not be disrupted by it. If we are to hope for more success, we must persist with the realization that any local changes leading toward accepting the wide-ranging concept of human rights as outlined in the UDHR can only happen gradually, by way of indigenously framed versions of rights that have some precedents in domestic cultural and political traditions, however eclectic such versions may be.[36] As in any translation, these new renditions must defer to the recipient culture's historically accrued repository of meanings.

NOTES

1. See Marie-Bénédicte Dembour, "What are Human Rights? Four Schools of Thought," *Human Rights Quarterly* 32, no. 1 (2010): 1–20; and Sally Engle Merry, *Human Rights and Gender Violence: Translating International Law into Local Justice* (Chicago: Chicago University Press, 2006), 228–229.

2. On legal recognition of cultural identity as a human right, see Marcella Ferri, "The Recognition of the Right to Cultural Identity under (and beyond) Human Rights International Law," *Journal of Law, Social Justice and Global Development*, forthcoming.

3. Jack Donnelly, *Universal Human Rights in Theory and Practice* (Ithaca: Cornell University Press, 2013), 10, 7.

4. Brooke A. Ackerly, *Universal Human Rights in a World of Difference* (Cambridge: Cambridge University Press, 2008), 116, 1.

5. See Richard D. Brown, *Modernization: The Transformation of American Life, 1600–1865* (New York: Hill and Wang, 1976).

6. Mary Ann Glendon, "The Rule of Law in the Universal Declaration of Human Rights," *Northwestern Journal of International Human Rights* 2, no. 1 (Spring 2004): 44.

7. "Drawing Closer to a Final Peace Deal–Colombia and FARC," *The Economist*, September 23, 2015.

8. Jane K. Cowan, Marie-Bénédicte Dembour, and Richard A. Wilson, eds., *Culture and Rights: Anthropological Perspectives* (Cambridge, UK: Cambridge University Press, 2001), Introduction. See also Ted Cantle, *Interculturalism: The New Era of Cohesion and Diversity* (New York: Palgrave Macmillan, 2012), 2.

9. Fred Dervin, "Researching Identity and Interculturality: Moving Away from Methodological Nationalism for Good?" in *Intersecting Identities and Interculturality: Discourse and Practice*, ed. Regis Machart et al. (Newcastle upon Tyne: Cambridge Scholars Publishing, 2013), 10, 16, 20.

10. Lynn Hunt, *Inventing Human Rights: A History* (New York: Norton, 2007).

11. Federico Lenzerini, *The Culturalization of Human Rights Law* (Oxford: Oxford University Press, 2014), 1–32.

12. See Gérard Bouchard, "What is Interculturalism?" *McGill Law Journal - Revue de droit de McGill* 56, no. 2 (2011): 461.

13. Michal Jan Rozbicki, "Cross-Cultural History: Toward an Interdisciplinary Theory," in *Cross-Cultural History and the Domestication of Otherness*, eds. Michal Jan Rozbicki and George Ndege (New York: Palgrave-Macmillan, 2015), 208–213.

14. Glendon, "The Rule of Law in the Universal Declaration of Human Rights," 33.

15. On worldwide values of "peace, democracy, and respect for human rights," see Philip L. White, "Globalization and the Mythology of the 'Nation State'," in *Globalization in World History*, ed. A.G. Hopkins (London: Pimlico, 2002), 280. On idiosyncrasies: William H. McNeill, "Afterword: World History and Globalization," ibid., 290.

16. J. R. McNeill and William H. McNeill, *The Human Web: A Bird's Eye View of World History* (New York and London: W.W. Norton, 2013), 20.

17. Glendon, "The Rule of Law in the Universal Declaration of Human Rights," 36.

18. Peter Onuf, "American Exceptionalism and National Identity," *American Political Thought: A Journal of Ideas, Institutions, and Culture* 1 (Spring 2012): 77–99.

19. Charles B. Guignon, *Heidegger and the Problem of Knowledge* (Indianapolis: Hackett, 1983), 157.

20. This dichotomy is masterfully elaborated by Anthony Giddens, *New Rules for Sociological Method* (London: Hutchinson, 1976).

21. Christian Jacob, *Qu'est-ce qu'un lieu de savoir?* (Marseille: Open Edition Press, 2014), generated on Internet November 5, 2014, available at: http://books.openedition.org/oep/423. ISBN:9782821834583. DOI:10.4000/books.oep.423.

22. Stanley Fish, *Is There A Text in This Class?* (Cambridge: Harvard University Press, 1980), 147–174.

23. Lawrence Venuti, *Translation Changes Everything: Theory and Practice* (Abingdon, UK: Routledge, 2013), 3, 4, 6.

24. On this dilemma, see Sanford Budick, "Crises of Alterity: Cultural Untranslability and the Experience of Secondary Otherness," in *The Translability of Cultures: Figurations of the Space Between*, eds. Sanford Budick and Wolfgang Iser (Stanford: Stanford University Press, 1996), 1–22.

25. Semahagn G. Abebe, "The Relevance of African Culture in Building Modern Institutions and the Quest for Legal Pluralism," *Saint Louis University Law Journal* 57, no. 2 (Winter 2013): 429–446.

26. Michal Jan Rozbicki, *Culture and Liberty in the Age of the American Revolution* (Charlottesville and London: University of Virginia Press, 2013), 165–178.

27. Abebe, "The Relevance of African Culture in Building Modern Institutions and the Quest for Legal Pluralism," 444–445.

28. Lefort, *The Political Forms of Modern Society: Bureaucracy, Democracy, Totalitarianism* (Cambridge: The MIT Press, 1986), 297.

29. Michele Graziadei, "On Learning from the Past: Universalism and Message Adaptation in Intercultural Translation," paper presented at the "Human Rights in Translation: Intercultural Pathways" conference at Saint Louis University, St. Louis, 2016.

30. Quoted in Richard Davy, "Helsinki Myths: Setting the Record Straight on the Final Act of the CSCE, 1975," *Cold War History* 9, no. 1 (2009): 7, 9.

31. See Glendon, "The Rule of Law in the Universal Declaration of Human Rights," 25.

32. On human dignity in non-Western conceptions of human rights, see Jack Donnelly, "Human Rights and Human Dignity: An Analytic Critique of Non-Western Conceptions of Human Rights," *The Political Science Review* 76, no. 2 (June 1982): 303–316.

33. On fictions, see Martin Jay, *The Virtues of Mendacity: On Lying in Politics* (Charlottesville and London: University of Virginia Press, 2010), 179–180.

34. Amartya Sen, *The Idea of Justice* (Cambridge: Harvard University Press, 2009), 387.

35. Lynn Hunt, *Inventing Human Rights: A History*, 19–31.

36. On eclecticism, see Patrick Chabal and Jean Pascal Daloz, *Culture Troubles: Politics and the Interpretation of Meaning* (Chicago: The University of Chicago Press, 2006), 309–310.

Chapter 2

Human Rights against Human Rights

Universal Declaration of Human Rights, Interpretive Discrepancies, and Intercultural Transpositions

Mario Ricca

HUMAN RIGHTS AND THE ACHIEVEMENT OF A LEGAL INTERCULTURAL GRAMMAR: DEFECTIVE REASONS

The early modern view on human rights identified them mainly with freedom and liberties. These were intended as features inherent to the natural and legal subject. Subsequently, the idea of social opportunities guaranteed by law sprung from the claims for freedom, and these were, in turn, considered as prerequisites for the democratic process. So, the universal right to political participation completed, in the end, the circle of modern legal constitutional subjectivity. Such movements along the pathways of rights converge into a broader and deeper process that coincides with the objectification of the Western sociopolitical subject. It was a dialogical cultural process, which comprised manifold interactions and dynamics of integration among people belonging to different classes, faiths, and ethnicities all across the world.[1] The contexts of signification and the combination of factors that fostered the genesis of human and/or fundamental rights and the increasing claims to them (as well as for the related institutional implementations) are to be found within this process. In this regard, it is to be observed that during the initial germination and advancing of human rights, individual prerogatives cannot be immediately and concretely envisaged as ends or practical patterns existing prior to the actual development of political integration (this is true even if this sort of ontological preexistence constitutes the axis of a rhetorical presentation of human rights). Concrete individual prerogatives are outcomes of political integration and its unfolding.

If considered along the historical pathway of their recognition, human and/or fundamental rights take the shape of processive ends, that is, semiotic means that—if skillfully and conveniently invoked—can trigger and legitimate the above dynamics of political and institutional integration. In other words, human rights cannot be read as predefined horizons of subjectivity, as such capable of aprioristically including all possible features and projections. On the contrary, every assertion or statement designed to claim or establish rights must relativize its linguistic absoluteness or universality. This is because rights enunciations have come to terms with a particular social context made of uses, symbols, and economical as well as technological constraints. Only the interactions with all these factors will shape, through a synergic relationship, the fashion and the sense of the subjectivities (legally) connoted by the "holding of human and/or fundamental rights." But the means for the fulfillment and achievement of rights differ according to the various cultural contexts. Consequently, the difference of means diversely situates and influences the signification of rights and ends. This is nothing but the means/ends dialectic that determines the processes of reification, something that the fulfillment of rights cannot easily escape.[2]

The issue of human rights' reification can serve as a sort of stress test to assess the distance between a multicultural and an intercultural approach to law. The multicultural reading of human and/or fundamental rights seems to be doomed to keeping a great distance from the sociopolitical integration processes mentioned above. It tends to ossify cultural differences in its attempt to maintain them in a condition of reciprocal isolation and non-contamination. But, in so doing, the multicultural legal gaze runs the risk of implicitly—sometimes even covertly—decontextualizing the alleged cultural difference of individual claims. Taken in this sort of conceptual isolation, the cultural difference, precisely because it is overtly claimed and recognized, alters the progressivity of any ongoing processes toward the composition of a pluralistic, democratic, and constitutional subjectivity in a way that is merely episodic and unsettled. Conversely, the generation of an intercultural grammar requires a deep interaction between the different social voices on the ground. An interactive dialogue and comparison should be focused on the center of the subject's constitutive meanings, and it needs to be sufficiently rich and open to allow a genuine processes of translation and integration among the different cultural viewpoints. By contrast, the assumption that human and/or fundamental rights hold an inherent ability to shape the meaning of social subjectivity is equivalent to transforming them into a sort of political and linguistic mallet. If so intended and used, rights statements will inevitably end up engendering apodictic stances or, in any case, growing impenetrable lines of conflict incompatible with any real perspective of dialogue.

And yet, claims and demands for recognition of culturally connoted prerogatives are constantly expanding. What is more, these requests often conflict with the legal categories that comprise the different branches of the Western law tradition (private law, penal law, etc.). In many cases, Western states and their legal systems react by flatly rejecting those claims for recognition, and arguing that they diverge from not only the statutory laws and the related institutions but also—through them—human and/or fundamental rights.

In this regard, we can identify two different ways to assess cultural claims and their legal relevance. The first mode of assessment, which could be termed "formal," is in tune with the open potentialities of semantic inclusion inherent in the universalism that resides in "human rights" formulas or other similar expressions. The second mode, which appears more substantial and culturally situated, seems to leave aside the universalism of rights and its ecumenical attitude, and wraps the constitutional signification of rights in the idiomatic traits of cultural orthodoxy. This tendency takes the shape of ethnocentric and aprioristic rationalism which in reality is not much more than a rhetorical device beholden to the exigencies of both identitarian self-preservation, and an indisputable as well as intransigent imposition of dominant group patterns of social and legal subjectivity. Most likely, the difference, emphasized by some scholars,[3] between human rights and constitutional rights comes from these differing ways of reading and considering the legal relevance of claims for recognition raised by cultural and social minorities. In this regard, given that the issue is rather peripheral to the argument of this essay, I would simply argue that any dichotomy between human rights and constitutional rights assumes a sort of ontological difference between local and global, national and international. But this distinction and its precarious historical stability are precisely the critical points from which the current intercultural experience seems to stem. In a circular way, the contemporary emergence of intercultural relationships as an inherent and unavoidable feature of social environments ultimately weakens the theoretical consistency of the distinction between national and transnational, constitutional and human declinations of rights.

I think that the actual *places* or *topics* from which conflicts arise coincide with the categories of subjectivity nestled in quotidian life rather than the abstract provisions or semantic potentialities of human rights.[4] Such categories are the same ones that give rhythm to the "lifeworld" and are coded by the statutory laws of each country. Diversities in such categories and their cultural backgrounds cannot be immediately transposed and projected at the level of human rights and the different conceptions or declinations of freedom, equality, solidarity, and so on. Such a conceptual displacement would be merely irresponsible and uncritical, the product of a deep cultural blindness and superficiality as well as a huge hindrance to any future peaceful coexistence. Rather, all of us have to grasp how the traditional distinctions between rights and institutional organizations, constitutions and statutory laws, and human rights and "common laws," inevitably change their signification if viewed from the perspective of intercultural experiences. The contemporary advent of social multiculturality caused the semantic and social cells previously underlying those distinctions to be filled with new meanings and expectations. These transformations are due to a deep, and even essential, transmutation of the overall social ground and the related cultural, economic, and political roles that its actors play within it. Consequently, we have to face a metamorphosis of social fabric that should be understood in qualitative terms, and not just through the demographic, quantitative tools of analysis.

The variation of the above legal distinctions along with the significance and effectiveness, let alone consistency, of their practical implications together cause dysfunction in the pluralistic patterns of coexistence among differences based on tolerance and privatization of individual diversities. It should be stressed again that the consequence of increasing cultural differences within our social fabric is that individual habits can no longer be considered to be peripheral with respect to the "semantic formants" of social life and its related legal categories. Conversely, the transformation of social landscapes (not infrequently caused by the spatial transpositions of people) encapsulates a critical and *estranging* attitude. It has a strong tendency to pierce the heart of the conceptual area that traditionally fostered the cultural, symbolic, and thereby legal structure of subjectivity in each national political context. This is exactly why the tolerance/freedom pairing is no longer efficacious as a general device to defuse the strong critical and conflictive charge of claims for legal recognition and protection arising from the multicultural galaxy.

The aims of such claims for recognition focus on the relational dimension of subjectivity that "scans" quotidian life as contract law, family law, forms of crime, and so on. Besides, the contemporary socio-economical cosmos has dramatically multiplied interdependence among individuals, social groups, and countries so as to increase the reciprocal influences between different and even geographically distant features of quotidian life as well as institutional choices. In this complex and integrated world, it is simply unrealistic to imagine relegating people's different cultural exigencies and connotations to a secluded do-it-yourself area formally secured by the traditional curtain of individual freedom. The attempt of nation states to adopt such a traditional liberal strategy would only raise a kind of smoke screen that maintains ethnocentric and dominant patterns of subjectivity. These patterns reveal themselves to be strongly asymmetrical, increasing every day with regard to the multifaceted symbolic universe seething within the social fabric. This is because they are culturally self-referential and therefore detached, if not even deaf, to the different ways in which people from different cultures and origins decline and represent their social and individual needs.

If nation states continue to engage in such defective strategies to include Otherness, which so far have been carried out with extraordinary ideological tenacity and political radicalism, they will end up fueling the collapse of the circuits of social communication. But this will inevitably bring about forms of contestation, perhaps expressed through unlawful means, against the dominant economic and legal structures. This future is here, it already contributes to the life of democracies everywhere, with all its threats. Only a dramatic cultural blindness makes people unable to see how such a future is with them, well nestled in their present. Terroristic attacks are only isolated waves rising from a whole ocean of psychosocial discomfort and discontent.

I believe that these observations are not merely an empty prophecy about possible dramatic social drifts. They seem to me, instead, the implication of a simple exercise of coherent thinking. I believe that it is nothing but an illusion to think that nation states can defuse the transfiguring impact stemming from the coexistence of cultural diversities only through a repeated implementation of the traditional vocabulary of liberal and tolerant constitutionalism. Those differences conflate ever more intimately and deeply with the circuits of quotidian life of different nation states. Such a conflation is the challenge directly posed by the global integration of economy and information, which inevitably also brings a transformation in the meanings of previous geographical and cultural borders. He who hopes to maintain the national citadels of the more economically advanced countries packed in a sort of vacuum on the inside of their sovereignty is harboring a delusion. This is because these economies—in order to assure their own continuous development and survival—are simultaneously engaged in a planetary distribution of information aimed to showcase goods and trigger a contagion of consumerist fever. Unfortunately, it is nearly impossible to sell goods and attract consumers while simultaneously keeping the latter at a distance. Recent history of capitalism has shown the utter inefficacy of such strategies to preserve the cultural purity of aspiring sellers' social spaces. Market is communication, and communication intrinsically tends to erase borders and spread everywhere. Certainly in the long term, commercial circuits cannot be divided into lots or compartmentalized. The flux of goods and trade-offs comes and goes, in the form of capital investments, but also involves human subjects that bring their symbolic universes with them. These mobile people, then, urge for their cultural, social, political, and legal integration in the host countries.

From a transnational constitutional point of view, market and cultural subalternity prove to be incompatible in the long run. As a consumer, every individual, wherever he is from, has acquired—mainly in psychological terms—an economic, global entitlement to reach the wealthy-country markets. He is, at least potentially, a migrant, and subject—sometimes psy-chosocially impelled—devoted to moving across national borders. But it is precisely this feeling, this dream of becoming economic world-citizens, so typical among contemporary global consumers, that can transform the legal strangeness and non-belonging of mobile people into a perception of social exile. This self-interpretation is, however, a prodromal symptom of an ensu-ing descent toward a fateful identitarian inward withdrawal: the main source of cultural radicalism and fundamentalism. But this kind of psychosocial phenomena is nothing more than the other side of the sociopolitical exclusion inherent to the denial of multilateral recognition and the intercultural transla-tion/transaction of Otherness.

In this scenario, the democratic institutions must absolutely resist the allure of the sirens of the assimilation approach. This political tendency emerges easily from a quick search for massive popular consent fostered by a sense of native cultural superiority: a choice, in the end, as irreflexive as it is irresponsible.

The popular question raised by ordinary people facing cultural claims for recognition, namely, "why should we, the nation, change?" should be responded to firmly asserting that this question—as well as other similar critical queries of this kind—is affected by a methodological flaw consisting in the personal pronoun "we." The identification of such a "we" with only those who allegedly belong to the nation or Western society has now become dangerously asymmetrical because of the current demographic and cultural changes within these states. The conditions that allowed for the political declination of the pronoun "we" as a synonym for national belonging to a homogeneous cultural strain or a dominant group seem to be a phenomenon of the past in most countries. Conditions have changed as a result of a meta-morphosis that has occurred on a planetary scale, which in turn requires an adequate "upgrading" of our cultural, political, symbolic, and legal templates. In its signification and scope, such a renewal should be gauged on the same geo-cultural dimensions of the phenomena by which it is prompted. The "we" that the fathers of European natural law theory were able to draw out from the Roman/Christian cultural and legal tradition is now obsolete. It proved to be incomplete and thereby unfit to meet the cultural exigencies and identities of non-Western people in the age of colonization and ended up being used as an instrument to legitimate plunder and exploitation. Today, the same "we" and its Western/Christian semantic declinations fail to reflect and include all the cultural subjectivities that populate the social landscape of these very democracies. At the same time, however, if taken as an abstract sociopolitical device, the modern idea of construing a "we," however multifaceted, urgently needs to be updated, relying upon cultural languages and religious traditions from all over the world. In this sense, a timely renewing of the semantic substance of the collective political "we" should be an aspiration and a commitment for all countries and peoples, whether they belong to the West or "the Rest." But in order for this updating to be real, each existing "we" must undertake a widespread process of reciprocal recognition and translation. Such a task, however, must be prior and not merely subsequent to the explosion of conflicts on a global scale. Unfortunately, all of us can see the early signs—and perhaps even something more—of a global cultural implosion. I think that it is to be considered as both cause and effect, stemming from the epochal breakdown of nation states' political order and the (already precarious) international economic (dis-)equilibrium it has produced so far.[5] Are we, whatever "we" might mean, ready to face such a huge transformation? Do we have the cognitive tools to invent and mold a global subjectivity capable of including cultural differences at an international scale as well as within local circuits of coexistence?

People cannot feel free when they are compelled to construe the meaning of their social life within a social cosmos that disregards their cultural codes and looks at them with self-righteous tolerance. When liberal democratic societies produce such psychosocial conditions, then they are betraying their own political prerequisites and the axiological assumption for their legitimacy. The recipe of liberalism cannot be passed off as a culture-based device of inequality and still preserve its ideal consistency. Cultural differences cannot be recognized merely by means of their relegation to the domain of private subjectivity. It would be nothing but a camouflaged conviction if people from different cultures or belonging to religious minorities were to spend their lives in a secluded area for the private exercise of freedom. Such conditions would be largely equivalent to a destiny of institutional irrelevance.

Subjectivity, even in its most solitary declinations, presupposes and consists of relationships and communication. A regime of freedom that is culturally amputated is bound to create only segregation and ghettoization at both a quantitative and a qualitative level, and as such is not sustainable in the long term. For all these reasons, the political agencies of nation states should urgently *invent* and provide a way to integrate the different kinds of subjectivity proposed by people from different cultures, through efforts that need to be carried out at anthropological and legal depths. To be actually accomplished, this task requires a cognitive/cultural attitude aimed at understanding and translating Otherness. It requires, however, taking into account the legal implications of Others' way of life, their habits and patterns of categorization. Combining cognitive and legal tools is an essential step to ensure that the processes of recognition and inclusion do not remain—as is all too often the case—devoid of any effectiveness. The target of a peaceful and fair coexistence among different cultural subjectivities cannot be achieved only by a generic readiness for political negotiation or through the accommodation of the various claims on the ground. Without knowledge it is impossible to understand Otherness. But without understanding it is impossible to translate, recognize, and supply effective protection for the "right reasons of difference."

A METHOD FOR THE INTERCULTURAL TRANSPOSITION OF HUMAN RIGHTS THROUGH THE SPECTRUM OF ARTICLE 30 OF THE UNIVERSAL DECLARATION OF HUMAN RIGHTS (UDHR)

A deep interpenetration between anthropological knowledge and legal skillfulness is the premise for the construction of a peaceful social coexistence under the law. In our age of increasing intercultural encounters and exchanges, law used without anthropological support runs the risk of remaining blind to people's real expectations and claims; anthropology without a legal awareness of its possible and actual implications runs the risk of remaining deaf to people's actual needs and their ability to make sense of their own lives. The lack of such a reciprocal "contamination" could transform both law and anthropology into cognitively and pragmatically crippled domains. Human Rights discourse, especially, demands a deep connection with quotidian life imaginaries and languages, but this is impossible to achieve without casting our gaze just where law and various anthropological habits converge in giving rhythm to people's experience.[6]

Interdisciplinary as well as intercultural translations and transductions are key ingredients for using human rights as "processive" horizons to produce (rather than merely to implement supposedly prior) new thresholds of an inclusive and non-essentialized universality. In other words, I think and hope that a combined anthropological and legal effort could finally help further the idea that universality is to be intended as the outcome of an aware and polyphonic exercise of human beings' creative cultural competence rather than as a synthesis from preexisting and, therefore, "cosified" cultures. This possibility includes, of course, historical awareness, without which it would be impossible to manage, negotiate, and transform one's own cultural "know how." I think that a very useful starting point to promote such creative approaches to universality (or better, the processes of universalization) could be a critical reading of an often-overlooked article of the Universal Declaration of Human Rights. Specifically, I refer to Article 30:

> Nothing in this Declaration may be interpreted as implying for any State, group or person any right to engage in any activity or to perform any act aimed at the destruction of any of the rights and freedoms set forth herein.

This is clearly a recursive and self-referential statement.[7] But, what are the authentic rights and the non-self-negating interpretations of articles included in the Declaration itself? *Res de re non predicatur*: Abelardo said. On the other hand, if questioned, the written word remains majestically silent. The Universal Declaration is not able to interpret itself. Nonetheless, the written word is a sign, and like all signs, is to be questioned and interpreted. But what interrogates a sign is, in turn, a sign, which is further questioned by the same sign that is to be interpreted. So, the true question is: who or what is being questioned by the Declaration?

The paradoxical recursivity of the whole Declaration, if read in light of its last, tautological article (precisely the 30th), can be unraveled only through an external factor. But the only way to avert the arbitrariness and partisan bent of external interpretations (namely, interpretant signs[8]) is to give voice to all the potential subjects called into play by the proclaimed universality of the Declaration. However, this multiplication of anthropological voices implies their reciprocal translation, mirrored in the semantic potentialities of human rights. To achieve such a level of translatability, the interpretants' voices must be *dis-composed* by narratively opening the connotative land-scapes that underlie their morphological aspects. This means that culturally based behaviors, symbolic expressions, and discourses that can be potentially inscribed in human rights and translated by using rights provisions as meta-phorical interfaces should be de-articulated in their connotative elements and then creatively re-composed and interculturally synthetized.[9] This is the only way to attain a universality that is co-construed within a horizon of sense that holds the potential to be used as a renewed ground for a peaceful coexistence among diversities and cultural differences.

A powerful pattern for carrying out a process of connotative *dis-composition* and its intercultural re-composition can be found in the cumulative heritage of four modern painters: Paul Gauguin, Juan Gris, Paul Klee, and Alberto Savinio. Further down in this chapter, I will analyze the ways in which the cognitive methods of this artistic avant-garde and their intercultural inspirations (from African, Asian, and American traditional artistic styles), and especially Paul Klee's work, can suggest the use of human rights in an intercultural way so as to face, through inclusive interpretation, the contemporary challenge of coexistence among cultures.

In order to trace a path of interpenetration between a legal-anthropological logic and an artistic logic through the experience of twentieth-century avant-garde painters, it is useful to first focus on the reasoning, the epistemological ground of this kind of parallel, and the related inter-semiotic translation across these two different domains. The point of departure coincides precisely with the conflicts of interpretation regarding human and/or fundamental rights statements. The 30th article referenced above implicitly, even if they are passed off as implementations of human rights, the eventuality of these conflicts. Its text states that anti-humanitarian activities or behaviors cannot be inscribed within the hermeneutical frame of the rights provided by the Universal Declaration. Such a provision, if it is to make sense, must necessarily exclude any semantic self-evidence of the statements on rights. Otherwise, how can we conclude that something preordered to destroy those rights could be (allegedly) categorized as an implementation of the same statements providing them? Excluding semantic self-evidence (in opposition to the maxim: *in claris non fit interpretatio*) implies, however, ambiguity, or better polysemy. But, ambiguity and polysemy are, in turn, consequences of the semantic vagueness of every generalization, even more so when it aspires to universality. Nonetheless, if a statement is vague, the assessment that something contrasts with it cannot be immediately obvious simply because of its morphological discrepancy. Quite the opposite, that evidence or obviousness is the conclusion, the final outcome of a hermeneutical process carried on creatively and according to axiological options. To put it differently, what is considered to be inside the category of "human rights" and what outside constitutes a divide that cannot stem from a formalistic distinction, somehow *more geometrico demonstrata.*

Yet, the law requires certainty (at least to a certain degree). Diversely, it loses its normativity; or worse, it legally legitimates a paradoxical anomic drift. This is why, inter alia, human rights, as every other statement endowed with constitutional efficacy, are assumed as the highest indexes, apical domes, or criteria of legal systems intended as hierarchical structures. They dwell on top of such deontic structures, while the social conducts remain at the base; in the middle, there is the whole discursive-pragmatic set of legal statements and behaviors relevant to law's application. He who intends to adopt a specific behavior and put forward claims for recognition can do so by invoking the law and, through a multilayered action sequence, reach the apex of the legal system within which he acts. Inscribing one's own behaviors within the semantic borders of human rights statements offers significant advantages relative to other kinds of claim strategies. Sometimes, such an advantage can even underpin criticism of the current legal system and, in this way, provoke the annulment or disapplication of the legal provision that contrasts with the claims made. However, the possibility of reaching such a significant outcome inevitably triggers many "desires," and therefore conflicts. Everyone will try to legitimate his own claims by inscribing them inside the semantic spectrum of national and international statements on human and/or fundamental rights. This race for humanitarian legitimacy, often evoking the natural law theory of rights, can engender distortions.[10] Even if the problem is, in this case, the separation of the wheat from the chaff.

The aim of avoiding incorrect exploitations and manipulations of human rights is surely both plausible and legitimate. The danger at stake, however, is precisely that of defining in the same inappropriate way what is to be assumed as a standard of authenticity in the interpretation of those rights. In our world, so culturally plural and populated by innumerable possibilities to decline the "human," it is all too likely that he who is different is marked as distorted or deviant. Besides, the virus of power can also find a home inside the body of human rights' hermeneutics. Power may manifest itself in the form of ethnocentrism or, more simply, take the guise of the cultural and political predominance of dominant groups. In this case, the danger that human rights statements are read through the eyes of the strongest subjects can produce a dialectic implication involving universality. This implication appears, often insidiously, through a metonymic inversion. Dominant groups or cultures assume their own interpretation of human rights statements, situated within their particular frameworks of experience and the related schemes of legal formalization, as if it were the necessary prototype of any possible implementation of those rights. Through this rhetorical device, the more powerful social actors end up passing off identification with the dominant group as universality. So, they transform their culturally rooted way of declining rights into the only semantic possibility in the related statements. In other words, they move (pass off) from the particular to the universal. The overall effect of this rhetorical substitution has been and remains dramatic. Human rights lose their inclusive bent and become, instead, a means to exclude, marginalize, and stigmatize Otherness.[11] This occurs because, as a consequence of the sleight of hand operated through the above metonymical substitution, anything found to be out of tune with the dominant prototype of human rights implementation can be labeled as inhuman.[12]

This rhetoric of exclusion takes shape through the reification of morphological appearances of claims for recognition and the related behaviors, words, symbols, and so on. What appears as morphologically different from the patterns of behaviors, the "knowing how to do"—that is, culture—of dominant groups or cultural circuits is now qualified as contrasting with human rights. The comparison is carried by means of a misleading (and sometimes shrewd) use of the hierarchical higher-level positioning of human rights statements. Actually, the real, formal, and morphological paradigm at work when the Others' customs are deemed illegitimate coincides with the dominant culture's habits.[13]

Within such games of hermeneutical tactics, the morphological appearance of "diversities" and the related claims for recognition are presented as data connoted by immediate evidence and universal perceptibility: in short, as objective facts. However, the key issue is that morphological appearance is not a datum but rather an outcome, precisely the conclusion of hermeneutical processes developed on the basis of a specific cultural point of view and by means of culturally connoted schemes of categorization.[14] Being unaware of the processive connotation of morphological objectifications necessarily dooms any effort intended to translate and, thereby, understand Otherness.

Averting such partisan misuses of human rights interpretation and assuring an equitably balanced implementation of Article 30 of UDHR requires a translational practice that is more knowledgeable and skilled from a semiotic and intercultural point of view. This implies, to begin with, that human rights should be situated along a process of translation between cultural differences. They should be used not so much as hierarchical axes, according to a systemic and semantic logic of pyramidal organization, but rather as interfaces of translation among the different connotative sets underlying words, behavior, claims of social actors.[15] The axiological and teleological ingredients encapsulated inside statements on rights can work, then, as metaphorical ground to manage transactional translations. And within legal language, these, in turn, can find their discursive platform as well as a socio-institutional instrument capable of giving their practical implications a concrete effectiveness.

To make all this possible, the work of intercultural translation is to be set by considering the following three channels, here logically distinguished and articulated—even if in practice they will operate almost simultaneously: (1) crossing narratives; (2) intercultural cross-contextualizations; (3) translations/transactions.[16]

Crossing narratives are helpful to bring to the surface the semantic/connotative landscape underlying single words or behaviors. This can support the avoidance of stereotyping attitudes, and readings of Otherness that have been forged exclusively in accordance with one's own schemes of judgment and cognition. The interpretation of narratives, in turn, constitutes the *sequel*, an ensuing process of that which each narrative represents in itself: that is, an engendering of history (through stories) as an inner consequence of the encounter with Other.[17] When mirrored in Otherness, everyone reflexively *recognizes* (namely, *again and anew*) herself/himself. It is a creative recognition, a result of the crossing between different experiential contexts and the generation—also by virtue of symbolic tools—of a new pragmatic and semantic context. When all of this occurs, then a *third* subjectivity begins to take shape. Inside this *thirdness*, just as in a metaphor, the connotative elements dug up and unveiled by means of the crossed narrative processes are re-composed so as to produce transactional translations. In these kinds of metaphorical transductions,[18] something *gets lost*, but something else is simultaneously *gained* (rather than merely "found"). The loss is to be considered, however, as an inner, dynamic, and instrumental aspect of the invention of a *third world*.

In order to select the connotation that is to be re-composed, metaphorical ground plays a crucial function. It comprises often axiological, qualitative, emotional, and teleological categories. This is because such categories are *plastic*, that is, capable of extending over and working across categorical analytical sets that might appear very distant when viewed morphologically. Now, human rights can serve as a horizontal interface/transducer for translation at the very moment when the process of intercultural translation between the habits of people from different cultures is taking shape. They—as noted above—will act as situated factors of semantic correspondence between connotative landscapes that are already dynamically interplaying. The axiological and teleological aspects, encapsulated in every enunciation about rights, will work, then, as a metaphorical ground. In this way, behaviors or symbols that are morphologically distant can converge; just as many behaviors or symbols that are morphologically close or analogous may prove to be pragmatically unrelated and semantically discontinuous.[19]

Article 30 of the UDHR and its application constitutes a sort of test case for intercultural translation; but, at the same time, this kind of translation can be seen as an indispensable means to avert exploitive, misleading, ethnocentric, and discriminatory uses of the same Article 30. Actually, if divorced from a situated intercultural translation of claims for recognition and the related interpretations of human rights, the vagueness of UDHR statements could render them senseless rather than productive. In this way, these rights enunciations could become a means of exclusion rather than of inclusion: they could become motors of morphological/symbolic/identitarian rigidity rather than cognitively creative dialogue. In short, to understand whether a claim and its related interpretation of human rights' statements embodies "disruptive implications" to the "substance" of the UDHR, the interpreters must look beyond its morphological appearance and features (as forged by each of the interpreting parties). Only in this way will the *production of universality* be possible. Besides, only if *universality* is assumed as a horizon, and thereby as a processive means, can it anticipate inclusion and avoid, instead, ethnocentric misuses and essentializing declinations of its iconic significance.

Despite possible expectations, when the process of universalization is grafted onto a legal dimension—as occurs in the case of human rights—it has the potential to improve the recognition of cultural differences through what can be designated from a semantic point of view as "categorical migration." The first move in this direction is that every legal statement conveys and indicates an "ought." This, in turn, is based on values. To put it clearly, something is to be made just because making it is considered to be good. Without such an axis of legitimation, deontic statements would be self-contradictory. "What is good to do," on the other hand, constitutes the minimal definition of "value." Values are the *clothes* of emotions and qualitative judgments. And, as shown above, axiological and qualitative categories are characterized by an idiomatic plasticity. Unlike descriptive and empirical categories—to the extent that they are viewed in analytical terms, namely through a checklist of properties and connotative elements—axiological-qualitative categories are endowed with a trans-categorical signification.

However, the checklists of descriptive-analytical categories are also, somehow, based on values. The decision about what is inside or outside a category is not an analytical determination but rather an axiological choice, and as such, is based on cognitive, ethical, esthetical values. So, the ability to grasp the axiological component inherent in rights statements can help to remold descriptive/empirical categories and, as a consequence, those schemes already forged to universalize experience and its phenomenal elements. This achievement can be reached, precisely, through the analysis of crossing inter-cultural narratives. Often the narratives and semiotic-relational webs underlying individual behaviors or words that are initially deemed morphologically incompatible instead show similar connotative features. The emersion of such continuities can produce the collapsing-in-on-themselves of the same descriptive-categorical assumptions responsible for previous incompatibilities. As a result, the justifications for maintaining the original categorical borders could also become insufficient. Such hermeneutical work can pave the way to the possibility of including Otherness and its features within the same categories that were previously considered to be inconsistent with them, and vice versa, perhaps even excluding what was previously taken to be compatible with or constitutive of the categorical checklist. The overall operation, moreover, will have practical effects. The guarantee of such effectiveness will be assured by the normativity of law. We can say, therefore, that an intercultural use of human rights, when grafted on processes of intercultural translation, allows for the forging of universalization, which is, ultimately, nothing but the source of sense.

The hermeneutical activity sketched out above might appear, perhaps, too creative and, therefore, at risk for anomic drift. Such anomie, however, can also be considered to be a predictable consequence of categorical rigidity and underlying schemes of judgment, precisely because these are often wielded as defense weapons against the changes imposed by experience. However, barricading ourselves in the shadows of forms forged in the past brings about nothing but the loss of their predictive potentialities. The heterogenesis of ends and meanings is the almost "assured" consequence that ensues from such a refusal of pragmatic dialectics, that is, what we could term—echoing a Bachelardian notion—as interculturally applied rationalism.[20]

In a world of radical change, creativity may be a risk, but it is a necessary one. There is no alternative to it. Otherwise we would be in danger of losing the crucial nexus between law and social meaning, rules, and subjects. This connection requires that legal knowledge be considered and practiced as an art: what could be considered, inter alia, as a sort of renewed follow-up on the idea of *ars iuris* that inspired the legal experience within the western ancient Roman tradition. An idea efficaciously synthetized by the definition of legal knowledge as *iuris prudential*, that is, an exercise of prudence and the sophisticated art of modulating its implications according to concrete life experiences.

INTERCULTURAL DIS-COMPOSITIONS AND RE-COMPOSITIONS OF CULTURAL HABITS BEYOND THEIR MORPHOLOGICAL APPEARANCES: EPISTEMOLOGICAL SUGGESTIONS FROM THE TWENTIETH-CENTURY ARTISTIC AVANT-GARDE

A sort of inter-semiotic toolkit for intercultural translation can be found in the cognitive paths traced by avant-garde artists, especially painters, in the late-nineteenth century and early twentieth century. The driving force behind avant-garde painting research can be considered a reaction against Impressionism. The subjectivist anti-realism approach of the Impressionists, in direct opposition to the perspectival-realist school that had developed after the Renaissance, drew a parabola, which soon led to the search for objective criteria underlying human perception. Assuming perception to be a phenomenological event resulting from a dynamic interpenetration between world and mind, the avant-garde movement followed the notion of *genetic determinants* giving rise to "the perceived." The result was an idiomatic commitment, an ideal and practical attitude toward dis-composing forms, that is, appearances taken in their *morphological fashion.*

The crumbling of the natural form and its usual meanings is achieved by virtue of representations that dis-compose, disaggregate, or factorize the connotative elements of images. This outcome is pursued either through figurative simplifications inspired by primitive art or the decontextualization of images and, as an alternative, a disarticulated/fragmented representation of their connotative components.

To illustrate the *common thinking* underlying intercultural translation and twentieth-century avant-garde artists, I have chosen select works from four painters: Paul Gauguin, Juan Gris, Paul Klee, and Alberto Savinio.

In Gauguin's paintings we can recognize the categorical crumbling produced by the juxtaposition of figurative elements belonging to different cultural, naturalistic or narrative contexts. As happens in our dreams, Gauguin shows us heteroclite fragments to trigger in the observer's mind a process of decontextualization of forms and figures. In this way, every portrayed object is engulfed in a sort of metaphorical vertigo.[21] Therefore, everything can, at the same time, signify something else and move across different categorical circuits. What supports such a process is the breaking free of connotative elements from predefined contextual frames established by and within specific cultural habits. But as soon as the connotative elements lose the link of semantic implications with a specific category and/or context of signification, they become potentially ubiquitous and omnipresent. As such, they serve as bridging factors, transducers of sense, liable to give rise to a process of categorical regeneration and new semantic synthesis. The paintings of Gauguin spur the observer's mind to operate connotative reworkings by means of markedly intercultural combinations and transposition. They are static representations only in appearance. On the contrary, they are designed to re-origin through their dynamic relation with the observer, the creation of new meanings, a new sense of the world.

The pioneering paths of Gauguin inspire, subsequently, Cubism and its different stages.[22] Echoing—as is well known—the *warnings* of Cézanne, who invited the painters to grasp *the real*, to be represented in constants and their geometrical features, Cubism opens the way to a connotative-perspectival *dis-composition* assumed as an interpretive criterion to analyze and portray the constitutive elements of every perceived form. Juan Gris, even more than Picasso or Braque, makes dis-compositions that unfold to synthetic re-compositions of new forms and meanings.[23] His paintings appear easily intelligible. This immediate but only apparent intelligibility—so much more pronounced than in Picasso's figurative dis-compositions—is, however, a result of the coordination of pure geometrical forms, assumed in a sort of Platonic fashion. Gris used to say that if Cézanne started from reality, with the aim of representing and rendering it to the observer as something reduced and transfigured in geometrical forms, he begins with geometrical forms to obtain, by means of their combination, recognizable images resembling the forms of living experience. Gris was somehow trying to have access to a sort of connotative-semantic repository, as if it enshrined the *building material* of the Platonic demiurge, to engender forms, to invite the observer to see the forms while they were still taking shape. Gris' synthetic representations actually remain open.[24] His images and figurations *are and are not* those which one might recognize at first.

This sort of saying but not saying, affirming and simultaneously veiling, are the constitutive canon of Paul Klee's conception of art. He thought that the main purpose of art was to make visible the invisible. But this is possible—he argued—only by putting in motion pictorial figuration through the active participation of the observer's mind. Klee's paintings bring to the surface the polyphony of connotative elements that lay beneath the form: which, in turn, is intended as a result, the conclusion of a hermeneutical/constitutive process ordered to produce sense.[25] Klee's influence on phenomenological thought (above all Heidegger and Merleau-Ponty) was remarkable.[26] He thought the artist's main commitment was as an educator. When the painting is observed,[27] the figurative transfiguration must be aimed to trigger the process of *Gestaltung*: a sort of writing of the world, a path of *re-origination* capable of showing reality as *forma formans* and not only, *figuratively*, as a *forma formata*. In Klee's poetics, the artist is committed to usher the observer into the forging of the world and its forms, giving him the creative pleasure of conjoining Heaven and Earth through the rite of re-categorization to which he is invited. Also in this case, the dis-composition is not static but rather designated to promote a dynamic movement.[28] Klee's works are as *sheets of notes*, almost recognizable figures barely sketched out, a door ajar toward the staging of semantic genesis, endlessly repeated, hence the constant regeneration of the world's sense.

My inter-semiotic overview concludes with Alberto Savinio. Brother of the more famous Giorgio De Chirico, he also inscribed his poetics along the lines of symbolism and the related tendency to juxtapose figures (objects, buildings, landscapes, individuals) apparently unrelated from a semantic point of view. However, the relationship extant between De Chirico and Savinio is somehow equivalent to that which is recognizable between Picasso and Gris. The former two dis-compose the forms (Picasso) or juxtapose them in a dystonic or heteroclite fashion (De Chirico); the latter two re-compose images starting from connotative singularities (Gris) or by means of a combination between real and well-known figures and fantastic elements (Savinio). Specifically, in Savinio the "fantastic" unfolds, as in a Bachelardian *rêverie*, the implicit semantic potentialities encapsulated within each categorical connotative set.[29] His iconic representations open the doors to a virtual maze of interpretations, re-configurations, re-semantizations.[30] In Savinio's paintings, rather than the invisible becoming visible, it is the unpredictable that opens the observer's mind to the regeneration of sense.

The lesson these great artists give us holds a very insightful cognitive meaning. The spectator of paintings—as well as the cultural agent involved in this intercultural relationship—is the co-construing actor of a dynamic *reality*. The painting functions as a mobile interface, a metaphorical fuel that bridges two reciprocal Others by producing a sort of genetic conjunction, a cooperative rewriting of signification and its paths. In the same way, an intercultural use of human rights could promote the elaboration of new traces, new plots of *experience and reality*. The outcome would be a new scenario, within which both the "symbolic" and the "pragmatic" would reciprocally inseminate, so engendering a new world obtained by writing, painting, and figuring new shapes of experience, the *real* that inhabits and makes itself throughout history. All of this would constitute, in other words, an open synthesis between word and object, minds and worlds, and natures and cultures.[31] But this would be also nothing but a "becoming," utterly in tune with the dialectics of sense, of the same human rights (epigones of natural rights), and the relations between the manifold natures generated by culture, indeed by the inner cultural and thus plural nature of human action. The paintings of the four artists cited above are, in a sense, like human rights statements. Both constitute discursive platforms, possible horizons of signification, semantic agendas that serve as means and thereby processive ends to draw polyphonically, through the unfolding of interpretive differences and their reciprocal translations, new inscriptions and declinations of sense, new plots of history written through an intercultural interweaving of quotidian life stories.

NOTES

1. See Gurminder K. Bhambhra, *Rethinking Modernity: Postcolonialism and the Sociological Imagination* (New York: Palgrave Macmillan, 2007).

2. See Peter Fitzpatrick, "The Revolutionary Past: Decolonizing Law and Human Rights," *Metodo. International Studies in Phenomenology and Philosophy* 2, no. 1 (2014): 117–133, specifically 127.

3. In this regard, within a vast literature, see Gerald L. Neuman, "Human Rights and Constitutional Rights: Harmony and Dissonance," *Stanford Law Review* 55, no. 5 (May 2003): 1863–1900.

4. I think that the imbrication of human/constitutional rights and "common civil rights" in Western legal experience is an overlooked feature of the overall problem regarding the contested universality of the former. Ethnocentricity and imperialism contested by the people from other cultures against the human rights discourse is a consequence of their interpretation and use: an interpretation but not the only possible one. Doubtless, human rights are a historically and geographically placed product. Their language shows its cultural wrinkles, for example, in the prevalence of the struggle for individuality and freedom. However, this does not definitively exclude their possible transposition and translation across cultures. Western people too have a long way to go in their discovery of the semantic potentialities of human rights. This is because such rights are simultaneously ends and means for human coexistence. In the same vein, I would like to emphasize how the semantic ambiguity of human rights language can allow for their intercultural use as metaphorical interfaces. In any case, for some examinations of the incompatibility of Western human rights and their cultural bent with other cultures' imageries and categories (especially regarding the oppositional couples subject/community, freedom/solidarity, etc.) see Brian Tierney, *The Idea of Natural Rights: Studies on Natural Rights, Natural Law, and Church Law 1550–1625* (Grand Rapids, Michigan – Cambridge, U.K.: Eerdmans, 1997); Cowan et al., eds., *Culture and Rights: Anthropological Perspectives*; Upendra Baxi, *The Future of Human Rights* (Oxford: Oxford University Press, 2002); Bonaventura de Sousa Santos, "Toward a Multicultural Conception of Human Rights," in *Moral Imperialism: A Critical Anthology*, ed. Berta Hernández-Truyol (New York: New York University Press, 2002), 44–45; Mark Goodale and Sally Engle Merry, eds., *The Practice of Human Rights: Tracking Law between the Global and the Local*

(Cambridge: Cambridge University Press, 2007); Stephen Hopgood, *The Endtimes of Human Rights* (Ithaca: Cornell University Press, 2013).

5. See Santos, "Toward a Multicultural Conception," 40.

6. Some interesting suggestions regarding the relationships between human rights signification and everyday life can be found, from different disciplinary standpoints, in Jim Ife, "Cultural Relativism and Community Activism," in *Challenges in Human Rights: A Social Work Perspective*, ed. Elizabeth Reickert (New York – Chichester (West Sussex): Columbia University Press, 2007), 86 ff., 90 ff.; Joseph A. Indaimo, *The Self, Ethics and Human Rights: Lacan, Levinas & Alterity* (Abingdon, Oxon – New York: Routledge, 2015); Mark Goodale, "Human Rights and Moral Agency," in *Human Rights: The Hard Questions*, eds. Cindy Holder and David Reidy (Cambridge: Cambridge University Press, 2013), 420 ff.; Sally Engle Merry, "Translational Human Rights and Local Activism: Mapping the Middle," in *Dialogues on Human Rights and Legal Pluralism*, eds. René Provost and Colleen Sheppard (Dordrecht – Heidelberg – New York – London: Springer, 2013), 207 ff.; Roderick A. Macdonald, "Pluralistic Human Rights? Universal Human Wrongs?" in *Dialogues on Human Rights and Legal Pluralism*, eds. René Provost and Colleen Sheppard (Dordrecht – Heidelberg – New York – London: Springer, 2013), 15 ff.; Liette Gilbert and Mustafa Dikeç, "Right to the City," in *Space, Difference, Everyday Life: Reading Henry Lefebvre*, eds. Kanishka Goonewardena, Stefan Kipfen, Richard Milgrom, and Christian Schmid (Abingdon, Oxon – New York: Routledge, 2008), 260–261.

7. The self-recursivity of art. 30 of UDHR is stressed by Torkel Opsahl and Vojin Dimitrijevic "Articles 29 and 30," in *The Universal Declaration of Human Rights: A Common Standard of Achievement*, eds. Gurdmundur S. Alfredsson and Eide Asbjørn (The Hague – Boston – London: Kluwer Law International, 1999), 648 ff.: even if the vicious circle is focused only on the possibility of a declaration of state of emergency. For a historical reconstruction of Art. 30, see Johannes Morsink, *The Universal Declaration of Human Rights: Origins, Draftings, and Intent* (Philadelphia: The University of Pennsylvania Press, 1999), 87 ff., who emphasizes the original connection between the drafting of this statement and the concerns for the possibility that Nazi experience could occur again in re-incarnated forms.

8. The term "sign-interpretant" is to be interpreted in a Peircean sense.

9. On this methodology see Mario Ricca, "Intercultural Law, Interdisciplinary Outlines: Lawyering and Anthropological Expertise in Migration Cases: Before the Courts," in: *www.ec-aiss.it EC. Rivista dell'Associazione italiana di Studi semiotici* (March 3, 2014), 1–53; Mario Ricca, "Errant Law: Spaces and Subjects" (June 30, 2016). Available at SSRN: https://ssrn.com/abstract=2802528 or http://dx.doi.org/10.2139/ssrn.2802528; Ricca, *The Intercultural Use of Human Rights and Legal Chorology* (July 9, 2016), available at SSRN: http://ssrn.com/abstract=2807424.

10. See Costas Douzinas, *The End of Human Rights: Critical Legal Thought and the Turn of the Century* (Oxford – Portland, OR: Hart Publishing, 2000; Başak Çali and Saladin Meckled-García, "Introduction: Human Rights Legalized: Defining, Interpreting, and Implementing an Ideal," in *The Legalization of Human Rights: Multidisciplinary Perspectives on Human Rights and Human Rights Law*, eds. Çali

and Meckled-García (Abingdon – New York: Routledge, 2006), 4. ff.; and "Lost in Translation: The Human Rights Ideal and International Human Rights Law," ibid., 21 ff.

11. See Mario Ricca, *Oltre Babele. Codici per una democrazia interculturale* (Bari: Dedalo, 2008), 114 ff., 126 ff.

12. See Xenia Chryssochoou, *Cultural Diversity: Its Social Diversity* (Malden, MA – Oxford – Carlton, Victoria: Blackwell, 2004).

13. As regards this slippage toward a discriminatory use of human rights and their (alleged) universality, see the collected essays edited by Tom Campbell, Keith D. Ewing, and Adam Tomkins, eds., *Sceptical Essays on Human Rights* (Oxford: Oxford University Press, 2003) and András Sajó, ed., *Human Rights with Modesty: The Problem of Universalism* (Leiden-Boston: Martinus Nijhoff Publishers, 2004).

14. An anthropological approach to this argument can be traced, in an enormous and multidisciplinary body of literature, in Michael Jackson, *Introduction:* "Phenomenology, Radical Empiricism, and Anthropological Critique," in *Things as They Are: New Directions in Phenomenological Anthropology*, ed. Michael Jackson (Bloomington – Indianapolis: Indiana University Press, 1996), 1 ff.

15. Ricca, "Errant Law."

16. A complete and broader discussion of these three steps of the intercultural translation/transaction can be found in Ricca, *Oltre Babele*, 216 ff.

17. As regards the encounter with Otherness as an event that is the source of stories and history, see the beautiful essay by Wolfgang Iser, "Coda to the Discussion," in *The Translatability of Cultures: Figurations of the Space Between*, eds. Sanford Budick and Wolfgang Iser (Stanford, CA: Stanford University Press, 1996), 294 ff.

18. I use the term "transduction"—from which the qualification of human rights as intercultural transducers comes—because it fits very well with the semantic and cross-contextual transformation that every translation between cultures implies. The Oxford Dictionary of English defines "transducer" as "a device that converts variations in a physical quantity, such as pressure or brightness into an electrical signal, or vice versa," and points out the derivation from *Latin trans-ducere* "lead across." More generally, we can say that "transduction" is the conversion of a signal, in a specific form, into another signal that materializes in another form: an example of transduction is the use of the microphone that converts sounds into electrical signals, which in turn are transformed into sounds by amplifiers and loudspeakers. From a semiotic, all-encompassing viewpoint, every sign encapsulates a possible enfolding of energy, which in turn is triggered by the encounter and relationship of that sign with other signs. Cultures can be considered, therefore, as aggregations of signs, so the process of their translation could be understood, in a broad sense, as a transduction. Human rights, in turn, can be considered and used as semantic interfaces and transducers that convey this process of signical transformation.

19. In this regard, see Ricca, "Intercultural Law, Interdisciplinary"; Ricca, "Errant Law"; Ricca, *The Intercultural Use of Human Rights*.

20. Gaston Bachelard, *Le Rationalisme Appliqué* (Paris: PUF, 1969).

21. See, for example, the following sequence of Gauguin's famous paintings: *D'ou Venons Nous, Oue Sommes Nous, Où Allons Nous (1897), The Broding Woman*

(1891), Contes Barbares (1912). In each of them there is a sort of extra-contextual and/or disturbing presence. It gives to the observer the estranging perception that a dystonic blending of forms and elements has taken place within the pictorial frame. The paintings of the four artists discussed here are widely available on the Internet.

22. On Gauguin as a precursor of Cubism, see Mariagrazia Messina, *Paul Gauguin: un esotismo controverso* (Firenze: Firenze University Press, 2006).

23. On Juan Gris, see Paz Gª. Ponce de León, *Juan Gris: La Pasión por el Cubismo* (Madrid: Libsa, 2008). But see also Juan Gris, *Posibilidades de la pintura* (Madrid: Casimiro, 2013 [orig. Paris 1946]).

24. See, for example, the subsequent series of Gris' paintings: *Botellas y cuchillo (1912), La mesa de café (1912), El lavabo (1912), El Velador (1918), Casas de Beaulieu (1918), Caveza de Hombre (1916), Naturaleza muerta con placa (1917), El Reloj (1912), Vista sobre la bahia (1921), La Ventana abierta (1921).*

25. In this regard, Marcia Sá Cavalcante Schuback, "In-between Painting and Music—or, Thinking with Paul Klee and Anton Webern," in *The Philosophical Vision of Paul Klee*, ed. John Sallis (Leiden – Boston: Brill, 2014), 124–125, makes some very insightful remarks: "Klee is not preoccupied in drawing lines but in drawing the drawing of lines. This drawing of the drawing shows that for him the question is not about movements but about the moving of movements, about movements in their 'being-moving.' In its continuous form, in its being-moving, a movement cannot be seized through a linear representation of movements as passage from one point or state to another. Thus while moving, movement comes from nowhere, not having anywhere to come from; it is moving. […] Klee's theory of the line is about the 'multidimensional simultaneity' of drawing lines that draw the drawing of lines, the appearing of the appearing in everything that appears. It unfolds his principle of principles, so to speak, in which 'to draw and to paint is to learn to see behind a façade, to grasp something in its roots, to recognize the underlying forces, to learn the pre-history of the visible, to 'unveil, to ground, to analyze.' What matters is the making visible of the meanwhileness and in-betweeness of the is-moving, is-drawing, is-painting, where the underlying forming forces can appear as such. Klee sees, that is, Klee makes visible, the impossibility of seizing in forms the meanwhileness and in-betweeness of the forming, Formende, since human senses, both sensible and sensitive, are usually accustomed to focus solely on formed forms, on Form-ende, on finished forms. Human senses are too conditioned to objectifying and reifying the is-being, so that first of all what they sense are beings and not the is-being, appearances and not the appearing as such, figures and not the drawing, the said and not the saying. In order to make visible the appearing as such, 'the underlying forces,' or 'pre-history of the visible,' in order to draw the drawing, to make visible the making visible, senses must un-learn habits of sensing, must de-form the formed. Thus it is while de-forming forms that forming forces appear in their 'being-forming.' This means that while the formed dis-appears, the appearing can appear as such, that is, in an 'it is appearing.' I proposed to define as sketch this appearing while dis-appearing, this making visible while detaching from the visualized forms, this becoming while in dissolution. The sketch is neither a preparation for a painting to come nor an unfinished drawing. It is the gesture of drawing the drawing of lines, of making visible the

coming to visibility in its own withdrawal. Understood in this manner, the sketch is a hovering in the gerundive in-between and meanwhile."

26. See Paolo Cappelletti, *L'inafferrabile visione. Pittura e scrittura in Paul Klee* (Milano: Jaca Book, 2003). As for a "tour" through the philosophical interpretations of Paul Klee's works, see Stephen H. Watson, ed., *Crescent Moon over the Rational: Philosophical Interpretations of Paul Klee* (Stanford, CA: Stanford University Press, 2009).

27. See Gottfried Boehm, *Genesis:* "Paul Klee's Temporalization of Form," in *The Philosophical Vision of Paul Klee*, ed. Sallis, 23: "The formations of the distinct configuration take place in a scene whose borders or whose totality respectively displaces the represented into an ambiguous space of the possible, of associations, of a surplus of meaning, and of interferences. It was of great importance to Klee not to restrict the genesis of form to the sphere of artistic activity: namely, not to treat it as a question of the 'aesthetics of production'. Genesis, after all, addresses at least equally the moving eye of the observer whose activity Klee quite literally characterized as the 'pasture of the eyes' (*Augerweide*), comparing it to the cow grazing on the pasture. Yet totalization brings the kinesis and stasis of formation into an interrelationship. Following the self-unfolding form, the observer recognizes a succession, while, in a totalizing turn, he mobilizes *simultaneity*. The two compositions of time (*Zeitgestalten*) never fully overlap. To the contrary, the image always gives the eye sufficient incentive to realize the suspenseful intersection of the two times anew and differently. The standstill that cosmic movement experiences in the image thus proves to be an impetus for an unending play of movement."

28. As regards the relationships of Klee with Cubism and his progressive distancing from this style of painting, consider the interesting observations of Michael Baumgartner, "Paul Klee: From Structural Analysis and Morphogenesis to Art," in *The Philosophical Vision of Paul Klee*, ed. Sallis, 72–74: "The process of artistic abstraction is accompanied by a growing tendency in Klee's theoretical reflections to conceive of his relationships to nature and natural processes in a wider metaphysical and at the same time analytical context. [...] This new analytical look at the visible world that the Cubists had presented manifested itself in Klee's oeuvre—as in When God Considered the Creation of the Plants, 1913, for example, a work whose title equated the idea of a new world created through artistic means with the idea of divine creation. It is clearly visible how Klee finds, by his own means, his (own) kind of synthetic Cubism, after having engaged himself in the previous years in possibilities on how to break down the world of objects into prism-like component parts and then recombine and interweave them in accordance with purely compositional requirements. Klee had seen Pablo Picasso's early Cubist works in Munich as early as 1910 at the exhibition of the Neue Künstlervererereinigung (New Artists's Association), and what impressed him about them was the boldness with which painting managed to gorge beyond the mere outward appearance of the visible to an analysis of inner structure. Although variously inspired by Cubism, Klee's attitude remained ambivalent. He certainly recognized Cubism as a breakthrough in modern pictorial construction; at the same time, however, he lamented the formal destructiveness that occurred when objects were reshaped. In this regard, he was especially critical of Picasso's

arbitrariness when reducing the human figure to 'primitive forms of projection such as the triangle, rectangle, and circle' that 'lose some of their viability with each conversion.' Klee's association with Cubism is limited almost exclusively to abstract constructions of space—from which he developed his metaphor of the 'crystalline'—and to occasional depictions of nature in which he dared to deconstruct the organic world, as in When God Considered the Creation of Plants. However after having dismantled the objects in the sense of analytical Cubism, it was rather the structural analysis of natural organisms that mattered to him in terms of the depiction of nature. It is what he described as a remote starting point of creation and a priori formulas for men, beasts, plants, and stones."

29. On Savinio's poetics, see Paolo Fabbri, "Transcritture in Alberto Savinio: il dicibile e il visibile," in *il Verri*, n. 33 (2007) "lettera/immagine"; also available at www.paolofabbri.it/saggi/savinio.html; Keala J. Jewell, *The Art of Enigma: The De Chirico Brothers and the Politics of Modernism* (University Park, PA: Pennsylvania University Press 2004); Alberto Savinio, *Alberto Savinio: Paintings and Drawings, 1925–1952* (Milano: Electa, 1992).

30. Savinio's synthetic and renewing approach to representations is well shown by the following series of paintings: *Objects dans la forêt (1927)*, *Abandonné (1929)*, *Marina (1929)*, *Ulisse e Polifemo (1929)*, *Paesaggio Tropicale (1931)*, *La notte della città (1950)*, *Il Fiume (1950)*.

31. Some suggestions on this view can be found in the Introduction to *Thinking through Things: Theorising Artefacts Ethnographically*, eds. Amiria Henare, Martin Holbraad, and Sari Wastell (London and New York: Routledge, 2007).

Part II

RIGHTS AND RELIGION

Chapter 3

Transgender Rights in Pakistan?

Global, Colonial, and Islamic Perspectives

Jeffrey A. Redding

On January 24, 2009, Pakistani police officers belonging to the city of Rawalpindi's police force received information that a peculiar marriage ceremony was going on within their jurisdiction during this day's early morning hours.[1] According to a police report filed in relation to this incident,[2] after receiving this information, the police entered the building where the marriage ceremony was transpiring and discovered that "a large number of persons were enjoying themselves by dance of women and castrated men in a vulgar manner."[3] These "dancing women" and "castrated men" were arrested by the police.

Three days later, a transgendered individual by the name of Almas Shah— also going by the name of "Boby"—delivered a petition to the Senior Superintendent of Police (SSP) in Rawalpindi, but only after first joining a violent protest of approximately 100 other transgendered persons outside the SSP's office.[4] Seemingly as a result of this protest, Boby's petition, and press coverage of the entire situation, the District Superintendent of Police in Rawalpindi "after thorough enquiry recommended that 3 dancing ladies and 5 dancing she-males were not involved in any kind of offence and recommended their discharge from the case."[5] Subsequently, all charges against these "dancing ladies" and "she-males" were dropped.

Soon thereafter, in early February 2009, a well-known activist and advocate by the name of Dr. Mohammad Aslam Khaki brought the circumstances surrounding these arrests—as well as the broader socio-legal position of "she-males"[6] in Pakistan in particular—to the attention of the Supreme Court of Pakistan via a legal petition. In response, and over the course of several years and several legal orders, the Court acted to remedy the injustice of transgendered life in contemporary Pakistan. As a consequence, since 2009, Pakistan has witnessed a flourishing of legal, political, and cultural activism by transgendered people living all over the country.[7]

Few people would have predicted this set of groundbreaking events in Pakistan. Indeed, the "suddenness" and "unpredictability" of the cascading set of events in Pakistan in 2009 seems akin to what Afsaneh Najmabadi has observed about developments in contemporary Iran. Writes Najmabadi: "Something happened in 2003–4: Transsexuals and transsexuality in Iran became a hot media topic, both in Iran and internationally."[8] Moreover, around the globe and in South Asia—not to mention within Pakistan itself— Pakistan has a particularly beleaguered reputation. The reasons for this poor reputation are many but, to be sure, Pakistan's poor record on gender justice and women's rights have figured highly.[9]

Yet now seemingly defying this record, Pakistan has become a sort of world leader in discussions of (trans)gender and (trans)gender rights. Moreover, it has done so by advancing a relatively radical conception of gender going beyond the male/female gender binary and the patriarchal practices commonly accompanying this binary. Indeed, Pakistani citizens now have *five* different formal gender options to choose from,[10] hence moving the discussion in Pakistan beyond *dichotomous* gender and into *transgender*.

This chapter aims to help explain this recent extraordinary set of gender developments in Pakistan. Simultaneously, this chapter aims to both ask and answer the following question: Why *transgender* rights in Pakistan *now*? Moreover, in asking and helping answer this Pakistan-focused question, this chapter aims to raise questions about other ongoing transgender rights movements around the world, including fundamental questions as to how to understand and interculturally translate these movements' meanings and implications. Where have all these rights come from, and what do they mean? Is their meaning singular? Are they really about transgenderism? If not, what alternative translations and understandings of "transgender rights"—both in contemporary Pakistan and elsewhere—can and should be made available?

The potential answers to these questions, like the questions themselves, are multiple, layered, and complex. Given the complexity of this chapter's inquiries, the remaining sections of this chapter work systematically to provide three different epistemological perspectives on recent events in Pakistan, each of which is suggested by different aspects of these events (explained in more detail below). In short, this chapter's three sections work to provide (1) an understanding of how recent transgender developments in Pakistan might be comparatively situated with—and understood as analogous to—contemporaneous developments in India and the United States alike; (2) a brief account of recent Pakistani transgender developments in which contemporary Pakistan is understood not only as a globally situated, contemporary, and complex state, but also an active legatee of the British colonial empire, and, finally, (3) a shorter and more speculative exploration of recent developments in Pakistan, seeing in them continuity with a set of longstanding Muslim discussions on gender, law, and society which differ (at least somewhat) from reigning Western discussions of these topics. Each of these epistemological lenses is taken up by the different sections below which, in the order of their respective appearance, are entitled "Global," "Colonial," and "Islamic." Given that each section's discussion opens up a different intercultural translational possibility for understanding contemporary gender developments within and without Pakistan alike, the conclusion to this chapter summarizes these possibilities and also suggests important, future areas of research and inquiry.

GLOBAL

The immediate aftermath of the events in Rawalpindi in the early morning hours of January 24, 2009, might be characterized as Pakistan's "Stonewall moment." And, indeed, echoing some of the more raucous scenes from the 1969 Stonewall riots in New York City, a riveting image accompanying a newspaper story shortly following the Rawalpindi police's early 2009 raid on a marriage party (where transgendered individuals were celebrating) showed an angry troupe of transgendered persons leading an assault on a police station where transgendered celebrants were being held.[11]

The use of a Stonewall-esque framing is certainly one way of telling the contemporary history of transgender rights discourse in Pakistan from a global perspective. Such a focus is also one that comports with common narratives about a seemingly recent and sudden upsurge of discussion and activism about transgender rights around the world—whether in Pakistan, India, the United States, Iran,[12] or elsewhere.[13] However, as attractive as commonplace "revolutionary moment" tellings of gender history appear to be, these accounts often elide important prerevolutionary developments that make the revolutionary moment either ordinary or relatively predictable. In short, while one way of globalizing our understanding of recent developments in Pakistan is to globalize Stonewall—perhaps akin to the international work of the well-known UK LGBT organization, Stonewall, itself[14]—this section aims to explore a different potential lens of globalization, namely, one that highlights the overall post-9/11 context of a fraught and paranoid world politics. During this time, the Pakistani state (along with many other states) became deeply enmeshed in a global struggle for legitimacy and life.

In the aftermath of 9/11, General Pervez Musharraf, the Pakistani military dictator, received massive financial and political support from the United States' military and intelligence apparatuses in order to help the United States fight its "Global War on Terror." As is well-known, key actors behind the 9/11 attacks were linked to Afghanistan, in relation to which Pakistan was both neighbor and proxy. As notorious as Musharraf became for helping the

United States fight this controversial and unconventional war against "terror," it was nevertheless not easy to simplistically categorize him as an "evil
tyrant." For example, during his rule from 1999 to 2008, Musharraf liberal-
ized the airwaves in Pakistan, allowing for the operation of privately owned
TV channels with (historically speaking) few content restrictions. On one of
these private TV stations, a talk show was started in 2005 by a transgendered
individual going by the (feminine) Begum Nawazish Ali name and identity.[15]
This talk show was the first of its kind in Pakistan—if not South Asia as a
whole[16]—and became incredibly popular.

In focusing on the Musharraf years here, and the connections Musharraf's
regime had with important geopolitical players enmeshed in the Global
War on Terror—including, most notably, the United States and India—this
section aims to suggest continuities not only between pre- and post-2009 gender developments in Pakistan, but also between these Pakistani developments
and developments in countries bound to Pakistan through fraught relationships involving conflict. This all suggests, in turn, the very real *possibility* of
translation of gender events and history across national and cultural borders,
albeit anxious ones. Without a doubt, this section is relatively optimistic
about the possibility of intercultural translation—a possibility that the next
section is more skeptical about. That being said, this section nonetheless aims
to complicate any easy notion that the appropriate translation of recent gender
events, whether in Pakistan or in the United States or elsewhere, relates to
the development of (liberal notions of) "transgender rights." How to alternatively (and convincingly) characterize what is going on globally is admittedly
difficult, and also suggestive of Talal Asad's point as to the unwillingness
of "powerful" contexts, such as the United States, to "submit to forcible
transformation in the [cultural] translation process [rather] than the other
way around."[17] Despite such unwillingness, this section's suggestion is that
the most appropriate understanding and translation of recent global gender
events could pertain not to "transgender rights" but, rather, to "the gendered
legal reaction of states immersed in the insecurity and paranoia accompanying endless war."

This is, to be sure, an unambiguously awkward and speculative mediating translation. However, it is perhaps better situated to explain (relatively)
contemporaneous developments in Pakistan and the United States both, for
example, than the use of any indigenous term from either specific context
is—for example, *"khwaja sira* rights" (Pakistan) or "transgender rights"
(United States).[18] That being said, the discussion in the remainder of this
chapter will often use—for the purposes of brevity, while also admittedly
risking inaccuracy and imprecision—the increasingly well-known Anglo
expressions "transgender," "transgendered," and "transgender rights." This
section itself will first outline the topsy-turvy (gender) developments of the

Musharraf era—which, importantly, preceded the 2009 transgender litigation at the Supreme Court of Pakistan—and then situate what followed these developments—namely, the 2009-and-onwards transgender litigation at the Supreme Court of Pakistan—alongside arguably related developments emanating from the simultaneously fraught contexts of a post-9/11 India and the United States.

The Musharraf Years

The future emergence of Pakistan as a haven for both transgenders and Taliban might be seen be as the result of a set of political events that the last days of the twentieth century witnessed. On October 12, 1999, Pakistan's highest ranking military commander, General Pervez Musharraf, ordered the overthrow of Prime Minister Nawaz Sharif's democratically elected government, placing key governmental institutions under military control in the process.

The first scenes from a coup have rarely been so queer. One of the first sites taken over by the military was the headquarters of Pakistan's government-controlled TV station, Pakistan Television (PTV), located in the capital city of Islamabad. Foreign news teams reaching the scene recorded scores of uniform-clad military men, backs to the cameras, their buttocks straining as these men struggled to surmount the locked gates surrounding PTV.[19] Footage and scenes of these contorting buttocks would be replayed for many days on international television.

The next nine years would witness many other contortions, both in relation to Musharraf's fortunes specifically, but also Pakistan's domestic politics and global relations generally. To be sure, 9/11 and its aftermath were deeply implicated in all of the above, seeing that this set of events resulted in Musharraf's regime receiving massive financial and political support from the United States and, hence, a longevity that few expected for Musharraf at the outset of his coup. Simultaneously, Musharraf was also at the receiving-end of much US criticism, largely centered around Musharraf's unwillingness to toe the US line on the need to eradicate the Taliban and their Pakistani sympathizers.[20] To be sure, Musharraf was a wily character, but even he could not completely escape history. And indeed, on August 18, 2008, a transformed *President* Pervez Musharraf, at risk of being impeached, would resign from his (now) civilian position[21] of leadership in Pakistan. At the end, Musharraf's decline was precipitous, overcome as he was by a series of crises coming from all directions.

One of the most alarming crises (from both the perspective of many Pakistanis and non-Pakistanis alike) was sparked by the actions of two Muslim cleric brothers, Abdul Aziz and Abdul Rashid Ghazi. Aziz and Ghazi, along with hundreds of female and male supporters, had operated from an established mosque in central Islamabad, the Lal Masjid, located just a stone's throw away from the Supreme Court. Two relatively longstanding goals of these Al-Qaeda-sympathetic brothers, or their supporters, had been the overthrow of the relatively secular (yet authoritarian) Musharraf regime, as well as a more robust imposition of *shari'a* in Pakistan.[22]

Perhaps toward these goals, on March 27, 2007, female students associated with a seminary attached to the Lal Masjid shocked the cosmopolitan capital city of Islamabad by conducting a raid on an alleged house of prostitution.[23] During this raid, these seminary students seized three Pakistani women working at this site, transporting them to the Lal Masjid grounds.[24] These three women were imprisoned on the grounds of the Lal Masjid for a couple of days, but were then released by the seminary students.[25]

Just a few months later, a similar episode transpired with stakes even higher than during the previous episode. In this next incident, Lal Masjid-affiliated seminary students conducted a raid on a Chinese acupuncture clinic[26] (also characterized as a massage parlor or, alternatively, yet another site of prostitution[27]) also located in Islamabad. In this raid, seminary students seized nine people including, notably, six Chinese women and one Chinese man.[28] All of these detainees were again taken to the grounds of the Lal Masjid, though this time they were released after a mere matter of hours.[29]

That Chinese nationals were seized here was deeply significant, and most likely the cause of their quick release. China has relatively recently overtaken the United States in becoming Pakistan's most important international ally, lending Pakistan a great deal of political, economic, and military support in the process.[30] As a result, journalistic reports of this raid took note of the fact that Pakistan's Interior Minister called the Chinese ambassador to Islamabad to keep the ambassador up to date on this crisis, as well as to apologize to the Chinese.[31]

Ultimately, it was this particular raid that seemed to breach the Musharraf regime's red-lines. In early July 2007, the Pakistani military laid siege to the Lal Masjid, eventually taking control of the mosque, but also resulting in the deaths of over 100 people[32]—including Abdul Rashid Ghazi, one of the firebrand brothers. As for Ghazi's brother, Abdul Aziz, he was captured alive as he attempted to sneak out of the battle-zone, ensconced in a woman's *burqa* and porting a woman's handbag.[33] While supporters of the state hailed the Musharraf regime's takeover of the Lal Masjid, the large number of casualties from the state's assault on the mosque angered many, and posed yet another set of insistent questions as to how long Musharraf could retain his office and perpetuate his regime.

Perhaps the most tragic crisis to undermine Musharraf's control of the Pakistani state was no less dramatically gendered than the Lal Masjid crisis, and also one in which the international community had an especially deep interest. This crisis arose as a result of the Musharraf regime's failure to ensure adequate security for former prime minister Benazir Bhutto's return from exile. Bhutto was the first elected female prime minister of Pakistan (and also any Muslim-majority country) but had left the country in 1999 shortly before Musharraf's coup ousting then-Prime Minister Nawaz Sharif. Despite the many setbacks she had suffered in her Pakistani political career, Bhutto had international celebrity and, to be sure, unparalleled grit and flair. She was also a favorite of many of Pakistan's transgendered citizens.[34] However, none of Bhutto's strengths could save her when, in an attempt to win the position of prime minister for yet another time, she was mortally wounded in an attack by an assailant while campaigning for votes in the city of Rawalpindi on December 27, 2007.

In the nine years separating General Musharraf's rise and President Musharraf's fall, then, more had transformed in Pakistan than just Musharraf's formal title. Since its inception in 1947 amid the decline of the British Empire and the murmurings of the Cold War, Pakistan had played an important role in international discussions and politics. Yet now this role had taken on a particularly unprecedented and unpredictable hue. Benazir Bhutto was dead, Taliban sympathizers were on the march, and transgendered people were about to win both cricket matches and significant legal attention.[35]

Comparativism, Conflict, and Unexpected Translations: Pakistan, India, and the United States

The emergence of Pakistan's transgender rights discussions in a period of high domestic turbulence and international intrigue suggests both traditional and untraditional sites of comparative inquiry. One traditional site of comparative inquiry for Pakistan has been India, which is not surprising given that modern India came into independence nearly simultaneously with Pakistan, and is linked with Pakistan geographically, historically, linguistically—and even legally[36]—all the while being engaged with Pakistan in an epic and often violent international contest for seventy years now. The geographical areas that now form Pakistan were, broadly speaking, formerly part of British colonial India. When most areas of colonial India achieved independence in 1947, Muslim-majority areas in India were "partitioned off" to form the independent country of Pakistan. However, this partition was hardly peaceful or orderly, and resulted in the migration of massive numbers of Muslims (to Pakistan) and Hindus (to India)—many of whom were murdered in communal violence along the way—and still unresolved disputes over which parts of colonial India (e.g., Kashmir) belonged to Pakistan versus India. As a consequence, since that uncertain time, contemporary Pakistan and contemporary India's entanglements have been both manifold and deeply fraught.

And arguably, regional and global developments in the wake of 9/11 have only further complicated this set of anxious entanglements.

Yet despite India's highly fraught relationship with Pakistan, transgender legal developments in India have recently begun to coincide with those in Pakistan. Notably, like the Supreme Court of Pakistan, the Supreme Court of India has also recently pronounced on transgender rights. Indeed, after the Supreme Court of Pakistan began issuing transgender rights pronounce-ments in 2009, the Supreme Court of India followed suit with its 2014 deci-sion in *National Legal Services Authority v. Union of India*.[37] This decision was a broad-based one, declaring multiple forms of social and governmental discrimination against India's transgendered citizens to be unconstitutional. For example, commenting on the shortcomings of India's legal treatment of different transgender communities, the Supreme Court of India took sharp cognizance of how "Indian Law, on the whole, only recognises the paradigm of binary genders of male and female, based on a person's sex assigned by birth, which [affects] the law relating to marriage, adoption, inheritance, succession and taxation and welfare legislations."[38] Ultimately, the Supreme Court of India's concluding directives to India's central and state govern-ments resonated with much of the Supreme Court of Pakistan's similarly multiple directives[39] and included commands for Indian state authorities to not only improve the formal legal situation of transgendered people, but also their broader social and cultural position.[40]

Compared to India, putting the United States into conversation with Paki-stan vis-à-vis the development of "transgender rights" perhaps needs more justification. At the very least, between the United States and Pakistan, there is no shared history of sovereignty or of historically shared (domestic) legal regimes—or the painful fracturing of either—as there is between India and Pakistan. Yet if Pakistan and India have moved, over time, *away* from their history of joint governance, Pakistan and the United States have arguably largely moved in the opposite direction—from separateness to mutuality, albeit also a fraught one. This was initially the result of the Cold War, with Pakistan geopolitically aligning itself with the United States in a bid for pro-tection from a hostile India, and India taking a non-aligned but sympathetic stance toward the Soviet Union.[41] But it has become perhaps even more the case with the Global War on Terror, commenced by the United States after the fateful events of 9/11. In the high drama of geopolitics, then, the United States and Pakistan have moved into a tighter and tighter orbit of—and anx-ious entanglement with—each other for some time now.

Moreover, these jointly authored geopolitical dramas have unfolded in a context infused with a politics premised on gender and sexuality. As to this kind of global politics, Jasbir Puar's work on "homonationalism" has highlighted how a wide range of nationalist political actors across the globe

have increasingly adopted ostensibly progressive gender and sexuality policies in order to give a cosmopolitan sheen to the otherwise ugly, racist, and
security-obsessed states in which these nationalist actors operate.[42] One tragic
consequence of all this, according to Puar, is a "dual movement" whereby
"patriotism momentarily sanctions some homosexualities, often through gendered, racial, and class sanitizing, in order to produce 'monster-terrorist fags'
[and then] homosexuals embrace the us-versus-them rhetoric of . . . patriotism and thus align themselves with this racist and homophobic production."[43]

While Puar's work contains many real-world examples of all this, one particularly striking example involves an episode from the animated US television series *South Park*. While this example is idiosyncratic—like the crude,
sexually explicit, yet politically incisive show itself—it is also deeply reve-
latory of a set of gendered and sexualized dynamics connecting the United
States and Pakistan, and especially in the post-9/11 context. This particular
South Park episode, dating from November 2003, concerned the antics of
a gay school teacher in the United States, Mr. Garrison, who was trying to
expose his employer to a sexual orientation-discrimination claim, with a presumed multimillion-dollar payout.[44] In doing so, Mr. Garrison

> uses sexual performativity to escalate discomfort and elicit disgust from his
> fourth-grade students. One day in class Mr. Garrison introduces a new teacher's
> assistant, Mr. Slave (who appears white), otherwise called the "Teacher's Ass."
> Mr. Slave, typifying a leather bottom, is a large strapping white man with a dark
> moustache, clad in a pink shirt, blue jeans, black leather chaps, vest, and boots,
> and a police cap. . . . After his introduction [to the class by Mr. Garrison,] Mr.
> Slave moves toward his seat, but not before being spanked by Mr. Garrison. As
> Mr. Slave sits down, Cartman and Craig, two white students in the classroom,
> confer about Mr. Slave. Cartman, whispering to Craig while glancing around
> furtively, states, "Dude, I think that Mr. Slave guy might be a . . . Pakistani."[45]

In a darkly humorous manner then, this *South Park* episode sharply
indexes the highly gendered relationship between the United States and Pakistan in the fraught, post-9/11 period. As Puar herself notes: "One can open up
[an] analysis [of this *South Park* episode] to the level of geopolitics as well.
It is notable that Cartman did not wonder if Mr. Slave was an Afghani or an
Iraqi. By naming him a Pakistani, the show astutely points to an understated
complexity in the war on terror, that of the liminal position of the nation of
Pakistan."[46] Or, even more specifically, "Pakistan . . . has been the pilfered
bottom to the United States' imperialist topping."[47]

To be sure, a gendered and sexualized relationship between the United
States and Pakistan pre-dates 9/11. For example, in the decisive Cold War bat-
tleground of Afghanistan, the (massively) US-backed Pakistani dictator, General Zia ul Haq, became internationally prominent for his important role in

helping the United States militarily bring down the Soviet Union. Zia also became internationally known for his campaign to Islamize Pakistan's legal system. This Islamization campaign, of which the infamous Hudood Ordinances[48] were one important result, infamously targeted the lives and life chances of so many Pakistani women. Both ironically and tragically, after the ouster of the Soviet Union from Afghanistan, the United States would itself invade Afghanistan just over a decade later, with the simultaneous goals of defeating Al-Qaeda and their Taliban hosts—but also saving Afghan women from the "Islamic excesses" of these actors.[49] Again, Pakistan would play a huge role in this Afghanistan campaign and its associated sexual politics.

However one looks at it then, when it comes to gender and sexuality, the United States and Pakistan arguably have shared and entangled trajectories of a degree not unlike that between India and Pakistan. To be sure, the discussions of transgender rights in the United States have often taken on a different hue than that in Pakistan (and also India). For example, the US Supreme Court has yet to speak to these rights in any truly paradigmatic way[50] akin to what has recently transpired in Pakistan (and India too). Furthermore, the transgender issues that have recently captivated the US public appear fairly unique, if not also peculiar. For example, recent efforts by several US states to legislatively restrict persons to using the sexed (i.e., male or female) restroom corresponding with the sex recorded on their birth certificate,[51] seems to many people distinctly odd. At first blush, at least, this kind of "toilet debate" seems to have little in common with the issues of access to education, jobs, the franchise, and inheritance/property rights that have been a prominent part of the recent Pakistani conversation.

Yet, at another level, overlaps, resonances, and similarities between recent discussions of gender in the United States and Pakistan emerge. For one, the US transgender toilet debate (in its most paranoid dimensions) has centered around the alleged need to protect children from "predator males" who allegedly will, if an "open toilets" regime is instituted, don women's clothes, enter women's bathrooms and locker rooms and, ultimately, sexually abuse women and girls.[52] While there is much that is going on in this contemporary US discussion, one important strand of it indubitably articulates a "concern" for children. In the contemporary Pakistan discussion of transgender rights, as well, there has been an idea/concern—one with long historical roots—that transgender communities recruit new members by kidnapping male children and, subsequently, castrating them.[53]

Moreover, in both the United States and Pakistan, recent Supreme Court discussions of gender have unfolded in a context of concern for property and inheritance rights. For example, in *United States v. Windsor*,[54] the US Supreme Court case shortly preceding and paving the way for *Obergefell v. Hodges*[55] (the more well-known US Supreme Court case constitutionalizing a right to same-sex marriage), the US Supreme Court took up a complaint by Edith Windsor as to the allegedly inequitable taxes she had to pay to the US federal government for property she had inherited from her deceased same-sex spouse. While the formal holding of the case was about the unconstitutionality of a key portion of the federal government's Defense of Marriage Act (DOMA)[56]—with Windsor successfully claiming that because of DOMA, Windsor's marriage to her *same-sex* partner was not federally recognized and, as a result, Windsor's spouse's transfer of property to Windsor was taxed at a much higher rate than the transfer of property between *opposite-sex* partners would be—this decision was also clearly preoccupied with maintaining privileges and norms concerning the transfer of property and wealth.[57]

Similarly, one key concern that the Pakistani Supreme Court has had for transgender individuals has been these individuals' disinheritance by their natal families.[58] This disinheritance, while widespread, is increasingly problematic in Pakistan because it occurs despite clear and firm Islamic legal prescriptions about the inheritance shares necessarily due offspring. This contemporary interest in the *enforcement* of transgender persons' property rights follows a deliberate choice by British colonial authorities during the nineteenth century to *not enforce* material privileges and rights that transgender people had in the pre-colonial period.[59]

In conclusion then, contemporary discussions of gender and sexuality in Pakistan, India, and the United States can be seen to overlap and intersect in significant ways. Moreover, in these shared trajectories, we see confirmation of this section's suggestion that comparative inquiry—and, moreover, inquiry that follow the sinews of contemporary geopolitical intrigue and conflict— might be important for understanding "transgender rights" developments not only in Pakistan but also elsewhere, including India and the United States. While the precise way to understand and interculturally translate all these recent gender developments is perhaps difficult and unwieldy, this section's discussions have suggested that engaging in this comparative exercise can be not only illuminating but perhaps also essential. This is especially the case given that neither law or gender or conflict appear to be easily cabined by contemporary borders. And, indeed, by "following the conflict," one may find new windows opening on to both law and gender, including the possibility that transgender law developments occurring contemporaneously in national contexts with highly fraught inter-relationships have something to do with the disruptions to society and gender that an apparently endless and particularly paranoid Global War on Terror has generated—and perhaps particularly so in Pakistan during the Musharraf years. Or, seen another way, that recent global conflict has done more to produce and disseminate discourses about transgenderism than any "peaceful" development and dissemination of liberal notions of gender, rights, or law has or can.

COLONIAL

The fuzziness of allegedly sharp national boundaries is not just a contemporary phenomenon. Indeed, the colonial period was also a time when the world witnessed massive transnational movements of peoples, ideas, politics, and laws between any number of geographic and cultural spaces. Moreover, the postcolonial period in many of these same spaces—whether colonial or metropole—continues to be deeply shaped (politically, culturally, legally) by colonial practices and procedures.

This section aims to suggest continuities between certain modes of colonial and postcolonial governance in Pakistan and, hence, the possibility of a very particular kind of intercultural translation of contemporary gender developments in Pakistan. This kind of intercultural characterization is one that might be, alternatively, considered "inter-historical."[60] Admittedly, in exploring the connections between the colonial and postcolonial in Pakistan, one result is an understanding of contemporary gender developments in Pakistan that is more siloed and less obviously "intercultural" than in the last section. That being said, given the connections between colonies and metropoles during both the colonial and postcolonial periods, the kind of "vertical" inter-historical analysis engaged in here does not completely preclude a more "horizontal" kind of intercultural translation for the contemporary period. Importantly too, this section's offering of a kind of inter-historical/intercultural analysis ends up challenging—as the last section did as well—any easy characterization of contemporary Pakistani gender developments as pertaining to (liberal notions of) "transgender rights."

To begin to see all of this, one important place to look is June 2009, four months after Dr. Khaki first filed his legal petition in the Supreme Court of Pakistan concerning the rights and welfare of transgendered people. In this month, the Supreme Court issued one of the first of a series of Court orders in what would turn out to be a protracted, multi-year litigation of the various issues raised by Dr. Khaki's petition. As part of this June 2009 order, the Supreme Court ordered Pakistan's various provincial governments to conduct a census of the numbers, names, and locations of "she-males" (as the Court initially termed them[61]) living in each province. Evidencing a degree of hostility and suspicion toward the "gurus" who typically govern "she-male" communities,[62] the Court also directed the provincial governments to "ensure that in future if any child is handed over to the 'Gurus', their particulars should be noted and intimated to the [provincial government] for the purpose of further probe with regard to the status of such child and also to know whether they are voluntarily handed over or under compulsion."[63]

Following this June 2009 order from the Supreme Court, Pakistan's most populous and wealthy province, Punjab, conducted a relatively extensive census of transgendered individuals residing within its borders, inquiring not only about their aggregate numbers, but also details as to how they became transgendered and different aspects of their well-being. And in a memo dated August 13, 2009, the Social Welfare, Women Development and Bait ul Maal Department of the Government of The Punjab reported to the Supreme Court "data regarding She-Males"[64] as part of a larger communication to the Supreme Court including "proposals and suggestions for social uplift of She-Males."[65]

This memo is interesting not only for the data it reports, but also because of its recounting of specific census questions asked of interview subjects. For example, this memo reveals that among the questions posed to census subjects were questions about each subject's own name, the name of their father, their place of residence, their occupation, and also their income. Other questions inquired about the "Nature of Eunuch" or, rather, how each interviewed person came to be transgendered.[66] The following options were available for checking,[67] each seemingly intended to provide exclusive means of how someone could come to be a "eunuch":

By Birth ___ By Accident ___ By Disease ___ By Force ___

Additionally, another set of questions seemed intended to get at each interviewed individual's non-natal familial living situation and, in particular, any living situation involving a *guru*. In this respect, the form asked the following questions (among others)[68]:

Name of Guru: _____

How the Eunuch reached to the Guru: _____

The area in which he/she[69] is living: _____

With Family ___ Independently ___ With Guru ___

His/her standard of living:

Good ___ Middle ___ Hand to Mouth ___

Whether he/she developed linkage with other eunuchs._____

Whether he/she is member of any eunuch association/body._____

In ordering this kind of counting and accounting of Pakistan's transgendered citizens, the Supreme Court of Pakistan's recent actions echo Foucault's observations about the modern state's biopolitical need to "qualify, measure, appraise, and hierarchize [its citizens], rather than display [the state] in its murderous splendor."[70]

Moreover, the Supreme Court of Pakistan's mandating of this kind of counting and accounting also has deep resonances with a well-known trope of British colonial governance—namely, the census.[71] In short, soon after the mid-nineteenth-century defeat of a major Indian uprising against the British East India Company, and then the consolidation of British rule in India under the formal authority of the British crown, colonial authorities began to organize (nearly) decennial counting and accountings of the people over which they hoped to continue to rule. Perhaps most infamously, the British census asked questions of subjects with the goal of trying to ascertain these individuals' religious and caste identities. Indeed, as to these types of questions, scholars now often trace the beginning of South Asia's religiously communalist politics—whether intra- or international, or intra- or interfaith—to colonial times and the objectification and reification of religious and caste identities instigated by British census practices.[72]

Arguably then, with the Supreme Court of Pakistan's ordering of a "gender census," the middle of 2009 witnessed the (re)emergence of important colonial governance techniques in a postcolonial Pakistan. As Arjun Appadurai has noted, the colonial census resulted in "new forms of categorization . . . which saw [colonial South Asia] as a museum or zoo of difference and of differences, and [a] project of reform [] which involved cleaning up the sleazy, flabby, frail, feminine, obsequious bodies of natives into clean, virile, muscular, moral, and loyal bodies."[73] With the 2009 Punjab census, similarly, we see efforts to exoticize, surveil, and reform transgendered persons and, also, their kinship/*guru* filiations.

This set of observations is confirmed by other actions around the same time by the Supreme Court of Pakistan, and also by other parts of the Pakistani state. In this respect, the Supreme Court of Pakistan issued an order in November 2009 (in the litigation instigated by Dr. Khaki's petition) relating to Pakistani transgendered persons' official registration as well as the issuance to them of official governmental identity documents. In this order, the Court ordered the Pakistani government's National Database and Registration Authority (NADRA)—the governmental bureaucracy responsible for issuing, to every adult Pakistani, a National Identity Card (NIC)[74]—to "adopt a strategy . . . to record [a transgendered individual's] exact status in the [identity document] column meant for male or female after undertaking some medical tests based on hormones etc."[75]

Why this concern—later repudiated[76]—with the "exact," hormonal status of various transgendered people? One reason appears to be that the Court had received information "that in the name of the [eunuchs] some male and female who . . . otherwise have no gender disorder in their bodies have adopted this status and commit crimes on account of which a bad name is brought to [eunuchs]."[77] While the source of this information is not clear from Supreme Court documents, Dr. Khaki has previously expressed his own personal experience to me of taking tea with and giving money to a teenaged "eunuch" who used to visit his law offices, and who was later revealed to be a "fake" when Dr. Khaki spotted him one day wearing "normal dress."[78] Moreover, in case anyone was mistaken that the Supreme Court was genuinely concerned about a real problem with "fake eunuchs," the Court repeated its concern with those "who in fact are not [eunuchs] but by using such status are committing the crimes and [as a result of which] the actual [eunuchs] are being blamed for the same" in a later December 2009 order in this litigation.[79] In short, it appears that one goal of the Supreme Court's mandate that NADRA issue more gender-nuanced NICs was to better identify individuals and, also, mitigate individuals' (alleged) attempts to commit any sort of confusing, destabilizing, and potentially dangerous "identity fraud."

In a manner not unlike their British colonial predecessors, then, the Pakistani state has also seemed interested in counting and identifying its citizens—admittedly along somewhat new axes—for the purposes of ensuring "clean, virile, muscular, moral, and loyal bodies."[80] As a consequence, an important "when question" is raised pertaining to *when* precisely transgendered people living in the geographic areas now constituting Pakistan became the object of state notice and (ostensible) solicitude. And to this issue, the redeployment of colonial governance tropes and techniques does put into doubt whether there is much "new" in the Supreme Court of Pakistan's "recent" notice of transgendered people. Indeed, one might be tempted to describe or translate this notice here as just "the latest postcolonial iteration of the colonial gaze."

The "when question" raised here is thus also intertwined with this chapter's "what question," namely: *What* do "transgender rights" in Pakistan mean or implicate? Alternatively, *what* liberty, if any, have transgendered people in Pakistan gained by the Supreme Court of Pakistan's recent notice of them? As well, what do Pakistan's gender continuities with the colonial period suggest about how to understand and interculturally translate recent gender developments in Pakistan—and elsewhere? The Conclusion will return to these questions, and the next section will raise similar ones.

ISLAMIC

The Punjab government was not the only provincial government in Pakistan to file a transgender census report with the Supreme Court of Pakistan in response to the Court's June 2009 orders. So did the province now known as Khyber Pakhtunkhwa, and then known as the North-West Frontier Province (commonly referred to as "the NWFP"). In a communication to the Supreme Court dated August 15, 2009, the Government of NWFP's Social Welfare & Women Development Department not only reported the results of the provincial government's census of the NWFP's transgendered population but also offered a more holistic and lengthy written analysis of the different kinds of transgendered people who could be found in the NWFP.[81]

The NWFP government's census efforts faced a number of noteworthy difficulties, not least being the security situation in the NWFP at the time, including in Swat Valley.[82] As a result, the NWFP government's communication to the Supreme Court took note of the fact that only a partial census could be conducted in that province. Indeed, summarizing the only partial success of its census efforts here, the NWFP government reported to the Supreme Court that "immediate actions for [transgender] Registration [were] taken in the districts of Peshawar, Nowshera, Charsadda, Mardan, Swabi, Kohat, Karak, Abbottabad, Haripur, Mansehra and Batagram,"[83] but that other districts under the jurisdiction of the NWFP could not be surveyed due to "the present Law and Order situation and the continued security operations within and the adjacent areas of NWFP."[84]

The NWFP government seemed to struggle with its census efforts in even more fundamental ways as well, however. These difficulties are suggested by the inclusion in the provincial government's census report to the Supreme Court of an extended qualitative analysis (mentioned above) of this province's complex gender geography—encompassing a wide variety of non-normative genders, including (among others) she-males, *hijras* of many varieties, *khwaja siras*, *khusras*, and *zenanas*.[85]

Interestingly, along with its extensive "gender mapping" of northwest Pakistan, the NWFP government's census report also included the following plea for social tolerance: "We must bear in mind that [the transgendered] community remained the guards and custodians of the second most sacred religious place of Islam, which is the Roza-i-Rasool [burial place of the Prophet Muhammad located in modern-day Saudi Arabia]. They have been recognized by Islam and our Holy Prophet."[86]

In this plea, this chapter's third (and perhaps most speculative) epistemological lens vis-à-vis the origins and meanings of Pakistan's transgender rights movement emerges, namely, a lens that sees contemporary Pakistan through the lens of a (pre-colonial) Islamic past. This past is vast both in temporal and geographical terms, stretching as it does from the seventh century (common) era immediately following the Prophet Muhammad's life in Arabia to the eighteenth century waning of the Muslim Mughal Empire in South Asia. Across this vast time and space, "eunuchs"—as much of the secondary English-language literature refers to them[87]—had Muslim social, institutional, and religious recognition.

The scholar David Ayalon, for example, narrates the employment of eunuchs by Muslim households belonging to notable figures in the history of Islam, including the first caliph in the Umayyad dynasty, Mu'awiya (d. 680 CE), and also the renowned jurist al-Shafi'i (d. 820 CE). With regard to the al-Shafi'i example, Ayalon concludes that "it shows that even the most religious persons, at a very early date in Islamic history, had no qualms in employing eunuchs in their own homes."[88] Ayalon also relays reports (of unascertainable reliability) that Mu'awiya employed eunuch soldiers in his army,[89] a military role that Shahzad Bashir's work indicates was consistent with other manifestations of eunuch power in other notable historical Islamic regimes.[90] For example, in the well-known Mamluk sultanate centered in Egypt from the early thirteenth to the early sixteenth centuries (CE), Shaun Marmon reports how "[t]he frequent government confiscations of the households of wealthy officials were usually supervised by eunuch 'police' drawn from the corps of eunuchs who served under the *muqaddam al-mamālīk*, the eunuch commandant of the sultan's elite slave cadets."[91] Similarly, K. S. Lal narrates a number of eunuch figures who served as powerful military commanders and advisors in a number of pre-colonial South Asian Muslim regimes, including those associated with the well-known Mughal Empire.[92]

Indeed, South Asia's Muslim Mughal era—at its height lasting from, approximately, the sixteenth to the eighteenth centuries (CE)—is very much relevant to current transgender nomenclatures in Pakistan, as the increasingly common usage across Pakistan of the Mughal-era term *"khwaja sira"* to describe (male-to-female) transgendered people suggests. As Claire Pamment describes this nomenclature development: "Contemporary hijras draw upon the history of khwajasaras as a source of political strength . . . [and] Pakistani hijras draw their esteem from Islam in general."[93]

Moreover, in the explicit referencing of Islam in recent Pakistani transgender discussions, the possibility of a larger difference between Islamic and non-Islamic discourses and interpretations of (trans)gender and (trans)gender rights—and, as a result, another view altogether on what the "recent" Pakistani "rights" developments mean—is arguably opened up. Of course, in any investigation of continuities between contemporary and pre-colonial Islamic legal and social regimes, one must be attuned to diversity: the seventh century Arabian Peninsula is a far cry from sixteenth century South Asia, and recent Pakistani prime ministers have had little resemblance to Mughal emperors. In short, there is a need here not to engage in any sort of essentialist reading of Islam, or Islamic law, or even "the West." Similarly, it is also important to not overdetermine Pakistan as an "Islamic state" only.[94]

Nonetheless, similar to the third section's tentatively siloed efforts to read postcolonial Pakistani gender developments in continuity with colonial-era governance techniques, there is arguably some benefit to engaging in something similar vis-à-vis Pakistan's Islamic heritage. This is the case even recognizing the difficulty of cabining a religious heritage as vast and old as Islam, or understanding contemporary Pakistan as necessarily in continuity with that heritage. However, in engaging in this admittedly speculative

enterprise, some historical Muslim practices relating to transgendered people—moreover, ones not fully coinciding with Western liberal norms of
rights and personhood—can be brought into relief. This, in turn, suggests the
possibility of a different valence to, and intercultural translation of, transgendered persons' recent "legal and social empowerment" in Pakistan.

While there is much more research to be done on all this—something
which the Conclusion will again discuss—it appears that Muslim practices of
"transgender" nomenclature are not only the difference between Islamic and
non-Islamic discourses in this area. Toward this suggestion, it is worth noting
the scholar Shaun Marmon's argument that eunuchs were, historically speaking, not just important vis-à-vis the world of the living, but also vis-à-vis the
world of the dead—hence their historical role in guarding Muslim households
and Muslim tombs alike.[95] With this historical insight in mind, there is an
argument to be made here that there are *necropolitical* dimension to Muslim
discussions of transgendered people which are different than the *biopolitical*
and Foucauldian aspects of contemporary law and (gender) governance—for
example, those discussed in the second section.[96]

And, in fact, one can find this kind of transgendered necropolitics arising
in the recent litigation in Pakistan, where one key issue that emerged was
the difficulty that transgendered individuals face (due to hostility concerning
their gender status from these individuals' natal families) when they attempt
to claim their shares of inheritance due to them under well-known Islamic
legal precepts relating to inheritance. *Enforcing* transgendered individuals'
Islamic legal rights to inheritance has been one focus of the Supreme Court
of Pakistan's interventions in 2009 and beyond.[97] Additionally, it is not only
the Supreme Court which has been concerned here with the legal consequences of death, but also non-state Islamic legal actors in Pakistan, with
some such actors also recently expressing sympathy for the Islamic rights of
inheritance and, also, proper Islamic funeral rites for transgendered Muslims
in Pakistan.[98]

CONCLUSION

The development and meaning of transgender rights in Pakistan is clearly
more complicated than it looks on first impression. This chapter has aimed
to offer views into this complexity, demonstrating the continuity of recent
developments in Pakistan with either global, colonial, or Islamic legal practices relating to persons who are not easily categorized as either "male" or
"female." Moreover, each of these chapter's sections has worked to challenge
conventional (liberal) narratives about gender and rights alike, whether in
Pakistan or elsewhere. The first section suggested that what we have recently

witnessed in Pakistan—and also India and the United States—is "the gendered legal reaction of states immersed in the insecurity and paranoia accompanying endless war." The second section suggested that recent developments in Pakistan are actually not so recent, and actually just the latest instance of South Asian authorities—whether colonial or postcolonial—attempting to both tame and police unruly subjects. Finally, the third section suggested that recent discussions in Pakistan are part of a longer necropolitical Islamic legal inclination, where law is just as much as about regulating death as it is about ensuring life.

Each of these intercultural translations of what we are seeing in Pakistan (and elsewhere) is likely controversial in its own way. And to be sure, this chapter has not offered to conclusively fix the meaning of what is very much an ongoing and dynamic set of developments around the world. Indeed, much more research is necessary and, in particular, on developments in Pakistan. For example, more research needs to be done on the issuances of NIC identity documents in Pakistan. Important questions vis-à-vis these documents include how common are requests for non-cisgender NICs? What kind of difficulties do non-cisgender persons in Pakistan face from governmental authorities in choosing their NIC gender? How easy is to change one's gender on one's NIC after its initial issuance? Answers to these questions would impact the analysis in all three of the above sections.

Additionally, much more research needs to be done on efforts by transgendered (Muslim) Pakistanis, both pre- and post-2009, to receive their due Islamic legal inheritance shares. Important questions vis-à-vis these efforts include how are transgendered Pakistanis classified gender-wise for the purposes of inheritance shares? What precedence do Islamic notions of and tests for gender have vis-à-vis the (elective) gender listed on (transgendered) persons' NICS when it comes to deciding inheritance shares? Are there instances of inheritance disputes being relitigated on the basis of a gender change? Answers to these questions would impact the analysis in the first and third sections, at a minimum.

Finally, Pakistan is not the only place where additional research and theorizing is necessary. Importantly, such theorizing can open up challenges to various suggestions made by this chapter itself, for example, this chapter's attempt to trace valences of transgenderism in Islam and Muslim-majority places which are *different* from those in the West. Toward this point, the Islamic necropolitical highlighted in this chapter's third section was also arguably on display in the first section,[99] where the US Supreme Court's recent *United States v. Windsor* decision explicitly concerning Edith Windsor's inheritance rights was discussed. And indeed, beyond the bare inheritance-taxation dispute central to this case, necropolitics were also on display elsewhere in that decision, most notably when Justice Anthony Kennedy, writing for the majority, took note of how the at-issue Defense of Marriage Act prevented same-sex couples "from being buried together in veterans' cemeteries."[100] In short then, Western legal discussions of gender and sexuality can be seen to be concerned with the legal consequences of death in a manner not totally dissimilar from their Islamic legal brethren. And more attention needs to be paid to this and other potentially disquieting possibilities.

In closing, it is also important to emphasize that each of the individual understandings and translations of what we are seeing in Pakistan (and elsewhere) offered by this chapter is, admittedly, simplistic on its own—even if the overall picture is one of complexity. No place is simply sedimentary. In other words, global, colonial, and Islamic discourses relating to transgenderism do not sit simply adjacent to or on top of each other, unsoiled and unmixed. As a result, any truly compelling intercultural understanding and translation of gender events—whether in Pakistan or elsewhere—will have to imbricate and weave together different epistemological lenses. In the construction of this "queer kaleidoscope," new and arguably better ways of seeing the world will be created, whereby both comparative and historical continuities—and discontinuities—will emerge, and commonplace gender narratives will lose any sense of innocence or obviousness.

NOTES

1. Jeffrey A. Redding, "From 'She-males' to 'Unix': Transgender Rights and the Productive Paradoxes of Pakistani Policing," in *Regimes of Legality: Ethnography of Criminal Cases in South Asia*, eds. Daniela Berti and Devika Bordia (New Delhi, India: Oxford University Press, 2015), 265. Information and quotes contained within this introduction and other places in this chapter are taken from this publication, with more specific references to primary documents used in the preparation of this earlier publication (and cited therein) also occasionally given.

2. "Report prepared by the Regional Police Officer, Rawalpindi for the Inspector General of Police" (report on file with author, Punjab, Lahore, 2009).

3. Ibid., 1.

4. "Eunuch Protest Leads to 3 Cops' Suspension," *Daily Times*, January 28, 2009 (article on file with author).

5. "Report prepared by the Regional Police Officer, Rawalpindi for the Inspector General of Police" (report on file with author, Punjab, Lahore, 2009), 2.

6. This nomenclature would change rapidly and multiple times over the course of the litigation instigated by Dr. Khaki. Redding, "From 'She-males' to 'Unix'," *supra* note 1; Shahnaz Khan, "What is in a Name? *Khwaja Sara*, *Hijra*, and Eunuchs in Pakistan," *Indian Journal of Gender Studies* 23, no. 2 (2016).

7. Earlier political efforts and cultural interventions by transgendered individuals in Pakistan are discussed in Claire Pamment, "Hijraism: Jostling for a Third Space in Pakistani Politics," *TDR: The Drama Review* 54, no. 2 (2010).

8. Afsaneh Najmabadi, *Professing Selves: Transsexuality and Same-Sex Desire in Contemporary Iran* (Durham, NC: Duke University Press, 2014), 1.

9. For example, for more than thirty years now, report after report has showered criticism on Pakistan's infamous "Hudood Ordinances"—severely criminalizing extramarital sex—and the detrimental impact of these "Islamic laws" on Pakistani women. Asma Jahangir and Hina Jilani, *The Hudood Ordinances: A Divine Sanction?* (Lahore: Rhotas Books, 1990); Shahnaz Khan, *Zina, Transnational Feminism and the Moral Regulation of Pakistani Women* (Vancouver: UBC Press, 2006).

10. These are male, female, khwaja sira (male), khwaja sira (female), and khunsa-e-mushkil (an Arabic-derived expression which can be translated as "hermaphrodite"). There is some difficulty in locating a precise statement of these options in the public literature, but the Lahore High Court did summarize the transgender options as follows in a recent litigation: "[T]ransgender for the purposes of the National Identity Card have been divided into three sub-categories:

(i)   Male Khawaja Sira;
(ii)   Female Khawaja Sira; or
(iii)   Khunsa-e-Mushkil.

It is the choice of the applicant to select one of the aforesaid categories and due to the shortage of space in the physical National Identity Card) the caption used for describing or identifying a transgender is 'X.'" Waqar Ali v. Federation of Pakistan, W.P. No. 37499/2016, Lahore High Court (Lahore), 09.01.2017 Order (on file with author). That being said, there has been a great deal of confusion and contestation over the nomenclature of these gender options, and also their meaning, as well as the ability of people to choose and move between these categories. "Dream come true: Transgender community celebrates CNICs, voter registration," *Express Tribune*, January 25, 2012, http://tribune.com.pk/story/326911/dream-come-true-transgender-community-celebrates-cnics-voter-registration/.

11. "Eunuch Protest Leads to 3 Cops' Suspension," *Daily Times*, January 28, 2009 (article on file with author).

12. See text accompanying *supra* note 8 (discussing Afsaneh Najmabadi's observations about recent transsexual discourse in Iran). To be sure, the rest of Najmabadi's groundbreaking work attempts to situate recent discussions and developments in Iran in broader historical, social, and comparative contexts.

13. Kyle Knight, "How Nepal's Constitution Got Queered," *Los Angeles Review of Books*, October 14, 2015, https://lareviewofbooks.org/article/how-nepals-constitution-got-queered. Notably, Knight summarizes the genesis of recent legislation of constitutional language protecting Nepalese "gender and sexual minorities" in the following manner: "The path to constitutional protection for a group at times openly derided as 'social pollutants' *was neither linear nor predictable,* and took a *unique* combination of courage and political wisdom. *It is reflected in the rise of Sunil Pant,* who in 2001 was an unemployed computer engineering graduate handing out condoms in a dusty Kathmandu park, and who seven years later became Asia's first openly gay national-level elected official when he was voted into the Constituent Assembly." Ibid. (emphasis added).

14. "International Work: Campaigning for Global LGBT Equality," *Stonewall*, accessed March 4, 2018, http://www.stonewall.org.uk/our-work/international-work-1.

15. For more on this show, see Pamment, *supra* note 7.

16. The first such show in India appears to date from 2008. "India's Transgender Talk Show Host," *BBC News*, March 5, 2008, http://news.bbc.co.uk/2/hi/south_asia/7265463.stm.

17. Talal Asad, "The Concept of Cultural Translation in British Social Anthropology," in *Writing Culture: The Poetics and Politics of Ethnography*, eds. James Clifford and George E. Marcus (Berkeley: University of California Press, 1986), 157–158.

18. I characterize the word "transgender" as "indigenous" to the United States, but am well aware of this term's relative newness to the United States, as well as ongoing uncertainty and contestation over its use and meaning. On this (recent) history more generally, see David Valentine, *Imagining Transgender: An Ethnography of a Category* (Durham, NC: Duke University Press, 2007).

19. "Watched by Foreign Journalists, Troops Seized the State TV Station," digital image, *BBC News*, August 23, 2007, accessed March 3, 2018, http://news.bbc.co.uk/2/hi/south_asia/6960670.stm.

20. Ahmed Rashid, "The Pakistan Paradox: U.S. Support for Musharraf Undermines War on Terror," *New York Times*, November 28, 2003, http://www.nytimes.com/2003/11/28/opinion/the-pakistan-paradox-us-support-for-musharraf-undermines-war-on.html.

21. Carlotta Gall, "Musharraf Resigns as Army Chief," *New York Times*, November 28, 2007, http://www.nytimes.com/2007/11/28/world/asia/28iht-28pakistan-resigned.8509070.html?_r=0.

22. Syed Shoaib Hasan, "Profile: Islamabad's Red Mosque," *BBC News*, July 27, 2007, http://news.bbc.co.uk/2/hi/6503477.stm; Carlotta Gall, "Siege of Red Mosque Highlights Pakistan's Malaise," *New York Times*, July 8, 2007, http://www.nytimes.com/2007/07/08/world/asia/08iht-islamabad.1.6547663.html?_r=0; Hasnaat Malik, "Lal Masjid Cleric Moves SC on Imposition of Sharia Law," *Express Tribune*, December 10, 2015, http://tribune.com.pk/story/1007500/lal-masjid-cleric-moves-sc-on-imposition-of-sharia-law/.

23. "Islamic Students Abduct Alleged Brothel Owner," *Associated Press*, March 28, 2007, http://www.nbcnews.com/id/11497286/ns/world_news-south_and_central_asia/t/islamic-students-abduct-alleged-brothel-owner/#.VzTxQPkrLIU.

24. Augustine Anthony, "Hard-line Pakistani Students Release Chinese Women," *Reuters*, June 23, 2007, http://www.reuters.com/article/us-pakistan-mosque-idUSSP14126820070623 (describing how "[i]n March [2007], [Lal Masjid seminary] students abducted three Pakistani women they accused of running a brothel and held them for several days before forcing them to confess and releasing them").

25. "Pakistan 'Brothel Woman' Released," *BBC News*, March 29, 2007, http://news.bbc.co.uk/2/hi/south_asia/6507205.stm.

26. "A Chronology of Lal Masjid Saga," *Dawn*, July 11, 2007, http://www.dawn.com/news/255802/a-chronology-of-lal-masjid-saga.

27. Anthony, *supra* note 24.

28. Ibid.

29. Ibid.

30. To be sure, this is not for unselfish reasons. With its Pakistan relationship, China gains significant economic and military advantages both globally and regionally. These advantages include trade-route access to the Arabian Sea via Pakistan's seacoast, and also a nuclear-armed ally who can keep India—also a Chinese adversary—militarily and diplomatically preoccupied.

31. Anthony, *supra* note 24.

32. Hasan, *supra* note 22.

33. "Mosque Leader in Burka Escape Bid," *BBC News*, July 4, 2007, http://news.bbc.co.uk/2/hi/6270626.stm. To be sure, much of the scorn surrounding this attempted escape echoes Jasbir Puar's observation that, for many contemporary nationalisms, "the terrorist is forever queer." Jasbir K. Puar, *Terrorist Assemblages: Homonationalism in Queer Times* (Durham, NC: Duke University Press, 2007), 14. For a more extended discussion of all this, see ibid., 37–78 (Chapter 1, "The Sexuality of Terrorism").

34. See Pamment, *supra* note 7, 41 for a discussion of reasons for low *hijra*-voter turnout in the 2008 national elections in Pakistan. According to Pamment, these reasons included the reality that "following the brutal assassination of Benazir Bhutto . . . who was a bold and beautiful icon for many hijras and the general populace, characterized by her vibrant rallies to the din of folk tunes, [*hijras*] lacked a leader to vote for." Ibid.

35. Declan Walsh, "Harassed, Intimidated, Abused: But now Pakistan's Hijra Transgender Minority Finds its Voice," *Guardian*, January 30, 2010, http://www.theguardian.com/world/2010/jan/29/hijra-pakistan-transgender-rights (noting how "[i]n October [2009] hijras in the southern city of Sukkur fielded the country's first hijras cricket team. After winning their inaugural match, the captain thanked the chief justice.").

36. Rohit De, "Mumtaz Bibi's Broken Heart: The Many Lives of the Dissolution of Muslim Marriages Act," *Indian Economic and Social History Review* 46, no. 1 (2009): 106 (noting that "the Dissolution of Muslim Marriages Act, 1939 [e]nacted by the colonial Central Legislative Assembly formed under the political reforms of 1935 . . . . still remains in force in India, Pakistan and Bangladesh.").

37. National Legal Services Authority v. Union of India, (2014) 5 S.C.C. 438.

38. Ibid., 484.

39. Redding, "From 'She-males' to 'Unix'," *supra* note 1.

40. For example, one of the concluding directives of the Supreme Court of India was that the "Centre and State Governments should seriously address the problems being faced by hijras/transgenders such as fear, shame, gender dysphoria, social pressure, depression, suicidal tendencies, social stigma, etc. and any insistence for [sexual reassignment surgery] for declaring one's gender is immoral and illegal." National Legal Services Authority v. Union of India, *supra* note 37, 508.

41. Vojtech Mastny, "The Soviet Union's Partnership with India," *Journal of Cold War Studies* 12, no. 3 (2010).

42. Puar, *supra* note 33.

43. Ibid., 46.

44. Ibid., 70–71.

45. Ibid., 71.

46. Ibid.

47. Ibid., 72 (paraphrasing the depiction of Pakistan and its relationship to the United States in an essay written by Arundhati Roy).

48. See *supra* note 9.

49. US First Lady Laura Bush became particularly emblematic of this politics. David Stout, "Mrs. Bush Cites Women's Plight Under Taliban," *New York Times*, November 18, 2001, http://www.nytimes.com/2001/11/18/us/a-nation-challenged-the-first-lady-mrs-bush-cites-women-s-plight-under-taliban.html.

50. It is certainly the case that the US Supreme Court has spoken on sex- and gender-based discrimination, including the relationship of "sex stereotyping" to sex-based discrimination. But the Court has not yet taken the opportunity to decide a case speaking broadly to transgendered people or the precarity of their legal and social situations. For the Court's most well-known and, arguably, most important ruling on sex stereotyping and the legal actionability of discrimination on the basis of non-normative gender expression, see Price Waterhouse v. Hopkins, 490 U.S. 228 (1989).

51. Tessa Stuart, "17 Anti-Trans Bills That Could Become Law Next," *Rolling Stone*, March 28, 2016, http://www.rollingstone.com/politics/news/17-anti-trans-bills-that-could-become-law-next-20160328.

52. Katy Steinmetz, "Why LGBT Advocates Say Bathroom 'Predators' Argument Is a Red Herring," *Time*, May 2, 2016, http://time.com/4314896/transgender-bathroom-bill-male-predators-argument/.

53. Redding, "From 'She-males' to 'Unix'," *supra* note 1, 261–262; Pamment, *supra* note 7, 46.

54. United States v. Windsor, 133 S. Ct. 2675 (2013).

55. Obergefell v. Hodges, 135 S. Ct. 2584 (2015).

56. United States v. Windsor (holding that Section 3 of the Defense of Marriage Act ("DOMA") was unconstitutional but not addressing Section 2 of the Act regarding the interstate recognition of same-sex marriages). Section 3 of DOMA legislated an explicitly heterosexual US federal definition of marriage which conflicted with several US states' less restrictive definitions of marriage. *See* Defense of Marriage Act, Pub. L. No. 104–199, § 3, 110 Stat. 2419, 2419 (1996) (codified at 1 U.S.C. § 7 (2012)).

57. On this point, see generally Jeffrey A. Redding, "Querying Edith Windsor, Querying Equality," *Villanova Law Review* (Tolle Lege) 59 (2013). I realize that I am conflating sexuality and gender here, but it is not clear to me that the two are as separable—in either the US or Pakistani context—as many theorists would have it.

58. Redding, "From 'She-males' to 'Unix,'" *supra* note 1, 268–269.

59. Laurence Preston's work, for example, describes pre-colonial, Western Indian regimes granting *hijras* certain rights to engage in begging and, moreover, certain government-provided financial and land grants. Laurence W. Preston, "A Right to Exist: Eunuchs and the State in Nineteenth-Century India," *Modern Asian Studies*

21, no. 2 (1987): 377–386. Importantly, some of these grants had also apparently been inheritable—indeed, through chains of *hijra* masters and disciples rather than blood- or heteronormative kin-premised chains of lineage! Ibid., 383. As Preston narrates, this situation caused the British much consternation given that British colonial authorities were forced to decide "whether, as the successor to indigenous states, it should uphold its predecessors' grants." Ibid., 381.

60. In making methodological connections between inter-historicism and inter-culturalism, I have the recent work of Monica Eppinger in mind. *See* Monica E. Eppinger, "The Health Exception," *Georgetown Journal of Gender & the Law* 17 (2016): 670 (observing that "Th[e] past is a foreign country.").

61. See generally Redding, "From 'She-males' to 'Unix,'" *supra* note 1, for a discussion of how terminology referring to the non-normatively-gendered individuals at the heart of this litigation changed over the course of the litigation.

62. See Gayatri Reddy, *With Respect to Sex: Negotiating Hijra Identity in South India* (Chicago: University of Chicago Press, 2005), 156–164, for a discussion of *guru* dynamics in a particular urban context in India.

63. Human Rights Const. P. No. 63 of 2009, 16.06.2009 Order (on file with author), 2.

64. "Government of the Punjab, Social Welfare, Women Development and Bait ul Maal Department, Memo to the Registrar, Supreme Court of Pakistan on Human Right Case No. 63/2009" (August 13, 2009) (memo on file with author), 1.

65. Ibid.

66. Ibid., 6. This is a quotation of the English text included on the survey form. The Urdu text on the form here referred to the *kaifiyat* ('condition,' or 'nature') of each *khwājah sirā*. Ibid.

67. Ibid. I have only included the English text of this part of the form here. However, there were accompanying Urdu translations for each of these boxes.

68. Ibid. I have only included the English text of this part of the form here. However, there were accompanying Urdu translations for each of these questions.

69. The "he/she" and "his/her" used throughout these questions seem to be referring to the gender of the eunuch being interviewed by the survey-takers and not about the gender of these eunuchs' *gurus*.

70. Michel Foucault, *The History of Sexuality, Volume 1: An Introduction*, trans. Robert Hurley (New York: Pantheon Books, 1978), 144 (noting how "[t]he law always refers to the sword. But a power whose task is to take charge of life needs continuous regulatory and corrective mechanisms. It is no longer a matter of bringing death into play in the field of sovereignty, but of distributing the living in the domain of value and utility. Such a power has to qualify, measure, appraise, and hierarchize, rather than display itself in its murderous splendor.").

71. For some of the more well-known works on the British colonial authorities' development and use of the census in colonial India, see Arjun Appadurai, "Number in the Colonial Imagination," in *Orientalism and the Postcolonial Predicament: Perspectives on South Asia*, eds. Carol Breckenridge and Peter van der Veer (Philadelphia: University of Pennsylvania Press, 1993); Bernard S. Cohn, "The Census, Social Structure and Objectification in South Asia," in *An Anthropologist Among the*

Historians and Other Essays, ed. Bernard S. Cohn (Delhi: Oxford University Press, 1987); Sudipta Kaviraj, "Religion and Identity in India," *Ethnic and Racial Studies* 20, no. 2 (1997).

72. For a version of this point, see Appadurai, "Number in the Colonial Imagination," 328. Cohn makes the more elemental point that the colonial census contributed to a "process of objectification," Cohn, 230, whereby Indian cultural and religious traditions have been transformed into "entit[ies]" that can be "polished and reformulated for conscious ends." Cohn, 229.

73. Appadurai, "Number in the Colonial Imagination," 335.

74. "National Identity Card (NIC)," *National Database and Registration Authority*, accessed March 13, 2018, https://www.nadra.gov.pk/identity/identity-cnic/.

75. Constitution Petition No. 43 of 2009, 20.11.2009 Order (on file with author), para. 2.

76. Azam Khan, "Transgender Rights: SC Tells NADRA to Amend Gender Verification Process," *Express Tribune*, April 26, 2011, http://tribune.com.pk/story/156256/sc-directs-nadra-to-include-eunuchs-in-gender-column/ (noting that "[t]he Supreme Court . . . directed the National Database and Registration Authority (NADRA) not to verify the gender of transgender people through a medical board").

77. Constitution Petition No. 43 of 2009, 20.11.2009 Order (on file with author), para. 5.

78. Dr. Mohammad Aslam Khaki, interview by Jeffrey A. Redding, March 10, 2012. Dr. Khaki also informed me that one reason that any number of people are "pretending" to be eunuchs these days is that, according to Dr. Khaki, it is possible to earn 20,000–30,000 Pakistani rupees per month—in other words, a Pakistani middle-class monthly salary—while begging on the streets, if one is recognized as a eunuch. Ibid.

79. Constitutional Petition No. 43 of 2009, 23.12.2009 Order (on file with author), para. 7.

80. Again quoting Appadurai here. See text accompanying *supra* note 70.

81. "Memorandum from the Government of NWFP Social Welfare & Women Dev: Department to the Registrar, Supreme Court of Pakistan & the Advocate General, NWFP, Peshawar on Petition under article 184(3) of the Constitution of the Islamic Republic Pakistan 1973" (August 15, 2009) (memo on file with author).

82. "Q&A: Pakistan's Swat Offensive," *BBC News*, May 20, 2009, http://news.bbc.co.uk/2/hi/south_asia/8044604.stm.

83. "Memorandum from the Government of NWFP Social Welfare & Women Dev: Department to the Registrar, Supreme Court of Pakistan & the Advocate General, NWFP, Peshawar on Petition under article 184(3) of the Constitution of the Islamic Republic Pakistan 1973" (August 15, 2009) (memo on file with author), 2.

84. Ibid.

85. Ibid., 4–7.

86. Ibid., 14. This guardian/custodial role is confirmed by Shahzad Bashir. Shahzad Bashir, "Islamic Tradition and Celibacy," in *Celibacy and Religious Traditions*, ed. Carl Olson (New York: Oxford University Press, 2007).

87. See, for example, David Ayalon, *Eunuchs, Caliphs and Sultans: A Study in Power Relationships* (Jerusalem: Magnes Press, Hebrew University, 1999); Shaun

Marmon, *Eunuchs and Sacred Boundaries in Islamic Society* (New York: Oxford University Press, 1995). For discussions of the gender situation in empires concurrent with and adjacent to early Islamic empires, see Kathryn M. Ringrose, *The Perfect Servant: Eunuchs and the Social Construction of Gender in Byzantium* (Chicago: University of Chicago Press, 2003).

88. Ayalon, 62. According to Ayalon, there was some religious disapproval of the castration process itself. However, "[s]ince most of the castration was carried out outside the boundaries of Islam, and mainly by unbelievers, the Muslim religious scholars could comfortably condemn the operation, but react much more mildly to the purchase of . . . eunuchs and their employment." Ibid., 61.

89. Ibid., 67.

90. As Bashir summarizes this typical eunuch role: "The most radical form of celibacy encountered in the setting of premodern Islamic societies is the widespread use of castrated slaves as trusted servants by ruling houses and the elites from the eighth century until the modern period. . . . After being bought, the slaves were vetted for innate aptitudes and then given extensive education and training to become the most trusted protectors and administrators of elite families." Bashir, *supra* note 86, 144. According to Bashir, these trusted roles included those of "highly placed military commanders and imperial officials in most dynastic empires that flourished in central Islamic lands from the eighth century to the coming of modernity." Ibid., 135.

91. Marmon, *supra* note 87, 7 (citation omitted).

92. K.S. Lal, *Muslim Slave System in Medieval India* (New Delhi: South Asia Books, 1994).

93. Pamment, *supra* note 7, 37.

94. For more on this, see generally Faisal Devji, *Muslim Zion: Pakistan as a Political Idea* (Cambridge, MA: Harvard University Press, 2013).

95. Marmon, *supra* note 87, 15–30.

96. See text accompanying *supra* note 70.

97. See discussion accompanying *supra* note 58; Redding, "From 'She-males' to 'Unix,'" *supra* note 1, 268–269; "Way Opens for Eunuchs' Right to Inheritance," *Dawn*, October 13, 2011, http://www.dawn.com/news/665914/way-opens-for-eunuchs-right-to-inheritance.

98. "Fatwa Allows Transgender Marriage," *Dawn*, June 27, 2016, http://www.dawn.com/news/1267491.

99. See discussion accompanying *supra* notes 54–57.

100. United States v. Windsor, *supra* note 54, 2694. For more on the necropolitics of *United States v. Windsor*, see Redding, "Querying Edith Windsor," *supra* note 57.

Chapter 4

The Off-centered Hub of Secularism

Religion inside Human Rights Projections and Quotidian Life

Melisa Vazquez

When we talk about human rights, notions of both universality and of faith are ever present. Famously, the United Nation's Universal Declaration of Human Rights states that its creators "reaffirmed their faith in fundamental human rights, in the dignity and worth of the human person and in the equal rights of men and women."[1] The Declaration, as well as the human rights discourse that has followed, presupposes and relies upon the possibility of universality. And yet this universality has been and continues to be called into question. As one scholar observes:

> Indeed the Declaration proved to spring from a particular conception of the human good. It only makes sense in certain kind of society and polity: that which its drafters knew. It is replete with concepts, such as legal personality (Article 6), nationality (Article 15), access to public service (Article 21), protection against unemployment (Article 23), and periodic holidays with pay (Article 24), which are simply not known to most human societies which have historically existed on earth. Significantly, it was drafted when a considerable portion of the world remained colonized and had no input into its formulation.[2]

The world is and has been populated by a plurality with clear differences from the "drafters of universality." Still, we can set these issues aside for a moment and concede that the declaration was, at the very least, intended as a call for universal human rights. Beyond mere aspiration, the declaration is part of international law. Further, individual liberal democratic states have attempted to map their laws, designed to reflect and regulate quotidian lives, in ways that are responsive to common-life needs as well as the moral projections emanating from human rights declarations. As societies have become increasingly diverse, however, it is ever more apparent that the moral projections that underlie both our rights statements and our laws are what Habermas calls "untapped moral intuitions,"[3] and they come from religion, more precisely, the anthropological projections of religious traditions.

And yet the neutrality of the secular State is taken as a fundamental tenet of modern societies. Elie Wiesel is frequently cited for having called human rights "the secular religion of our time."[4] Secularism, for its part, depends on the neutrality of politics and law with regard to religion, at least in its theoretical conception. Today it is generally assumed that secularism is indeed neutral. However, this chapter comes from the viewpoint that secularism today is neither neutral nor complete, and that this lack of completion is at the core of the conflicts lately erupting in the contemporary world within the realms of religion and law. There are entire bodies of research by important scholars on these topics writ large coming from an increasingly diverse range of fields including philosophy, religious studies, sociology, anthropology, and political science, just to name a few. A comprehensive consideration of human rights through the prisms of religion and law is beyond the scope of this chapter. However, since human rights seem to depend—at the very least—upon the concept of secularism, I would like to assume a particular critical perspective encapsulated well by the book title *Secularization and Its Discontents*,[5] to further investigate how some "underground features" of current day conflicts in religion and law might help shed light on human rights projections in European quotidian life today.

Over the last few years, the secularism concept, crown prince of the Western religion/law divide, has been increasingly present in the public discourse. The year 2015 saw a violent attack on the French satirical magazine "Charlie Hebdo," bombings in Paris and Tunis, and in Brussels in 2016, all claimed by Islamic State. The war in Syria and the related massive influx of Muslim migrants into Europe during this time period have led to issues of religion and law, religiosity and secularism, Europeans and Muslims, Us and Them, being splashed all over the news and debated in circles of every dimension. The dominant narrative, sketched in the broadest of terms, runs, "(We) Europeans were perfectly at peace, conducting (our) successfully secular European lives, until (you) Muslims destroyed (our) peace with your hyper-religiosity that has no place in (our) rational, secular world. You attack our way of life, our values." There are, of course, also oppositional voices calling for rational analysis and nuanced consideration. And yet walls continue to go up, borders to close; migrants are attacked, benefits cut, and mass protests held. Anti-migration parties are enjoying unprecedented popularity in multiple European states. The French state has been in a declared state of emergency for nearly a year. These could be characterized as political and/or sociological responses. And yet there is a strain of religiosity across both public and state responses that is hard to miss. To take just one example, after the Charlie Hebdo attack in Paris, President Hollande declared that France would "lead the fight, and it will be *merciless*." "This was an *abomination*," he continued, "because it was a *barbaric* act."⁶ The most popular social media tag was "*Pray* for Paris." It seems that alongside the politics of war and violence, there is also an increasingly pronounced conflict of values and of religion. It begs the question: Why is a self-declared secular society so enmeshed in responses bearing a religious cast?

One striking aspect of these events has been the consistency of "message,"—in the marketing sense—from politicians and even academics on what these trying times call for from good liberal citizens. What is at stake, we continue to hear, are the *values of our secular way of life*, namely "human reason," and "freedom." Most are in agreement that the correct descriptive dialectical poles are peaceful-liberal-secular-Europeans against violent-extremist-religious-Muslims. Clearly each of these terms can immediately be problematized. And yet there seems to be a deep commitment to these oppositions. The conflict is not framed as one between Christians and Muslims, but rather Europeans and Muslims, or better, Europeans and Muslim terrorists. Beyond merely statements, these positions translate into concrete state actions. In response to the November 2015 attacks in Paris, the French government activated a 1955 law (originally enacted during the war with Algeria) authorizing a declared "state of emergency" that gave the interior minister and local government officials the power to search homes and premises and restrict people's movements without a judicial warrant. This emergency state remains in place nearly one year later. Human Rights Watch reports that according to the French Ministry of the Interior, during the first three months of the state of emergency, "French law enforcement officials conducted more than 3,200 raids and placed between 350 and 400 people under house arrest. . . . As a result of the 3,289 searches, only five investigations into terrorism-related offenses were being conducted by the Paris prosecutor's office."⁷ Rights groups have reported widely on the targeting and discrimination against Muslims that these efforts have entailed, leaving many without work, injured, with damage to their homes and in one extreme case, with their children taken from them.⁸

These actions are held to be wholly secular actions of the State to protect the people. It is the law that enables them, that solid, majestic institution that is intended to safeguard and defend our freedoms. It is the law that separates Church and State in Europe, the law that is the shining beacon of rationality, protecting us from the murky morass of an ignorant past where magic ruled and science was yet to be discovered. But can we count on the law's secularity? On its neutrality? Leaving responses to violent conflicts aside, and turning more to the management of everyday life, is the law in Europe showing itself to be secular, intended as a neutral stance toward all religious positions? Perhaps the most recently cited case in this regard is the European Court of Human Rights' ruling in 2014 in *SAS v. France* which supported the ban against wearing the niqab and burka in public in the name of "living together." The idea was that wearing these religious garments in public was disturbing, was bringing religion into a public square that must instead, remain religion-free, in line with, once again, our values of humanity and freedom. As French-Bulgarian critic Tzvetan Todorov put it:

> Even if its application in particular cases can pose a problem: in a democracy, law is higher than custom. . . . The values of a society find their expression in the Constitution, the laws, or indeed the structure of the state; if custom transgresses them, it must be abandoned.[9]

But what if we consider that the law also *is* custom or, at least, includes it? And, indeed: How could the law not include custom? We see this in the way people know how to follow laws while simultaneously having very little awareness of what they know. We see it in the value concepts that serve as pillars to the law, such as truth, good faith, right to property, right to privacy, and yes, "living together." These are not material things "out there," universal, indisputable, but instead are epitomes of long historical processes. They do not exist a priori, nor does the way in which society interprets them remain fixed over time. Children, women, and slaves have all moved from objects of possession to human beings with rights, over time, in the eyes of the law. Laws are not "inspired" by values, they are *constituted* by values, they embody them. These values are not orphans (even when orphaned). On the contrary, as has been repeatedly shown in the last decades, at least some among such legal Western values (and these are not the lesser ones) come from none other than the Christian roots of the West. The fervor ubiquitous to public discourse on free speech, to take just one example, is rooted in the Christian idea of Truth. As Talal Asad notes, "Free speech—truthful speech—releases the human subject from his or her servitude. . . . Of course the liberal principle of free speech does not depend on the proviso that speech to be free must be literally true, but the Christian idea of Truth as applied to speaking and listening freely helps [. . .] to explain why that principle has come to be thought of as 'sacred.'"[10]

Asad and other prominent scholars of secularism (Casanova[11], Calhoun[12]) have made convincing cases that there is not a single secularism but rather secularisms, that secularism is infused with religious features that endure, and that religious entities contain secularisms within them; in short, this tidy dialectic is anything but tidy. Casanova and others are careful to point out the differences in terms used to discuss the secular. Grace Davie put it succinctly:

> Let's start by taking apart *secular, secularity, secularism* and *secularization*. They all have different meanings. Secular is an adjective. It shouldn't be loaded, but it often is. Secularity is a state of affairs. Secularism is an ideology, like rationalism or communism, and there's very little of that in Britain, but much more in France. And secularization is a process.[13]

In the face of mounting societal evidence (from large-scale studies, such as the one done by the Pew Research Center[14]), theories regarding the decline of religiosity in the West have been reconsidered; new frameworks have been devised, such as Davie's "believing without belonging,"[15] which makes the case that in Western Europe, many who do not go to church or consider themselves to be religious nonetheless share basic ideas regarding faith and morality with those who technically belong to the church. Peter Fitzpatrick takes it one step further in his work on legal theology, in which he employs Nietzsche's idea of "active forgetfulness." As Fitzpatrick puts it, in order to understand the present, there must be "a bringing forth of what had to be forgotten so as to affirm the putative completion that is, for example, the triumph of a modernist secularism." This forgetting, he goes on to say, "is continuous with, and constituent of, what is remembered."[16] His analysis of the institution of law is complex and beyond the scope of this chapter, but with the idea of active forgetfulness hovering above us, we can consider a few small examples, using the eruption of conflict as a kind of flashlight that illuminates contrasts. What is of interest here is not so much institutional religion, but rather the anthropological traces of religion that can be seen in the vestiges of Christianity extant in the everyday behaviors of the inhabitants of even the most evidently secular societies. A few examples may be illuminating.

In one anthropological study on women in Turkey, the authors reference a cartoon in which a middle-aged woman in a headscarf is riding a city bus. She calls out to the driver, "Sir, let me get off before coming to a public sphere."[17] The conflicts over the headscarf in Europe have highlighted notions of public versus private space that are infused with Christian conceptions stemming from the Reformation, if not before. As referenced earlier, it has been ruled that the public sphere must be protected from overt signs of religiousness such as the niqab or burka. The same public space, presumably, that draws millions of visitors from around the world because of the vast number of historic cathedrals that fill it. The same public space, that in the wake of both the Paris and Brussels attacks, was marked by huge altars of flowers and candles, candle-lit vigils, and moments of silence.

After *SAS*, the most oft cited case regarding state and religion in Europe is surely *Lautsi v. Italy* (2011), which addressed the presence of the crucifix on the walls of an Italian public school. The European Court of Human Rights supported the Italian court's claim that the crucifix is not a religious symbol, but rather a cultural one, adding that it was "essentially a passive symbol" that could not be deemed to have "influence on pupils." What we find is a kind of "pushing to the side" of the anthropological projections of religious traditions, even when they are expressed in material religious symbols. This response is not unique to Italy or even Europe. In the United States, for example, as recently as 2015 New Jersey Supreme Court justice David F. Bauman dismissed a case against a regional school district brought by a student who argued that the phrase "under God" in the Pledge of Allegiance (whose daily recitation is mandatory in many US schools) created a climate of discrimination against nonbelievers. The United States has been a perplexing case for many a religious and legal scholar because of its unique mix of the official "separation of church and state" alongside a pervasive religiosity of culture which requires swearing on the Bible before testifying in court among many other Christian-based cultural habits and traditions. While it is commonly argued that the United States is a model nation when it comes to modern, secular societies, the claim is also made that the Christian legacy of the nation was instrumental to the American version of secularism and continues to produce very blurry boundaries between the religious and the secular.[18] To wit, Judge Bauman stated, "As a matter of historical tradition, the words 'under God' can no more be expunged from the national consciousness than the words 'In God We Trust' from every coin in the land, than the words 'so help me God' from every presidential oath since 1789, or than the prayer that has opened every congressional session of legislative business since 1787."[19] In the *Lautsi* case, the argument was that the crucifix is a cultural symbol that cannot be supposed to proselytize; in the Pledge of Allegiance case, the argument is that religion as expressed in the words "under God" is so pervasive and entrenched in the national culture that it makes no sense to try to remove it. In both cases there is an overarching mindset that the anthropological traces of Christianity within these Western societies are simply part and parcel of those societies and need not to be questioned. When the niqab, instead, makes an appearance in the public sphere, it is another story altogether.

Thomas Luckmann wrote about "invisible religion" as early as 1967[20] and noted sociologists (Schutz[21], Lefebvre[22]) preceded scholars of secularism in their calls for a meaningful examination of what has been termed, "the sociologies of the unnoticed."[23] Insofar as secularism has been characterized as the removal of religion from the public space, and given that this removal has not succeeded in expelling "the religious" from the public, in all of its undeniable anthropological diversity, behaviors developed from Christian roots continue to go unnoticed; that is, until behaviors with non-Christian roots seem to suddenly pull them out of hiding. Do we stop to really consider why Sunday is a day of rest? Fish on Fridays, Christmas caroling, Easter egg hunts, and candle-lit vigils are for the most part experienced as standard features of "secular" lives. From the school holiday calendar to the consistency of how births, weddings, and deaths are marked, it seems impossible to "remove" religious roots, anthropologically connoted, from quotidian behaviors. The concepts that are fundamental to our institutions, including the law, are perhaps even more significant in this vein. After a person has served time for committing a crime it is said that he has "paid his debt to society," but where does this concept of redemption come from? The concept of truth, again, is perhaps the most fundamental of all to the legal system: the truth, the whole truth and nothing but the truth, is the sacred vow taken in the witness stand, and yet anthropologists, sociologists, and even jurists have shown how concepts of truth can vary radically from one culture to another. This is not to speak of relativism, but rather of the complexity of what is routinely and pervasively taken for granted. What of the legality of our personal names? What about image, and the issues of privacy therein? Concepts of legal person? John Dewey perhaps said it best when he wrote, "discussions and theories which have influenced legal practice have, with respect to the concept of 'person,' introduced and depended upon a mass of non-legal considerations: considerations popular, historical, political, moral, philosophical, metaphysical and, in connection with the latter, theological."[24] Can we successfully address the legal issues regarding the integrity of the body and related matters regarding, for example, organ transplants (these fragments of humanity) without values? And is there evidence that values can successfully be stripped of all traces of (anthropologically rooted) religion?

One response might be that all of this is not important, that the roots of values in Europe and the United States may well have Christian traces, but that this need not be an impediment to a peaceful social life. Returning to human rights discourse, we might say that concepts borrowed from Christianity are strengths for human rights, that universal freedom and other like concepts are irrefutably to the benefit of humanity. I would argue that it is not where values come from or whether they are beneficial that is at issue. Rather, it is the lack of reflection or acknowledgment of these roots that creates conflict.

The challenge is that the very division between "out there in the world" and "in here in our interior lives," which seems so self-evident, as do true/untrue, religious/secular, is itself the historical consequence of a particular set of conditions evolved from St. Francis to Luther[25], to today's self-proclaimed religion-free societies. How do we know this? We bump into it, as it were, every time we confront the Other. In the Jyllands-Posten Muhammad cartoons controversy in 2005, European responses were largely unified in characterizing Muslim responses as inappropriate and even ridiculous. As Saba Mahmood elucidates,

> One source of bafflement emanates from the semiotic ideology that underpins their sense that religious symbols and icons are one thing, and sacred figures, with all the devotional respect they might evoke, another. To confuse one with the other is to commit a category mistake and to fail to realize that signs and symbols are only arbitrarily linked to the abstractions that humans have come to revere and regard as sacred. As any modern sensible human being must understand, religious signs—such as the cross—are not embodiments of the divine but only stand in for the divine through an act of human encoding and interpretation.[26]

This, however, Mahmood goes on to show, is a conception with decidedly Christian roots. The notion of an image or icon as an embodiment of the divine is an altogether different conception for many Muslims. Again, the argument could be made that these are minority conceptions, minority concerns, and should not stand in the way of majoritarian visions for society. To be concrete, Muslims who are upset about the cartoons should simply learn, as residents of Europe, to take them less seriously since they are a part of the world of material symbols and signs and are separate from the *forum internum* of true religious belief. But this response "crucially depends . . . upon a prior agreement about what religion should be in the modern world." It depends upon a "normative understanding of religion internal to liberalism,"[27] and normative understandings are not universal.

The binaries that inform, suffuse, and define that which we call "living together" are constitutive processes, despite all textual insistence to the contrary. That the post-Enlightenment world has been formed, in discourse, via these binaries does not make them "real," "true," or, importantly, universal. The same notion has been effectively argued in the field of anthropology. The seminal work *Thinking through Things* by a group of anthropologists at Cambridge including Ameria Henare summarizes the matter with aplomb:

> The point is not that anthropologists might be wrong (or indeed unique) in their predilection for structuring the world according to proverbial "binary oppositions," but simply that such notions are not universally shared (even within "the West"), and therefore may not be particularly useful as a lens through which to view other people's lives and ideas.[28]

That ordinary Muslims describing their feelings about the cartoons mocking the prophet as personally painful were summarily dismissed across Western media is a direct consequence of "the presumptions of the civil law tradition in which the epistemological status of religious belief has come to be cast as speculative and therefore less 'real' than the materiality of race and biology" (Mahmood). To be sure, this demotion of religious belief is also fragile, and tends to wobble in the winds of asymmetrical politics. When, for example, it comes to conscientious objection to military participation based on religious belief, Western courts have protected freedom of conscience. Or when the population thought to be a victim of religiously offensive materials is Christian, the courts have ruled in their favor, for example the European Court of Human Rights decision in *Wingrove v. United Kingdom*, which supported the censorship of a film that was found to be offensive to devout Christians. What we find is a conflagration of politics, morals, and a specific semantic and conceptual field that insists on its own consistency while simultaneously being blind to its own contours: in a word, modernity.

Bruno Latour, in his work *We Have Never Been Modern*[29] is at the forefront of an upending of traditional modern theory. He argues that implicit in modernity's separation or *purification* of objects from subjects (e.g., the Danish comic vs. the Prophet), nonhumans from humans (e.g., terrorists vs. European citizens) is a denial of what he terms "hybrids" or "quasi-objects," that is, "things that are simultaneously natural and cultural, subject and object, ideal and material." The anthropological question posed by Henare, Holbraad, and Wastell reveals this issue concisely: *Why would purification be necessary if there was no contamination in the first place?* This question is directly applicable to the issue of secularization. If the values and principles that suffuse legal systems and human rights declarations alike are universal and secular, meaning completely "uncontaminated" by religion, then why does such discord around these issues continue? In the interest of seeking solutions rather than identifying problems we might ask: Is a complete secularization possible? What about human rights? Aren't human rights conceived of precisely in order to avoid the limitations of state political institutions so that we may find more universal ways of protecting people? As John T. Noonan, Jr., poetically reminds us, "declarations are not deeds, a form of words by itself secures nothing, . . . the same words pregnant with meaning in one cultural context may be entirely barren in another."[30] Human Rights, in short, are only as strong as their implementations. Implementations, for their part, come from state institutions. State institutions, as we have seen, take a stance of neutrality toward values—and especially religiously connoted values—in their declarations, but often not in their deeds. Whether the justifications are overt, as in the Bauman ruling claiming that it is impossible to "expunge" the historical tradition of the presence of God in American legal and political language, or more subtle as in the French defense of "living together" to exclude the burqa/niqab from the public sphere, state institutions repeatedly show themselves to be "contaminated" with values of a religiously traced provenance. The very concept of secularism, as has been shown, is itself the product of a Christian heritage. How then can we address the universality of human rights in the absence of an analysis of secularism? Self-awareness is only possible before a mirror, and that mirror is provided by the plurality of perspectives that continues to multiply in modern societies. The "hidden Christianity" of Western legal concepts is only visible when Others fail to see themselves in its interfaces. The theological origins of modern secular concepts of political thought is not a new idea, of course; Carl Schmitt's *Political Theology*[31] was perhaps the seminal work on the topic, addressing the public dimension of theological concepts within the legal order. In crucial absence, however, is an intercultural analysis of serious challenges regarding the civil and penal law dimensions (contract law, succession, categories of crimes, corporations and associations law, and of course family law), which, in turn, are fundamental to any implementation of human rights. It is in the private sphere that people's quotidian life needs are addressed, and it is here that we find the most resilient strains of religious traces, which again, only surface when confronted with difference.

Perhaps we simply have not yet reached the end of the secularization process. If so, might our state laws continue to develop ways to keep religion (in all of its various manifestations) out of public sphere? Perhaps we are still on a universal trajectory of growth and development which moves away from the religious (broadly intended) and toward a rational secular modernity. This idea has been nestled within secularization studies and scholarship in general for quite some time. Following sociologist Gurminder Bhambra, I submit that this theory of development has been a kind of keystone to the very concept of modernity and with it secularization.

Bhambra identifies two fundamental assumptions on which modernity rests, "*rupture* and *difference*—a temporal rupture that distinguishes a traditional agrarian past from the modern industrial present; and a fundamental difference that distinguishes Europe from the rest of the world."[32] This framing is closely aligned to the idea of "stages of civilization," in which Europeans lead the world in all "rational" measures of success while the rest of the world struggles to catch up. It also aligns well with what Charles Taylor has described regarding the application of secularization frameworks by the West to the rest of the world. Describing how the secular came to be distinguished from the religious in Europe, he writes:

> The hiving off of a specifically "earthly" criterion figured within a broader distinction, that which divided "this world," or the immanent, from the transcendent. This very clear-cut distinction is itself a product of the development of Latin Christendom and has become part of our way of seeing things in the West. We tend to apply it universally, even though no distinction this hard and fast has existed in any other human culture in history.[33]

As for modernity, Bhambra questions the Western story about "stages of civilization," by pointing to historical events such as the Haitian Revolution. The Haitian Revolution included the self-emancipation of its slaves, the abolition of slavery, and the institution of suffrage across the color bar, as part of a revolution that led to the unique creation of a state ruled by nonwhites and former captives. And yet it is a story that has been, until relatively recently, largely silenced. Might there be some benefit to a reflection on the fact that slavery continued, to name just one European example, in Danish colonies until 1848, a full forty-four years after its abolition in Haiti? Can we learn from this discrepancy (and others like it) in the "stages of civilization" story?

To summarize, there seems to be a growing consensus among a wide range of scholars that the stories and frameworks upon which scholarship has depended to explain "the West and the rest" with regard to secularism and modernity are no longer adequate to address today's conflicts. We do not appear to be approaching the end of a secularization process, not only because the facts don't bear it out, but because such a thing is not actually possible. Once we tug on any of the loose threads of these frameworks (secularism, modernity, neutrality, universalism) the fabric pulls apart. We find that neither the historically girded arguments about progress nor the universalistic arguments defining secularism are able to hold together. Also, "religious" behaviors by both individuals and institutions persist despite everything.

One might ask, then, what is this "idiom of religion"? One etymological dictionary states that an early definition of "idiom," placed in the 1580s, is that of, "a form of speech peculiar to a people or place." I would say this is certainly an apt description and indeed, that if we are to attempt to step away from endless identitarian conflict in the realm of religion and society in the West, we would do well to pay close attention to the word "peculiar," defined as "belonging exclusively to." Until we are able to consider just how profoundly Western universalism is not universal, but rather belongs to the Western project of modernity, we will continue to be baffled, to use Mahmood's word, when faced with conflict and violence. It is modernity's insistence on its own universality and neutrality that appears as in bas-relief in the face of Other perspectives. Western violence is characterized as humanitarian. Muslim violence is characterized as terrorism. As is clarified in the introduction to *Thinking through Things*,

> [O]ur concepts, (not our representations) must, by definition, be inadequate to translate different ones. This, it is suggested, is the only way to take difference—alterity—seriously as the starting point for anthropological analysis. One must accept that when someone tells us, say, that powder is power, the anthropological problem cannot be that of accounting for why he might think that about powder (explaining, interpreting, placing his statement into context),

but rather that if that really is the case, then we just do not know what powder he is talking about. . . . The world in which powder is power is not an uncharted (and preposterous!) region of our own [and, I would dare say, is not "untrue."]. It is a different world, in which what we take to be powder is actually power, or, more to the point, a third element which will remain ineffably paradoxical for as long as we insist on glossing it with our default concepts—neither "powder" nor "power" but, somehow, both, or better still, the same thing.[34]

To return to Mahmood's arguments regarding the comics of the Prophet, the only way to take difference seriously is to accept that if the icon of the Prophet really is something with which some believers identify in a bodily way, then we just do not know what identification they are talking about. It's a different world. What we uncover, if we take alterity seriously, is something that for us is a "third element," an as-of-yet undiscovered angle which cannot be simply a "pluralized" version of what came before. If we are to have any hope of understanding it, it must be radically de-composed. We must explore, investigate, dig beneath, to see what its constituent parts are. Once we acknowledge that taken-for-granted neutrality, or "cultural symbols," are perceived and felt in radically different ways by different people, then we need to try to understand how and why, if we are at all interested in peaceful pluralistic societies. The kind of de-composition being referenced is part of the theory of "intercultural trans-lation," as addressed in depth in this volume by Mario Ricca. It calls for a breaking down of the connotative elements of value-based positions, a movement simultaneously backward in time and down-to-the-foundations in direction, that seeks to trace the storylines and roots that constitute our present. The idea is to dig beneath our discourse, to "splinter" our hardened ideological stances into their constitutive elements. And what are we looking for? Possible continuities. Because after the end of World War II when European powers drafted the Declaration of Human Rights, their faith was in the "dignity and worth of the human person," and is this not still an aim worth pointing toward? Human rights are not doomed because the grand narratives behind secularism, universalism, and modernity are being questioned. Rather, if they are to be effective, they must necessarily be reconfigured to involve processes of exploration, of opening up to the stories and projections of the humans they are intended to protect, in all their complexity.

The realities of so-called subaltern lives are increasingly visible as the globe shrinks and digital recording, and therefore visibility, grows exponentially. One can only hope that perhaps an unintended consequence of these changes will be to bring to light the ways in which the Western European secularism concept, viewed through the experiences of people's everyday lives (and the laws that rule them), is no longer adequate to help us address conflicts that emerge in the realms of religion and law. Stockpiles of unexamined assumptions are weighing down the terrain where we cohabitate in ever closer quarters. Until the values and contours of these assumptions are unearthed, it will be impossible to decipher where or what religion is or means, inside or outside of the states that stand for "universal human rights." This does not mean that human rights are no longer useful as a tool to manage the conflicts emerging in our plural societies, quite the contrary. What I believe is called for is a new approach, one that does not hide behind unexamined claims of universality but instead engages in deliberate acts of exploration and understanding that seek to connect rights statements and laws to the realities lived by the people who are beholden to them. Until then, the wheel of secularism will presumably continue to wobble on an asymmetrical axis.

NOTES

1. United Nations Universal Declaration of Human Rights, Preamble, paragraph 5.

2. Marie-Bénédicte Dembour, *Who Believes in Human Rights? Reflections on the European Convention* (New York: Cambridge University Press, 2006), 156.

3. Jeffrey Flynn, *Reframing the Intercultural Dialogue on Human Rights: A Philosophical Approach* (New York: Routledge, 2014).

4. Elie Wiesel, "A Tribute to Human Rights," in *The Universal Declaration of Human Rights: Fifty Years and Beyond*, eds. Yael Danieli, Elsa Stamatopoulou, and Clarence J. Dias (Amityville, NY: Baywood, 1999), 3–4.

5. Robert Warner, *Secularization and Its Discontents* (London: Continuum International Publishing, 2010).

6. François Hollande, speech by the president of the Republic before a joint session of Parliament Versailles, November 16, 2015, available at: http://www.diplomati e.gouv.fr/en/french-foreign-policy/defence-security/parisattacks-paris-terror-attacks-november-2015/article/speech-by-the-president-of-the-republic-before-a-joint-se ssion-of-parliament.

7. Human Rights Watch, "France: Abuses Under State of Emergency, Halt Warrantless Search and House Arrest", published February 3, 2016; available at https:// www.hrw.org/news/2016/02/03/france-abuses-under-state-emergency.

8. Ibid.

9. Tzvetan Todorov, *Fear of the Barbarians: Beyond the Clash of Civilizations*, trans. Andrew Brown (Cambridge: Polity Press, 2010), 84.

10. Talal Asad et al., *Is Critique Secular? Blasphemy, Injury and Free Speech* (Berkeley: University of California Press, 2009), 34.

11. José Casanova, "The Secular, Secularizations, Secularisms," in *Rethinking Secularism*, eds. Craig Calhoun, Mark Juergensmeyer, and Jonathan VanAntwerpen (New York: Oxford University Press, 2011), 54–74.

12. Ibid., *Rethinking Secularism*, 75–91.

13. Grace Davie, *Believing Without Belonging: Just how Secular is Europe?* transcript, Pew Research Center bi-annual Faith Angle Conference, December 5, 2005.

14. See, http://www.pewforum.org.

15. Grace Davie, *Religion in Britain Since 1945: Believing Without Belonging* (New Jersey: Wiley, 1994).

16. Peter Fitzpatrick, "Legal Theology: Law, Modernity and the Sacred," 32 SEATTLE U. L. REV. 321 (2008).

17. Banu Gökariksel and Ann Secor, "Post-Secular Geographies and the Problem of Pluralism: Religion and Everyday Life in Istanbul, Turkey," *Political Geography* 46 (2015): 26.

18. "On the contrary, the United States has always been the paradigmatic form of a modern secular, differentiated society. Yet the triumph of "the secular" came aided by religion rather than at its expense, and the boundaries themselves became so diffused that, at least by European ecclesiastical standards, it is not clear where the secular ends and religion begins," Jose Casanova, "Rethinking Secularization: A Global Comparative Perspective," *The Hedgehog Review* (Spring/Summer 2006): 6.

19. Judgment of New Jersey Supreme Court Justice David Bauman, February 4, 2015, available at: http://www.becketfund.org/wp-content/uploads/2015/02/American-Humanist-v-Matawan-Aberdeen-Regional-School-District.pdf.

20. Thomas Luckmann, *The Invisible Religion: The Problem of Religion in Modern Society* (Boston: MacMillan, 1967).

21. Alfred Schutz, *The Phenomenology of the Social World* (Evanston: Northwestern University Press, 1932/1972), 10.

22. Henri Lefebvre, *Critique of Everyday Life*, Volume 2, trans. John Moore (London: Verso, 1961/2002), 4.

23. Michael Hviid Jacobsen, ed., *Encountering the Everyday: An Introduction to the Sociologies of the Unnoticed* (New York: Palgrave MacMillan, 2009).

24. John Dewey, "The Historic Background of Corporate Legal Personality," *Yale Law Journal* 35 (1926): 655.

25. Following phenomenology and pragmatism, cognitive scientists such as George Lakoff, Mark Johnson, and Antonio Damasio have written extensively about the relationship between body and mind, mounting a formal critique of Decartes' dictum, "I think therefore I am." They are major contributors to an extensive literature that includes embodiment theory which argues (following William James and John Dewey) that body and mind are continuous and co-constructive of environment. As such, every perception we have is a result of "organism-environment interactions" (Johnson) that are "qualities in the world as much as they are in us." Though these ideas continue to encounter resistance, extensive empirical research bears them out; the line between out there in the world and inside us is simply not an absolute. See, George Lakoff, *Women, Fire and Dangerous Things: What Categories Reveal About the Mind* (Chicago: The University of Chicago Press, 1987), Mark Johnson, *The Meaning of the Body: Aesthetics of Human Understanding* (Chicago: The University of Chicago Press, 2007), and Antonio R. Damasio, *Decartes' Error: Emotion, Reason and the Human Brain* (New York: Avon Books, 1994). For a thoughtful and germane analysis of the influence of

Christian precepts on today's legal conceptions of truth in western societies, see Talal Asad et al. Regarding the origins of the secular/religious divide, John Witte Jr., for example, has written extensively about Luther's two kingdoms theory as being the most impactful (of his many dialectical theses) on the division of the immanent from the transcendent which subsequently became the division between the secular and the sacred. In Luther's formulation, all matters related to God and spirituality belong to the heavenly kingdom, while everyday material matters belong to the earthly kingdom. Christians, according to Luther, were beholden to the laws of both kingdoms. See Witte Jr., *Law and Protestantism: The Legal Teachings of the Lutheran Reformation* (Cambridge: Cambridge University Press, 2002), 88–117. Of course, this division does not originate only with Luther. The Catholic Church also divided Christians into clergy and laity along these lines. The subsequent tasking of states with the management of earthly affairs leaving religious institutions and individuals to manage spiritual affairs was an understandable corollary.

26. Asad et al., *Critique*, 73.

27. Ibid., 74.

28. Amiria Henare, Martin Holbraad, M., and Sari Wastell, eds., *Thinking Through Things: Theorising Artifacts Ethnographically* (London: Routledge, 2007).

29. Bruno Latour, *We Have Never Been Modern*, trans. Catherine Porter (Cambridge: Harvard University Press, 1991/1993), 51, 89.

30. John Noonan, Jr., "The Tensions and the Ideals," in *Religious Human Rights in Global Perspective: Legal Perspectives* (The Hague: Kluwer Law International, 1996), 595.

31. Carl Schmitt, *Political Theology: Four Chapters on the Concept of Sovereignty*, trans. George Schwab (Chicago: University of Chicago Press, 1932/1985).

32. Gurminder K. Bhambra, *Rethinking Modernity: Postcolonialism and the Sociological Imagination* (Basingstoke: Palgrave Macmillan, 2009), 1.

33. Craig Calhoun, ed., *Rethinking Secularism* (New York: Oxford University Press, 2011), 33.

34. Henare et al., *Thinking Through Things,* 2007, 12.

Chapter 5

"Migration" as a Metaphor for Religious Conversion

A Reinterpretation of Freedom of Conscience and Belief in Colonial India and Pakistan

Shazia Ahmad

Rights related to religious liberty, contained in Article 18 of the Universal Declaration of Human Rights (UDHR), have come to be viewed as a particularly intractable area of conflict between Islamic law and the supposedly Western cultural norms embodied in the UDHR.[1] This conflict seems nowhere more evident than in Pakistan. Created as a Muslim-majority nation after the British decolonized India in 1947, Pakistan inherited many of the laws and institutions established under colonial rule. Included among these, it would seem, was the principle of religious liberty. In 1948, the newly created nation strongly supported Article 18 in the United Nations General Assembly.[2] Shortly thereafter, Pakistan's constitution guaranteed religious freedom to its citizens among other civil liberties. Since the 1970s, however, Pakistan has introduced a number of laws restricting religious freedom, just as it ostensibly shed its colonial past and moved toward a program of "Islamization."[3] In the 1990s, a Pakistani-led block of Muslim states drafted the "Cairo Declaration on Human Rights in Islam." While echoing much of the UDHR, it did not recognize religious liberty, conversion, and missionary work as individual rights.[4] It seemed that Article 18 was less of a universal value than a Western imposition.

An interpretation of legal developments in Pakistan as simply the result of "Islamization," the replacement of Western and secular legal principles with Islamic ones, obscures the contested nature of Islamic law itself. The position of Pakistan's early administration was not that human rights, and civil liberties that mirrored them, must be pursued in place of Islamic law. Rather, they vigorously argued that human rights derived from Islamic law.[5] Moreover,

93

contestations around Islamic law, and its compatibility with religious freedom in particular, began before the creation of Pakistan in the colonial period.
For Pakistan's founding fathers, whose experience was with the administration of colonial law, these contestations around Islamic law had implications
that are lost to human rights theorists who take a cultural perspective toward
understanding international law.

This paper will examine the legal context from which the first administration of Pakistan emerged. Under colonialism, Islamic law was confined
to the domain of "personal law," which like international law was a plural
legal system. Whereas international law encompasses the domestic laws of
nation-states, personal law in India encompassed the laws of "communities"
defined by caste and religion. By fixing an individual's civil rights to his or
her religious and caste identity, personal law created jurisdictional boundaries
between Muslims and non-Muslims.

Restrictions on religious freedom (and the right to religious conversion
in particular) seemed to have been intrinsic to the functioning of personal
law as a plural legal system. This paper will examine two cases in which the
Lahore court upheld "orthodox" interpretations of Islamic law that restricted
religious freedom against attempts by Indian Muslims lawyers to reform
Islamic law. It will also look at legislative assembly debates around Islamic
law, which suggest reforms to bring Islamic law in line with rights related to
religious freedom were improbable without also reforming the personal law
of non-Muslim communities, and Hindu personal law in particular. Perhaps
counter-intuitively, only after the creation of a Muslim-majority state could
Islamic law be brought in line with this secular principle.

Within the context of personal law, "migration" is a useful metaphor to
conceptualize religious conversion as the movement of individuals across
jurisdictional boundaries. Freedom of religion compromised jurisdictional
boundaries of caste and religious community, and the unequal distribution of
rights they maintained, by making conversion (i.e., "migration" across these
boundaries) an individual right. In colonial India, freedom of conscience and
belief implied not only the right of an individual to leave Islam, but also the
right of an individual to join Hinduism across caste barriers.

PERSONAL LAW

Colonial law in India treated Hindus and Muslims as distinct communities
over whom separate bodies of personal law operated. Hindu and Muslim
personal law operated in civil suits "regarding inheritance, marriage, caste
and other religious usages and institutions."[6] In such matters, courts adhered
to scriptural law: the Quran (for Muslims) and the Vedas (for Hindus), on

which commentaries had been compiled and translated by the British in the late eighteenth century. Additionally, caste communities were defined by religious law modified by custom. Colonial courts applied a similar logic as used to define caste communities to interpret the personal law of minority religious communities that were not Hindu or Muslim. Jains, Buddhists, and Sikhs were conceptualized as arising from Hinduism and following Hindu personal law modified by custom.

As David Washbrook has argued, personal law cut against legal principles based on individualism, utility, and equity, which were embodied in statutory law in India.[7] Personal law had material implications: it differentiated individual property rights according to the community into which an individual was born and it regulated the devolution of wealth within communities through rules of property inheritance and succession. The 1793 Permanent Settlement established the foundation of real property law in India according to principles of private ownership and a free market in land.[8] Hindu personal law operated against these principles by recognizing property rights to be shared among members of the "Hindu joint family."[9] Interpreted as a sacred institution under Hindu personal law, the Hindu joint family functioned like a trust that impeded the individual's absolute right over property.[10]

Muslim personal law had different economic implications than Hindu law because it recognized individuals' absolute ownership rights and distributed them widely among heirs.[11] Raymond West, a Bombay judge and eminent authority on Hindu law, described Islamic laws of family and inheritance as having a "centrifugal dispersive character."[12] "Dispersive" elements within Islamic law included laws allowing up to four wives, legitimizing the offspring of concubines, and placing sons on equal legal standing. Islamic law opposed the law of primogeniture, succession of property through patrilineal descent, upon which English economic theories on the wealth of nations were based.[13]

Colonial law did not allow Indian Muslims to keep their estates intact by creating endowments called "waqfs" either.[14] For centuries, waqfs in the Middle East and South Asia allowed their creators to place their estates under the management of a designated heir, bypassing Muslim rules of inheritance. Colonial law made a novel distinction between "private" waqfs and "public" waqfs. Only public waqfs in which income was designated for charitable and public use were recognized as valid. As endowments made for the benefit of family members, private waqfs were treated as invalid, both because they violated the Islamic law of inheritance and British laws against perpetuities.[15] Private waqfs only became valid after 1913 with the passage of Muhammad Ali Jinnah's *Mussalman Wakf Validation Act.*[16]

Colonial law recognized caste difference among Indians, which cut across religious difference and further differentiated property rights.[17] Caste

was understood to organize Indian society hierarchically. The higher caste
Brahmins, Kshatriyas, and Vaishyas were organized on top, Sudras below.
Dalits (those who were described in colonial sources as "Untouchables"
or "depressed classes"), pastoralists, and forest dwellers fell outside of this
system. British interpreted caste in India according to racial theories, with
higher castes being of Aryan descent and lower-caste Sudras and dalits being
of indigenous descent.[18] They understood caste ideologies as a mechanism
for maintaining racial purity by creating exclusionary conventions, such as
restrictions on marriage and food handling.[19] British Indian courts invalidated
marriages and adoptions between castes and recognizing caste communities
to be regulated by separate rules of succession, adoption, and marriage.[20]
Severe restrictions on commensality between castes, based on conceptions of
purity and pollution, were validated in criminal as well as civil court cases.[21]

Although caste was understood as a Hindu institution, colonial law interpreted caste as extending beyond religious boundaries to include Indian
Muslims. By the late nineteenth century, British ethnography had come to
interpret the majority of Muslims in India as descended from lower-caste and
depressed-class Hindu converts.[22] In the Punjab, the province from which
Pakistan's first administration was overwhelmingly drawn, the majority of
Muslim were designated as belonging to "agriculturalist" tribes and legally
defined as lower caste (Sudra).

Personal law in the Punjab developed peculiarly from other provinces in
India. In other provinces, Muslim and Hindus were assumed to follow scriptural law unless caste custom could be proven. Under the Punjab Laws Act of
1872, Punjabi Muslim agriculturalists were assumed to follow customary law
in common with Sikh and Hindu agriculturalists. For them, rules of inheritance were interpreted to be more akin to Hindu law and the joint family than
Muslim law. This categorization of Punjabi society around caste made possible land laws designed to protect the economic status peasant landowners.
These included the Punjab Land Alienation Act of 1900, which restricted the
transfer of land from castes designated as agriculturalist to those not designated as agriculturalist.[23]

Punjab land laws, underpinned by a peculiarly structured system of personal law, were also relevant to representational politics. A system of political representation in which political rights were attached to land ownership,
gave agriculturalists a disproportionate amount of political representation.
This contributed to the rise of the Punjab Unionist Party. This majority-
Muslim party depended upon non-communal alliances between Muslim and
Hindu politicians in support of agriculturalist interests, and it came to represent Muslims in all-India politics in the 1930s.[24]

For the majority of Muslims in the Punjab, including the most politically influential, inheritance and property rights were defined by their caste

identity but Islamic law continued to define other areas of personal law. Marriage for Hindus and Muslims continued to be treated as different institutions. While personal law in the Punjab was based on a concept of agriculturalist communities that transcended religious boundaries, it continued to regulate social relations between Hindus and Muslims as separate communities. This is relevant to the two cases examined below, which were brought before Punjab's chief court in Lahore. These civil disputes arose as a consequence of religious conversion of one partner in a married pair, in one case Muslim and in the other case Hindu. The issue of religious conversion was complicated by the fact that personal law did not allow for the interreligious marriages that resulted.

ISLAMIC LAW AND RELIGIOUS FREEDOM

The British administration ruled according to a principle of religious freedom (enunciated by Queen Victoria in an 1858 proclamation that guaranteed her subjects security in the practice of their religion). However, this principle was liable to be interpreted as protecting "orthodox" interpretations of Hindu and Muslim personal law that restricted an individual's freedom of conscience and belief (or right to convert between religious communities) against interpretations that embodied this principle.

Colonial law in India interpreted Islamic law as punishing apostasy from Islam through death. This "orthodox" interpretation of Islamic law was contained in Charles Hamilton's *Hedaya*, among other authoritative legal texts: death for the male apostate and imprisonment for the female apostate. The source for this law was an interpretation of Quranic verse translated by Hamilton as "slay the man who changes his religion."[25] Colonial courts adapted the punishment for apostasy to Muslim personal law by recognizing apostasy by one or both of a married pair to invalidate their marriage immediately and without requiring a judicial decree.[26] However, rather than being a punishment, the dissolution of marriage for apostasy was used by Muslim women to bypass otherwise restrictive divorce laws.[27]

This law fed into a perception, supported by British ethnography, that Islamic conversion happened by force. Hindu associations supported the law as protecting Hindu women from being abducted and forced into marriage by giving them an easy release from their marriage ties. Islam, as interpreted by the British, was a religion of compulsion not conviction.

At the same time, late nineteenth-century evolutionary legal theories (made influential over British administrative policies in India by Sir Henry Maine) interpreted Islamic law as amenable to progressive reform. Lahore Chief Justice William Rattigan described "orthodoxy" in Islam not as correct belief but the product of the codification of Islamic law by Muslim lawyers during the eighth and ninth centuries, when the traditional schools of law were founded. Islamic law had developed from an elastic law based on ethical precepts to a rigid code of law due to curtailment of *ijtihad* by Muslim lawyers.[28] *Ijtihad* is an Islamic legal term that means independent reasoning. Within the tradition of Islamic jurisprudence, it was used to arrive at a legal decision when none could be reached through the Quran and traditions of the Prophet Muhammad (hadith). According to Rattigan, restoring the use of ijtihad to Islamic law turned it into a rational science, developing it back into a progressive and enlightened legal system.[29]

Maine's evolutionary legal theories were taught to Indian law students in the Punjab as "a set of consistent generalizations from known facts in the growth of legal institutions and ideas" that were necessary to understanding the evolution of society.[30] They provided for Indian Muslim legal reformers a means to reform apostasy laws, even if to close the loophole in divorce laws. In his 1904 digest on Islamic law, Muslim legal expert Ameer Ali interpreted the punishment for apostasy in Islamic law as analogous to the position taken by the Christian churches in Europe, which had condemned heretics to the stake. He understood the automatic dissolution of marriage as replacing the death penalty according to a natural progression that all religious systems passed through.[31] With the expansion of European people's conscience, the death penalty was replaced by the forfeiture of civil rights and social ostracism. This interpretation implied that all societies would progress toward a norm that valued religious liberty, endorsed by the British administration but not recognized under colonial law as being contained in Islamic law.

LEGAL CASES

Although evolutionary legal theories posited that Indian laws would develop under British influence according to progressive legal principles, in the two cases examined below, *Imam Din v. Hasan Bibi* (1905) and *Jamna Devi v. Mul Raj* (1906), the Lahore court upheld "orthodox" interpretations of Islamic and Hindu law against attempts at progressive reform by Punjabi Muslim lawyer (and later founder of the Punjab Unionist Party) Fazli Husain.[32]

In the first case, *Imam Din v. Hasan Bibi* (1905), Hasan Bibi converted from Islam to Christianity and understood her marriage to Imam Din as having been dissolved as a consequence of her apostasy.[33] Imam Din, the husband, brought a suit against Hasan Bibi for the restoration of his marital rights, and Fazli Husain provided his legal counsel. Rather than using the standard textbooks on Islamic law—Hamilton's *Hedaya* and Baillie's *Digest of Muhammadan Law* based on the *Fatwa-i-Alamgiri*—Husain's argument relied upon the opinions of eminent Islamic jurists from Samar-kand and Balkh.[34] According to these sources, apostasy laws that made the life of a male apostate *mobah* (free to be taken away) did not apply to women. Husain argued that the court should adopt this interpretation and not recognize the marriage of a female apostate as being automati-cally dissolved, thus fixing the loophole apostasy laws created in Muslim divorce laws.

The court rejected Husain's argument and upheld the "orthodox" interpre-tation of the punishment for apostasy as a matter of principle. In his ruling, Justice Chatterji upheld "divine law" against amendment: "Muhammadans do not admit the right of the Sovereign power to amend or alter that law."[35] In Chatterji's judgment it was "beyond the province of British Courts to deduce that law by such methods from original texts and sources."[36] His judg-ment equated "orthodoxy" with correctness, and made it the court's preroga-tive to apply "correct" laws: "There is no allegation that [the Samarkand and Balkh] opinion is accepted by [Muslims] generally as the more orthodox and correct. On the contrary, the authority of *Fatawa-i-Alamgiri* the most impor-tant Digest of Muhammadan law of the Hanafite School prepared in India and promulgated under the authority of the most orthodox Muhammadan Ruler India ever had, is against it."[37]

The second case, *Jamna Devi v. Mul Raj* (1906),[38] closely followed after the first. Jamna Devi was married to Mul Raj under Hindu personal law, but separated from him after converting to Islam. Mul Raj applied for a decree of custody of Jamna Devi from a lower court, which at its discretion dissolved the marriage, determining that Devi was a sincere Muslim who would not willingly reconvert to Hinduism, while Raj was likely to coerce Devi into renouncing Islam and was even a threat to her life should they remain mar-ried. The case was brought to the Lahore High Court on appeal, and Fazli Husain argued in Jamna Devi's defense.

Husain argued that the dissolution of Devi's marriage was necessary to protect her religious liberty. He argued that under Hindu law the effect of conversion to Islam was to cast Devi beyond the pale of Hinduism. Accord-ing to the principles of Hindu law quoted by Husain, Devi's husband lost his conjugal rights as a consequence of her conversion: "He cannot eat food cooked by her or let her touch his food or drink; he cannot let her join him in any religious ceremony or seat of worship, and so forth."[39] Devi lost the rights granted to her in marriage but did not relinquish her "already existing liabilities."[40] Husain argued that Raj's only recourse to restore his conjugal rights and make Devi fulfill her marital obligations was for him to force her to renounce Islam. This, concluded Husain, was "tantamount to laying it down that a Hindu woman has no right to freedom of conscience and can never renounce Hinduism, whatever her real sentiments might be."[41]

Husain also attempted to apply the principles of "conflict of laws" (private international law) to the operation of Hindu and Muslim personal laws in this case.[42] British statute enabled the Supreme Court to determine suits related to inheritance and succession of lands, rent, and goods, and matters of contract according to Muslim law in cases involving Muslims, and Hindu law in cases involving Hindus. In cases where one party was Muslim and the other Hindu, the laws and usage of the defendant was to determine the decision.[43] Husain argued that the conversion of Devi from Hinduism to Islam meant that she was now governed by Muslim law, while her husband continued to be governed by Hindu law. If decided according to Muslim law, the law of the defendant in the suit, Devi's marriage to Raj would be invalidated because Islam prohibited the marriage of Muslim women to non-Muslim men.[44]

The presiding judges, Justice Johnstone and Henry Rattigan, ruled in favor of the restoration of Mul Raj's conjugal rights. Johnstone's judgment affirmed the distinctive nature of the institution of Hindu marriage: "the Hindu law being so entirely opposed to the Muhammadan in this matter."[45] Hindu marriage was defined by an entirely different set of rights and duties that formed the basis of a "social fabric." To grant a Hindu wife powers of divorce as a consequence of her conversion to Islam would be to fundamentally alter that fabric by rendering her "virtually independent of her husband."[46] Johnstone did not refute Husain's argument that Devi's marriage deprived her of freedom of conscience. Rather, he stated that it was enough to assume that he would "simply keep her in some part of his house and try to persuade her to abjure her faith."[47] He acknowledged that Raj had expressed his intention of trying to reconvert her. Justice Rattigan's judgment noted that the degradation occasioned by Devi's conversion to Islam "can be atoned for and the convert re-admitted to her status as a Hindu, if she hereafter renounces Islamism and performs the right of expiation of her caste."[48] Mul Raj, he noted, "would be entitled, if he so wished, to desert his wife by reason of her apostasy and, under the personal law which must be taken to govern the case, he need do no more than allow her what is called a 'starving maintenance.'"[49]

LEGISLATIVE DEBATES

In 1938, a Muslim member of the India's legislative assembly introduced the Muslim Dissolution of Marriage (MDM) Bill. The Bill's objective was to reform divorce laws to provide Muslim women with the widest grounds for divorce allowed under Islamic law. It also included a clause that apostasy from Islam was not in itself grounds for the automatic dissolution of marriage.[50]

The MDM Bill was passed, but the caveat was added that apostasy still operated to automatically dissolve marriages in cases in which the female apostate was returning to her original faith. This caveat was the result of intense opposition to the clause relating to apostasy from Hindu members of the legislative assembly, who argued that it would adversely affect Hindus and allow forcible conversion to Islam to take place. Bhai Parma Nand, a Hindu member of the Select Committee for the Bill, objected to the Bill on account of the "fear prevailing in the minds of Hindus" that it would adversely affect them.[51] Nand quoted from the opinion of the Rajputana Provincial Hindu Sabha that the Bill opposed the principles of Hindu law. According to the Sabha, it also prevented Hindu women "who have been converted to another faith" from returning to the Hindu fold: Hindu widows, wives, and virgins were enticed away from Hinduism by Muslims and married to Muslims immediately after conversion. The Bill would prevent Hindu women from releasing themselves from "the clutches of Muslims."[52] Babu Baijnath Bajoria objected to the Bill as according to him it would bring about the breakdown of Hindu society. He read a letter from his Hindu constituents that the Bill would "interfere with the established laws of Hindu society and Hindu religion" and would "inject the poison of communal animosities into the body politic of the Indian nation."

Within the legislative assembly debates over this Bill, Pakistan's early interpretation of Islamic law can be found in the comments of Zafrullah Khan, who spoke on behalf of the government of India as the Muslim member of the Executive Council.[53] Khan was a lawyer in the Lahore High Court circuit, a member of the Punjab Unionist Party, and Fazli Husain's protégé. He was Pakistan's first foreign minister and its delegate to the United Nations General Assembly during the drafting of the UDHR, lobbying among other majority-Muslim state delegates for support of Article 18.

During Khan's speech to the Indian legislature, he interpreted Islamic law in a manner that accorded with freedom of conscience and belief. Firstly, he defined Islam as a religion of inner conviction. Religion, synonymous with "faith," was "a matter of the heart." Conversion from Islam was not a matter of leaving one community to join another, as it was interpreted under personal law, but believing one faith to be true over another.

According to Khan's interpretation of the Quran, any punishment for apostasy was a violation of the Islamic precept that there was no compulsion in religion.[54] While British Indian law had not distinguished between sincere and insincere conversion from Islam for automatic dissolution of marriage, the sincerity of conversion was of primary importance to Khan's argument. Khan quoted Quranic verse to argue that hypocrisy (munafikin) in Islam was morally worse than honest disbelief. According to the Quran, "hypocrites shall be consigned to the nether most regions of fire."[55] To illustrate how the law of apostasy did not conform to Islam in this regard, Khan described the conversion to Christianity of a Muslim woman married to a Muslim man. If she wished to remain married, the law would operate to either dissolve their marriage as a consequence of her conversion or compel her to live as a hypocrite.

Khan's interpretation of Islamic law as according with freedom of conscience and belief was disconnected from the legislative debates surrounding the MDM Bill. How Islamic law was to be interpreted was contested by Muslim as well as non-Muslim legislative assembly members, and these contestations did not resolve in the interpretation of Islamic law given by Khan. Rather, Khan's interpretation that there is no punishment for apostasy in Islam, one that aligned with Pakistan's early interpretation of Islamic law and Article 18 of the UDHR, was a radical departure from the compromising nature of colonial reforms.

NOTES

1. On Islamic law and human rights, see Bassan Tibi, "Islamic Law/Shari'a, Human Rights, Universal Morality Ad International Law," *Human Rights Quarterly* 16, no. 2 (1994): 277–299; Abdullahi Ahmed An-Na'im, *Towards an Islamic Reformation: Civil Liberties, Human Rights, and International Law* (Syracuse, NY: Syracuse University Press, 1990); Heiner Bielfeldt, "Muslim Voices in the Human Rights Debate," *Human Rights Quarterly* 17, no. 4 (1995): 587–617. For broader cultural critique of human rights, see Melville J. Herskovits, *Cultural Relativism, Perspectives in Cultural Pluralism*, ed. Frances Herskovits (New York: Random House, 1972) and Ruth Benedict, *Patterns of Culture* (Boston: Houghton Mifflin Co., 1934).

2. Eileen Waltz, "Universal Human Rights: The Contribution of Muslim States," *Human Rights Quarterly* 26, no. 4 (2004): 817; Ann L. Mayer, *Islam and Human Rights: Tradition and Politics* (Boulder, Colorado: Westview Press, 2012), chapter 7.

3. For analysis of these laws, see Martin Lau, "The Legal Mechanism of Islamization: The New Islamic Criminal Law of Pakistan," *Journal of Law and Society* 11 (1992): 43–58.

4. Paula Schriefer, "Remarks by Paula Schriefer," *Proceedings of the Annual Meeting (American Society of International Law)* 106 (2012): 352.

5. Muhammad Munir, *Punjab Disturbances of 1953: Report of the Court of Inquiry* (Lahore: Government Printing, 1954), 149–202.

6. Warren Hastings 1772 framing of the Regulation of 17 April 1780, section 27. Cited in Faiz Badruddin Tyabji, *Principles of Muhammadan Law*, 2nd ed. (Calcutta: Butterworth & Co., 1919), 36. On personal law in colonial India, see Duncan Derrett, *Religion, Law and the State in India* (London: Faber and Faber, 1968); B. Hooker, *An Introduction to Colonial and Neo-colonial Laws* (Oxford: Clarendon Press, 1975), ch. 1.

7. David Washbrook, "Law, State, and Agrarian Society in Colonial India," *Modern Asian Studies* 15, no. 3 (1981): 649–721.

8. Ranajit Guha, *The Rule of Property in Bengal* (Mouton: Paris, 1963).

9. Washbrook, "Law, State, and Agrarian Society," 653–655.

10. Ibid., 669; Derrett, *Religion, Law and the State*, 113–114.

11. Muslim inheritance laws were derived from the Hanafi text *al-Sirajiyya*. See, Gregory C. Kozlowski, *Muslim Endowments and Society in British India* (Cambridge: Cambridge University Press, 1985), 128–131. For how the Islamic legal tradition was codified by the British, see Scott Alan Kugle, "Framed, Blamed, and Renamed: The Recasting of Islamic Jurisprudence in Colonial South Asia," *Modern Asian Studies* 35, no. 2 (2001): 257–314; Michael Anderson, "Islamic Law and Colonial Encounter in British India," in *Institutions and their Ideologies: A SOAS South Asia Reader*, eds." David Arnold and Peter Robb (Richmond, Surrey: Curzon Press, 1993), 165–185.

12. Raymond West, "Mohammedan Law in India: Its Origins and Growth," *Journal of the Society of Comparative Legislation* 2, no. 1 (1900): 40.

13. Adam Smith, *An Inquiry into the Nature and Causes of the Wealth of Nations* (London: Electric Book Co., 2001), 507–510. For a background on the European debate relating to primogenitor, see Joan Thirsk, "The European Debate on Customs of Inheritance, 1500–1700," in *Family and Inheritance: Rural Society in Western Europe, 1200–1800*, eds. Jack Goody, Joan Thirsk, and E.P. Thompson (Cambridge: Cambridge University Press, 1976), 177–191.

14. Kozlowski, *Muslim Endowments.*

15. Ibid., 194–196.

16. Ibid., 156–187. Prior to this legislation, Raymond West and prominent Muslims Syed Ahmad Khan and Ameer Ali had argued for the recognition of private waqfs.

17. Washbrook, "Law, State, and Agrarian Society," 655.

18. Ibid., 4.

19. Susan Bayly, *Caste, Society and Politics in India* (Cambridge: Cambridge University Press, 1999), 127.

20. Ibid., 187–232.

21. Ibid.

22. Peter Hardy, "Modern European and Muslim Explanations of Conversion to Islam in South Asia: A Preliminary Survey of the Literature," *Journal of the Royal Asiatic Society of Great Britain and Ireland* 2 (1977): 178–179.

23. Gerald Barrier, *The Punjab Alienation of Land Bill of 1900. Monograph and Occasional Paper Series Number Two* (Durham: Duke University Program in Comparative Studies on Southern Asia, 1966).

24. Ian Talbot, *Punjab and the Raj, 1849–1947* (Manohar: New Delhi, 1988); Ayesha Jalal and Anil Seal, "Alternative to Partition: Muslim Politics between the Wars," *Modern Asian Studies* 15, no. 3 (1981): 415–454.

25. *The Hedaya, or Guide: A Commentary on the Mussalman Laws,* Vol. II, trans. Charles Hamilton (London: T. Bensley, 1791), 226.

26. N. B. E. Baillie, *The Digest of Moohummudan Law* (London: Smith, Elder, & Co., 1875), 182.

27. On apostasy from Islam as a means for obtaining a divorce, see: Rohit De, "The Two Husbands of Vera Tiscenko: Apostasy, Conversion, and Divorce in Late Colonial India," *Law and History Review* 28, no. 4 (2010): 1011–1041.

28. Raymond West, "Modern Developments of Mohammedan Law," *Journal of the Society of Comparative Legislation* 2 (1900): 271–275; William Rattigan, "The Scientific Study of the Muhammadan Law," *The Law Quarterly Review* (October 1901): 401–414.

29. W. H. Rattigan, "The Scientific Study of Muhammadan Law," *The Law Quarterly Review* (October 1901): 412.

30. Ibid., 90.

31. Ameer Ali, *Mahommedan Law, Vol. II* (Calcutta: Thacker, Spink, and Co., 1908), 429.

32. Anderson, "Islamic Law," 165.

33. Imam Din v. Hasan Bibi (1905) 7 PLR 148.

34. Ibid., at 490–491.

35. Ibid., at 492.

36. Ibid.

37. Ibid., at 493.

38. Jamna Devi v. Mul Raj (1906) 9 PLR 83.

39. Ibid., at 200. Husain is quoting Jogendra Chandar Ghose, *Principles of Hindu Law*, 2nd ed. (Calcutta: S. C. Ruddy & Co., 1906), 664.

40. Ibid.

41. Ibid.

42. Ibid., at 199.

43. Statute 21 Geo. III., c. 70, § 17, quoted in Raymond West and Johann Georg Buhler, *A Digest of the Hindu Law of Inheritance, Partition, and Adoption,* Vol. 1, 3rd ed. (Bombay: Education Society's Press, 1884), 5.

44. Jamna Devi v. Mul Raj (1906) 9 PLR 83, at 201.

45. Ibid., at 199.

46. Ibid.

47. Ibid., at 201.

48. Ibid., at 202.

49. Ibid., at 203.

50. Muhammad Kazmi, 'Extract from the Legislative Assembly Debate', Vol. V, no. 1, 26 August 1938, at 1–3, Public and Judicial Department Records, IOR L/PJ/7/1065.

51. Bhai Parma Nand, 'Extract from Legislative Assembly Debate', Vol. V, no. 1, 26 August 1938, at 9, ibid.

52. Babu Baijnath Bajoria, ibid.

53. Zafrullah Khan, 'Extract from Legislative Assembly Debates', Vol. V, no. 11, 9 September 1938, at 13–22, ibid.

54. Ibid., at 18: Khan quoted the following Quranic verses to argue that there was no compulsion in religion: "say (to these people) the Truth is from your Lord, then let whosoever desires believe, and let whosoever desires disbelieve." "Had thy Lord

desired to force people to believe, then everyone on earth would have believed. Then dost thou (O Prophet) desire to compel people to believe?" and "There shall be no compulsion in faith; guidance has become manifest from error."

55. Ibid., at 20.

Part III

RIGHTS AND MIGRATION

Chapter 6

Protestant Work Ethic Revisited

The Ephemeral Nature of Commitment to Human Rights

Hisako Matsuo and Rachel Santon

The United Nations Convention on Refugee Status[1] defines "refugee" as someone outside his/her country of nationality or former habitual residence who is unable or unwilling to return based on a well-founded fear of persecution regarding race, religion, nationality, social group, and/or political affiliation.[2] According to the United Nations High Commissioner for Refugees (UNHCR), there are more than 20 million refugees scattered worldwide, and about 300,000 of them residing in the United States.[3] To effectively resettle and help refugees achieve economic self-sufficiency in the United States, the Refugee Act of 1980 created the Federal Refugee Resettlement Program. Since then, major conflicts have occurred in many parts of the world, including Bosnia and Herzegovina, the Republic of Somalia, Sudan, Afghanistan, and Latin America, which led to waves of Bosnian and Somali refugees resettling in the United States. For example, International Institute of St. Louis sponsored 706 refugees in 2015. International Institute expected that the omnibus bill passed by Congress in October 2015 would provide funding to increase refugee resettlement by 10,000 during that fiscal year.[4]

St. Louis, Missouri's long history of assisting refugees dates back to waves of European refugees in the early 1900s.[5] While St. Louis is ranked only 60th among American municipalities for foreign-born population size, the city is ranked 21st for highest refugee resettlement, with 22,046 refugees arriving from 1983 to 2004.[6] In the 1990s, over 13,185 refugees were initially resettled in St. Louis and an additional 41,073 foreign-born residents entered due to secondary and tertiary migration.[7] In 2015, refugees from the Democratic Republic of the Congo (DRC) were on the top of the list of refugees sponsored by the International Institute of St. Louis. Due mainly to the conflict in the eastern part of the country, approximately 430,000 refugees from the DRC remain in neighboring countries, including Burundi, Rwanda, Uganda, and Tanzania. In March 2015, the Institute sponsored its first Syrian refugee family, and thirty-nine Syrian refugees had arrived by the end of the year.[8]

While refugees entering host societies receive sympathetic attitudes from the public in general, people's perceptions toward refugees vary depending upon the racial, ethnic, and religious backgrounds of these refugees. On the one hand, many believe that Americans have responsibilities to these refugees from the perspective of human rights; on the other hand, some argue that certain groups of refugees are not welcome. The recent international development regarding Syrian refugees is a typical example of this ambivalent sentiment of "human rights," which is not only due to the diverse cultural backgrounds of refugees and people in the host countries but also to the ever changing circumstances and conditions that host societies face.

The Syrian refugee crisis has captured international attention and has elicited emotional responses from people all around the world. However, the responses and human rights conceptions of the public and state leaders toward refugees have been transitory. The heart wrenching and harsh realities forcing Syrian refugees to flee their homeland have not changed since the Syrian Civil War began in 2011. Rather, surrounding circumstances, such as the wide publication of the image of the Syrian refugee boy who drowned in the Mediterranean Sea and the Paris terrorist attacks, have shifted people's attitudes regarding appropriate human rights definition and response toward these individuals.

In fall of 2015, media headlines around the world described the horrific drowning of Aylan Kurdi, a three-year-old Syrian boy who died during his family's attempted escape from violence near the Turkish border to a safe haven in Greece. The image of the lifeless child evoked international outrage, discussions of the violation of refugees' human rights, and calls to action for both ordinary citizens and state leaders. This story and its accompanying image prompted worldwide petitions to national leaders to accept more refugees along with pledges by leaders, such as the UK prime minister David Cameron's promise to fulfill Britain's moral responsibility to accept more refugees and the French prime minister Manuel Valls's call for urgent action across Europe.[9] In response to this shocking photo, the Turkish National Security Council, echoing the views of numerous individuals and national agencies across the world, emphasized that the refugee "issue should be taken up in a basic human rights perspective."[10]

The publication of Aylan's death highlighted the humanity of the refugees fleeing for their lives and produced responses from national governments to increase the number of Syrian refugees accepted into their borders. Days after the image of the child surfaced, US president Barack Obama, yielding to international and internal pressure, increased the number of Syrian refugees for US resettlement from under 2,000 for the previous fiscal year to 10,000 for the next fiscal year.[11] In September, 2015, the United Kingdom also announced that it would accept 4,000 more Syrian refugees.[12] In the same month, Germany pledged to take in 500,000 Syrian refugees every year[13] and France agreed to accept 24,000 refugees over the next two years.[14] These pledges demonstrated strong support for refugees as fellow humans who deserved to have their human rights protected.

The Islamic terrorist attacks in Paris on November 14, 2015, quickly shifted international responses on the basis of human rights and common humanity to widespread fear and security concerns. Immediately following the Paris bombings, US governors expressed outright refusal to accept Syrian refugees into their states.[15] Throughout Europe, countries from Austria and Hungary to Greece and Italy, promptly enacted plans to close their borders to restrict further entry of Syrian refugees.[16] In addition to national leaders' responses of border closings, public protests against accepting Syrian refugees and Islamophobic backlashes have spread across Europe and the rest of the Western world.[17] In the wake of the Paris attacks, public opinion has swung sharply against Syrian refugees, with increased racist attacks against refugees throughout the world and opinion polls, such as a poll showing that 70 percent of Dutch people believe their borders should close, demonstrating waning support for refugees' human rights.[18]

Since the Paris attacks, fierce debate has broken out in the United States regarding the implementation of policies to ban Syrian refugees from entering the country. By the middle of November, thirty-one governors publicly stated their refusal to allow refugees to enter their states, and the House of Representative approved a bill to block Syrian refugee resettlement in the country.[19] Reports that one of the Paris attackers had entered Europe by posing as a Syrian refugee further intensified rhetoric to prevent alleged security threats posed by Syrian refugees entering the country. Republican factions have rallied against accepting Syrian refugees who are Muslim and have expressed a commitment to only provide refuge for Christian refugees.[20] Fearmongering and an emphasis on American security have taken hold since the Paris bombings and have largely shifted the country's focus from protecting the Syrian refugees to supporting an anti-refugee platform that would all but ensure a disregard for human rights. Even Democratic leaders in the United States have softened their human rights–based arguments and pronouncements of common humanity to accept refugees from Syria and have taken to stressing the importance of strengthening security checks before refugees are admitted. Although Senate Democrats successfully blocked the House bill that would have enforced a total ban on Syrian refugee entry, the fifty-five to forty-three vote conveyed deep divisions over policies to accept and protect those fleeing wholesale degradation of their rights and dignity.[21]

In the midst of the international shift in emotional response from the human rights characterization of the refugee crisis evoked by the drowned Syrian child to the alarmist rhetoric of security threats, refugees came to bear the increasing weight of human inaction. With the war in Syria intensifying, estimates of up to 1 million Syrian refugees have been stranded at the now-closed Turkish border.[22] Frozen in time with waning hope for the future, they wait with bated breath for European pronouncements on human rights interpretations and the consequent policies that will determine their fate. Although Articles 13 and 14 of the Universal Declaration of Human Rights specifically state refugees' and asylees' rights, the current situation that Syrian refugees face cannot be reduced to a monolithic interpretation of human rights. Several questions need to be explored; first, who is considered to be acceptable as a refugee to come to the United States; second, who decides which group is acceptable; and third, how do changing attitudes toward certain groups of refugees transform the identity of refugees themselves? We explore these questions, using the framework of contact theory,[23] and we juxtapose this theory with Biernat and colleagues' work on Protestant work ethic (PWE) and humanitarianism.[24] Further, we explore refugees' identity shift from the perspective of circumstantialism and primodialism. Although refugees are one of the three subcategories of immigrants who enter the United States (labor-based, family-based, or policy-based), we use the term "immigrants" in order to broadly capture the migration of people across borders. Findings from the Hisako Matsuo's previous studies will be used to illuminate intercultural aspects of attitudinal change of Americans[25] and identity shift of refugees in response to the changing circumstances.[26]

AMERICANS' ATTITUDE TOWARD IMMIGRANTS[27]

The contact hypothesis is based on the notion that prejudice originates from unfamiliarity and separation between groups and that contact among the groups will lead to more positive intergroup attitudes.[28] Brown, Vivian, and Hewstone suggested that positive contact between groups as a means to reduce prejudice is one of the most enduring ideas in the study of intergroup relations.[29] Beginning with the work of Allport, research on the effects of social contact has examined the conditions under which social contact results in reduction of prejudice.[30] Pettigrew suggests that cross-group friendship potentially addresses necessary conditions of the contact hypothesis, and thereby represents the optimal situation for prejudice reduction.[31] Further, personal contact with individual outgroup members may generalize, thereby making attitudes toward the outgroup more positive.[32] Conversely, impersonal contact refers to passive and superficial contact with outgroup members. Such experiences may actually lead to more negative attitudes toward the outgroup in that these interactions may be difficult, such as when individuals speak different languages.[33] In the recent case of Syrian refugees, we argue that the mass media have served as a prominent means of impersonal/secondary contact, creating negative images of this group.

The discordant nature of American values, attitudes, and behaviors toward immigrants has been the subject of a substantial body of research. The literature suggests that attitudes toward racial and ethnic outgroups, including immigrants, are best characterized as ambivalent; that is, they contain both positive and negative elements.[34] The sympathy and antipathy that individuals express toward these groups is hypothesized to be due to two strong, but conflicting American values.[35] While on the one hand, Americans value humanitarianism, characterized by social equality, social justice, and concern for others in need, they also value the PWE, an individualistic belief in hard work, self-discipline, and individual achievement.[36] Biernat and colleagues suggest that humanitarianism is negatively associated with all forms of prejudice, whereas adherence to the PWE is positively associated with prejudice toward those outgroups viewed to violate the PWE.[37] This finding is consistent with other research on prejudice that shows that perceived value violations by outgroups are associated with increased prejudice.[38]

Research on Americans attitudes toward immigrants consistently shows that a large percentage of Americans hold prejudiced views of immigration regardless of the means of entry to the United States.[39] Further, immigration may be viewed as both a realistic threat (i.e., as competition for resources or attack toward national security) and a symbolic threat (i.e., threat to worldview).[40] The present study further tested this notion by examining the relationship of humanitarianism and PWE with attitudes toward immigrants of different ethnic origins.

The data set collected a few years after the 9/11 incident consisted of 382 St. Louisans (174 male, 202 female, 6 missing) with 288 whites, 42 blacks, 40 participants from other racial minority groups, and 12 missing. The mean age of the sample was 50.10 ($SD = 13.82$), and 360 of the participants were born in the United States. Scales were used to measure some constructs, including social contact,[41] general attitudes toward immigrants,[42] attitudes toward specific ethnic groups,[43] humanitarianism,[44] and PWE.[45]

The results showed that people consistently perceived Middle Easterners more negatively than other groups on semantic differential items (e.g., colder, more unfriendly, less welcoming). Further, while contact with outgroup members played an important role in determining attitudes toward these groups, impersonal contact lead to negative attitudes toward immigrants. As expected, while humanitarianism was associated with positive attitudes, PWE was associated with negative attitudes toward immigrants. Unexpectedly, Christians (we contrasted Christians vs. non-Christians) showed more negative attitudes toward immigrants than non-Christians, particularly toward immigrants from the Middle East. In sum, the results suggested that the interplay between humanitarianism and PWE was dependent on the ethnicity of the outgroup. These results provide initial evidence that people in St. Louis hold ambivalent attitudes toward immigrants and that these attitudes are based upon the maintenance of dual conflicting values of humanitarianism and PWE.

IDENTITY SHIFT AMONG REFUGEES[46]

A substantial number of Muslims from Africa and Europe, due to ethnic conflicts on these two continents, came to the United States toward the end of the twentieth century. There are about 3.5 million Muslims in the United States. As noted in the previous section on American's attitude toward immigrants, Middle Easterners are perceived more negatively by Americans than other ethnic groups of immigrants. Although Islamophobia existed not only in the United States but also in the world before 9/11 in 2001, following 9/11, many Muslims, particularly those in the West, found themselves as the object of suspicion, harassment, and discrimination. A 2006 Gallup Poll found that while about 2/3 of Americans never met Muslims in person, many of them thought Muslims were not loyal to the United States.[47] The media portrayed Muslims as terrorists especially after 9/11 which led to rising anti-Muslim sentiments and attitudes.

Hisako Matsuo has been studying the process of resettlement and adaptation of Bosnians refugees since the early 2000s. The majority of Bosnian refugees in the United States are Muslims, although they are cultural Muslims. She noted "Bosnians' religious backgrounds as secular Muslims and their racial backgrounds as Europeans seem to have contributed to their acceptance by the mainstream society, rendering Bosnians racially 'invisible' in American society, which continues to appreciate whiteness."[48] Many Bosnians who first resettled in North St. Louis quickly learned the racial hierarchy of American society and emigrated from that area. Now the majority of Bosnians reside in a community centered around Kings Highway and Gravois. Similar findings on Bosnian resettlement were reported by other scholars who studied Bosnians in Australia.[49] This process of dissociating themselves from racial minorities parallels the experience of German settlers in the St. Louis area almost 200 years ago. Anderson argues that immigrants from European countries learned the privilege of being white, even though they showed sympathy to African American slaves in the beginning. She coined the term "lessons in whiteness" to describe immigrants' identity formation along the racial hierarchy in the host country.[50] Whiteness is seen as a social capital in the United

States, and it also translates into economic capital for upward mobility.[51] Bosnians dissociated themselves not only from other racial minority groups but also from their religious background. Some Bosnian refugees mentioned, "I am proud of being Muslim but I do not identify myself as Muslim."

Matsuo contrasted Bosnians' resettlement process and their identity shift in response to the conditions surrounding them against that of African refugees, particularly those from Somalia.[52] African refugees are visible in American society because of their skin color and their strong adherence to their religious background as well. Many African Muslim refugees practice their religion in their everyday lives (e.g., praying at certain times), and many women wear hijabs which are the symbol of modesty and dignity. As we might recall, right after the 9/11 incident in 2001, many Muslim female students on campuses in the United States started wearing hijabs even though they did not wear them before. They were sending a statement to society that they were proud of being Muslim and they identified themselves as Muslim. Their statement was also that they were not affiliated with terrorists and they were loyal to the United States.

The differences between Bosnian refugees and African refugees in their identity formations were explained from the perspectives of circumstantialism and primodialism.[53] Circumstantialism argues that ethnic identity fluctuates according to the circumstances and situations; ethnic identity is not given but it is a function of position in a social structure and a response to rapidly changing social conditions.[54] Primodialism argues that ethnic identity is a given reality; ethnic identity binds members of the ingroup, creating solidarity among them despite the changing nature of their surroundings.[55]

CURRENT RELEVANCE TO REFUGEES' SEARCH FOR HUMAN RIGHTS

This chapter has illuminated some of the issues involved in American perceptions toward immigrants in general and immigrants from different ethnic groups. These ambivalent perceptions suggest that human rights views of refugees may change based on current events as well as the ethnic groups they are directed toward. A few important recent events stand out as examples of variations in the way refugees' human rights are viewed as well as the practical implications of those variations.

In a seminar given in early 2016, Michnik emphasized the need for the European Union (EU) to present a "coherent response" to the refugee crisis it is facing.[56] However, concerns over security and cultural identity greatly spurred the United Kingdom's vote to leave the EU in June 2016. The United Kingdom's decision to exit the EU demonstrates the United Kingdom's wish to separate itself from the EU's response to refugees and immigration.

In electing to take a different path regarding refugee and immigration policy than its European counterparts, the United Kingdom has chosen to distinguish itself with the freedom to construct a different cultural narrative of the refugee influx. Ultimately, the United Kingdom's decision to leave the EU, or "Brexit" as it has been coined, represents a failure of the EU to create a truly European identity.[57] Brexit was a vote to declare and further establish the United Kingdom's unique national and cultural identity separate from the rest of Europe. Quite significantly, this identity includes perceptions of and attitudes toward refugees and immigration. Whiteley and Clarke argue that "the immigration issue is primarily about threats to identity and culture resulting from people coming into the country without any apparent controls."[58] Brexit unequivocally sent a message to the EU and the rest of the world that Britain has a unique cultural identity with an accompanying unique cultural view of refugee and immigration issues.

In a similar vein to Brexit, the United States' election of Donald Trump as the Republican Party's presidential nominee for the 2016 election conveys distinct perceptions of American cultural identity in relation to other cultures. In Trump's acceptance speech at the Republican National Convention, he emphasized that "the most important difference between our plan and that of our opponents, is that our plan will put America First. Americanism, not globalism, will be our credo."[59] This statement represents a stance that sharply diverges from intercultural translation and instead emphasizes ethnocentrism.

A recent study found that people with higher than average incomes, less education, and little contact with diverse racial and ethnic groups are more likely to support Trump and his anti-immigration policies.[60] These findings support this chapter's own application of contact theory to understand variations in Americans' attitudes toward immigrants. Essentially, those who have less contact with immigrants are less likely to hold positive perceptions of immigrants, and that is exactly what is happening with Trump supporters. Instead of promoting a universal, intercultural view of intergroup relations, the Trump campaign is evoking an isolationist, culturally homogenized American identity. Such an identity leaves little space for intercultural cooperation or translation of human rights and other norms.

Contrary to the previous two incidents, people throughout the world witnessed the refugee team marching in at the opening ceremony of the 2016 Summer Olympic Games. This is the first time in the history of the Olympic Games that a group of refugees with different nationalities was recognized as a team. The authors of this chapter wonder what was going through the minds of people watching TV in their living rooms. While the refugee team reminded the world of the Universal Declaration of Human Rights, people' attitudes toward immigrants, and more specifically toward refugees, are circumstantial and ephemeral. St. Louis in Missouri boasts a large population of Bosnian refugees, creating the largest Bosnian population in the world outside of Bosnia and Herzegovina. The area with a large Bosnian refugee population is called "Little Sarajevo," following the name of the town where the 1984 Winter Olympic Games were held. Ironically, wars broke out in the former Yugoslavia only several years after this Olympic event, with over 100,000 fatalities and 2 million people displaced.

CONCLUSION AND LIMITATIONS

Three questions were raised: (1) Who is considered to be acceptable as refugees to come to the United States? (2) Who decides which group is acceptable? and (3) How do changing attitudes toward certain groups of refugees transform identity of refugees themselves? We argue that while Islam is a religion, Muslims are treated as a racial group similar to Jews, who have been persecuted for thousands of years. As evidenced in the quantitative study, refugees from the Middle East are perceived negatively in general. We further argue that Americans hold ambivalent attitudes toward refugees and immigrants in general; while many hold humanitarian attitudes toward those who are underserved, a dominant ideology of individualistic attitudes prevails. Additionally, there is an intersection between religious and racial hierarchies in American society; immigrants who whiten the society and who show adherence to PWE are perceived as more welcoming. Interestingly, some immigrants, who are able to melt into American society, internalize a dominant ideology of rigid racial and religious hierarchies by shifting their identities in response to the changing circumstances.

This chapter has several limitations. The studies used in this chapter were conducted in the St. Louis area which is not as diverse as other larger cities like New York, Los Angeles, or Chicago. While the studies demonstrate some experiences of Muslim immigrants since 9/11, the latest information is lacking to address the current issues. Further, the sample sizes are not large enough to generalize over the St. Louis population. More importantly, the studies did not include experiences of Muslims from the Middle East in addressing intercultural issues surrounding human rights. As the number of Syrian refugees to the United States is expected to increase, there will be ample opportunities for scholars to explore different resettlement processes among refugees with Muslim backgrounds and Americans' response to this group.

NOTES

1. Portions of this chapter were previously published as H. Matsuo, L. Willoughby, K. McIntyre, and E. Uwalaka, "Attitude Toward Immigrants: Test of

Protestant Work Ethic, Egalitarianism, Social Contact, and Ethnic Origin," *IAFOR Journal for the Social Science* 1, no. 1 (2013): 11–21.

2. "Convention Relating to the Status of Refugees," United Nations, accessed February 5, 2016, http://legal.un.org/avl/ha/prsr/prsr.html.

3. "Figures at a Glance," UNHCR, accessed February 5, 2016, http://www.unhcr.org/en-us/figures-at-a-glance.html.

4. "Resettlement Year at a Glance," International Institute, accessed February 5, 2016, http://www.iistl.org/newsbriefjanuary16.html.

5. Audrey Singer, Jill H. Wilson, and Brookings Institution, *From 'There' to 'Here': Refugee Resettlement in Metropolitan America* (Washington, D.C.: Metropolitan Policy Program, Brookings Institution, 2006).

6. Ibid.

7. Ibid.

8. International Institute, "Resettlement Year at a Glance."

9. Joe Parkinson and David George-Cosh, "Image of Drowned Syrian Boy Echoes Around the World," *The Wall Street Journal*, September 3, 2015, accessed February 5, 2016, http://www.wsj.com/articles/image-of-syrian-boy-washed-up-on-beach-hits-hard-1441282847.

10. Daren Butler and Ece Toksabay, "Troubling Image of Drowned Boy Captivates, Horrifies," *Reuters*, September 2, 2015, accessed February 5, 2016, http://www.reuters.com/article/us-europe-migrants-turkey-idUSKCN0R20IJ20150902.

11. Gardiner Harris, David E. Sanger, and David M. Herszenhorn, "Obama Increases Number of Syrian Refugees for U.S. Resettlement to 10,000," *The New York Times*, September 10, 2015, accessed February 5, 2016, http://www.nytimes.com/2015/09/11/world/middleeast/obama-directs-administration-to-accept-10000-syrian-refugees.html?_r=0.

12. "EU Migrant Crisis: UK will Accept more Syrian Refugees," *BBC*, September 4, 2015, accessed February 5, 2016, http://www.bbc.co.uk/newsround/34152641.

13. Matt Dathan, "Germany says it can take in 500,000 Syrian Refugees Every Year – as David Cameron Insists on Accepting no more than 20,000 in 5 Years," *The Independent*, September 8, 2015, accessed February 5, 2016, http://www.independent.co.uk/news/uk/politics/germany-says-it-can-take-in-500000-syrian-refugees-every-year-as-david-cameron-insists-on-accepting-10491080.html.

14. Sarah Elzas, "Syrian Refugees Agree to Stay in France, Despite Negative Reputation," *RFI*, September 21, 2015, accessed February 5, 2016, http://en.rfi.fr/europe/20150921-syrian-refugees-agree-stay-france-despite-negative-reputation.

15. Mary Troyan, "After Attacks in Paris, Governors Refuse to Accept Syrian Refugees," *USA Today*, November 16, 2015, accessed February 6, 2016, http://www.usatoday.com/story/news/politics/2015/11/16/alabama-refuses-syrian-refugees-paris-terror-attack/75857924/.

16. "After Paris, Drawbridges Up?" *The Economist*, November 21, 2015, accessed February 6, 2016, http://www.economist.com/news/europe/21678832-schengen-system-open-borders-was-already-under-pressure-latest-terrorist-attacks-may.

17. Anna Sauerbrey, "Paris and Europe's Anti-Refugee Backlash," *The New York Times*, November 16, 2015, accessed February 6, 2016, http://www.nytimes.com/2015/11/17/opinion/paris-and-europes-anti-refugee-backlash.html.

18. "After Paris, Drawbridges Up?" *The Economist.*

19. Ruth Sherlock and Harriet Alexander, "US Politicians Vote to Ban Entry to the Country for Syrian Refugees," *The Telegraph*, November 19, 2015, accessed February 6, 2016, http://www.telegraph.co.uk/news/worldnews/northamerica/usa/12006741/US-politicians-vote-to-ban-entry-to-the-country-for-Syrian-refugees.html.

20. Sharon McAnear, "What it Means to be a GOOD SAMARITAN," *U.S. News & World Report*, December 9, 2015, accessed February 6, 2016, http://www.usnews.com/opinion/blogs/faith-matters/2015/12/09/calls-to-ban-muslims-and-only-accept-christian-refugees-arent-christian.

21. Ted Barrett, "Senate Democrats Block Syrian Refugee Bill," *CNN*, January 20, 2016, accessed February 6, 2016, http://www.cnn.com/2016/01/20/politics/syrian-refugees-senate-vote-2016/.

22. Corey Charlton., "Turkey Warns It Now Expects Up to One Million Syrians to Arrive at its Borders," *Daily Mail*, February 9, 2016, accessed February 15, 2016, http://www.dailymail.co.uk/news/article-3438558/Turkey-warns-expects-600-000-Syrians-arrive-borders-warns-goal-host-refugees-OUTSIDE-Turkey.html.

23. Marilynn B. Brewer and Samuel L. Gaertner, "Toward Reduction of Prejudice: Intergroup Contact and Social Categorization," in *Blackwell Handbook of Social Psychology: Intergroup Processes*, eds. Rupert Brown and Samuel L. Gaertner (Malden, MA: Blackwell, 2002).

24. Monica Biernat, Theresa K. Vescio, Shelley A. Theno, and Christian S. Crandall, "Values and Prejudice: Toward Understanding the Impact of American Values on Outgroup Attitudes," in *The Psychology of Values: The Ontario Symposium on Personality and Social Psychology,* eds. Clive Seligman et al. (Mahwah, NJ: L. Erlbaum Associates, 1996).

25. Matsuo et al., "Attitude Toward Immigrants: Test of Protestant Work Ethic, Egalitarianism, Social Contact, and Ethnic Origin," 11–21, accessed August 20, 2016, https://issuu.com/iafor/docs/social-science-journal-vol1-issue1.

26. Hisako Matsuo, Kathryn Kuhn, Emmanuel Uwalaka, Cynthia Wessel, Thu Do, Wala Almostadi, and Candace M. Ruocco, "Refugee Resettlement in St. Louis, Missouri: Race, Religion, and Identity," *Journal of Humanities and Social Sciences* 4, no. 11 (2014): 207–216, accessed August 20, 2016, http://www.ijhssnet.com/journals/Vol_4_No_11_1_September_2014/22.pdf.

27. Matsuo et al., "Attitude Toward Immigrants." This section is from Matsuo et al. by permission of the editors of *IAFOR Journal for the Social Sciences* 1, no. 1 (2013): 11–21. Minor revisions were made in the original paper.

28. Brewer and Gaertner, "Toward Reduction of Prejudice."

29. Rupert Brown, James Vivian, and Miles Hewstone, "Changing Attitudes through Intergroup Contact: The Effects of Group Membership Salience," *European Journal of Social Psychology* 29 (1999): 741–764, accessed February 16, 2016, doi: 10.1002/(SICI)1099-0992(199908/09)29:5/6<741::AID-EJSP972>3.0.CO;2-8.

30. Gordon W. Allport, *The Nature of Prejudice* (Reading, MA: Addison-Wesley, 1954).

31. Thomas F. Pettigrew, "Intergroup Contact Theory," *Annual Review of Psychology* 49 (1998): 65–85, accessed February 16, 2016, doi: 10.1146/annurev.psych.49.1.65.

32. Miles Hewstone and Rupert Brown, "Contact is Not Enough: An Intergroup Perspective on the 'Contact Hypothesis,'" in *Contact and Conflict in Intergroup Encounters Social Psychology and Society*, eds. Miles Hewstone and Rupert Brown (New York: Blackwell, 1986); Thomas F. Pettigrew, "Generalized Intergroup Contact Effects on Prejudice," *Personality & Social Psychology Bulletin* 23 (1997): 173–185, accessed February 16, 2016, doi: 10.1177/0146167297232006.

33. Christian S. Crandall and Amy Eshleman, "A Justification-Suppression Model of the Expression and Experience of Prejudice," *Psychological Bulletin* 129 (2003): 414–446, accessed February 16, 2016, doi: http://dx.doi.org/10.1037/0033-2909.129.3.414; Hewstone and Brown, "Contact Is not Enough."

34. Biernat et al., "Values and Prejudice"; Crandall and Eshleman, "A Justification-Suppression Model"; Irwin Katz and Glen Hass, "Racial Ambivalence and American Value Conflict: Correlational and Priming Studies of Dual Cognitive Structures," *Journal of Personality & Social Psychology* 55 (1988): 893–905, accessed February 17, 2016, doi: 10.1037/0022-3514.55.6.893; Irwin Katz, Joyce Wackenhut, and Glen Hass, "Racial Ambivalence, Value Duality, and Behavior," in *Prejudice, Discrimination, and Racism*, eds. J. F. Dovidio and S. L. Gaertner (Toronto, ON, Canada: Academic Press, 1986); Gregory R. Maio, D. W. Bell, and Victoria M. Esses, "Ambivalence in Persuasion: The Processing of Messages about Immigrant Groups," *Journal of Experimental Social Psychology* 32 (1996): 513–536, accessed February 17, 2016, doi: 10.1006/jesp.1996.0023.

35. Biernat et al., "Values and Prejudice"; Katz and Hass, "Racial Ambivalence and American Value Conflict."

36. Ibid.; Katz, Wackenhut, and Hass, "Racial Ambivalence."

37. Biernat et al., "Values and Prejudice."

38. Crandall and Eshleman, "A Justification-Suppression Model"; Milton Rokeach, *The Open and Closed Mind: Investigation into the Nature of Belief Systems and Personality Systems* (New York: Basic Books, 1960).

39. Walter G. Stephan, Oscar Ybarra, and Guy Bachman, "Prejudice toward Immigrants," *Journal of Applied Social Psychology* 29 (1999): 2221–2237, accessed February 17, 2016, doi: 10.1111/j.1559-1816.1999.tb00107.x.

40. Ibid.

41. Hisako Matsuo, "Identificational Assimilation of Japanese Americans: A Reassessment of Primordialism and Circumstantialism," *Sociological Perspectives* 35 (1992): 505–523, accessed February 18, 2016, doi: 10.2307/1389332.

42. Alberto Voci and Miles Hewstone, "Intergroup Contact and Prejudice toward Immigrants in Italy: The Mediational Role of Anxiety and the Moderational Role of Group Salience," *Group Processes & Intergroup Relations* 6 (2003): 37–54, accessed February 17, 2016, doi: 10.1177/1368430203006001011.

43. Paul D. Starr and Alden E. Roberts, "Attitudes toward New Americans: Perceptions of Indo-Chinese in Nine Cities," *Research in Race & Ethnic Relations* 3 (1982): 165–186, accessed February 17, 2016, http://psycnet.apa.org/psycinfo/1983-25519-001.

44. Katz and Hass, "Racial Ambivalence and American Value Conflict."

45. Ibid.

46. Matsuo et al., "Refugee Resettlement in St. Louis, Missouri." This section is partially from Matsuo et al. in *International Journal of Humanities and Social Sciences* 4, no. 11 (2014): 207–216. The journal states 'Copyrights for articles published in IJHSS are retained by the authors, with first publication rights granted to the journal.'

47. "Anti-Muslim Sentiments Fairly Commonplace," Gallup, accessed February 17, 2016, http://www.gallup.com/poll/24073/antimuslim-sentiments-fairly-com monplace.aspx.

48. Hisako Matsuo, "Bosnian Refugee Resettlement in St. Louis, Missouri," in *Homeland Wanted: Interdisciplinary Perspective on Refugee Resettlement in the West*, eds. P. Waxman and V. Colic-Peisker (New York: Nova Science Publishers, Inc., 2005).

49. Val Colic-Peisker, "At Least You're the Right Colour: Identity and Social Inclusion of Bosnian Refugees in Australia," *Journal of Ethnic and Migration Studies* 31 (2005): 615–638, accessed February 17, 2016, doi: 10.1080/13691830500109720.

50. Kristen Anderson, "Lessons in Whiteness: German Immigrants and Racial Ideology in Nineteenth-Century America," in *Cross-Cultural History and the Domestication of Otherness*, eds. Michal Jan Rozbicki and George O. Ndege (New York: Palgrave Macmillan, 2012).

51. Pierre Bourdieu, *Distinction: A Social Critique of the Judgement of Taste* (London: Routledge, 1979); Maria Cristina Morales, "Ethnic-Controlled Economy or Segregation? Exploring Inequality in Latina/o Co-Ethnic Jobsites," *Sociological Forum* 24 (2009): 589–610, accessed February 17, 2016, doi: 10.1111/j.1573-7861.2009.01121.x.

52. Hisako Matsuo, Emmanuel Uwalaka, Kathryn E Kuhn, Candace Ruocco, Thu Do, Wala Almostadi, Cynthia Wessel, Savitri Grover, and David Githinji, paper presented at the Annual Conference sponsored by the Center for Intercultural Studies of Saint Louis University, St. Louis, MO, 2014.

53. Ibid.

54. Daniel Glaser, "Dynamics of Ethnic Identification," *American Sociological Review* 23, no. 1 (1958): 31–40, accessed July 5, 2016, http://www.jstor.org/stable/2088621.

55. Stanley B. Greenberg, *Race and State in Capitalist Development* (London: Yale University Press, 1980); Matsuo, "Identificational Assimilation of Japanese Americans."

56. Wojciech Michnik, "Beyond Fortress Europe: European Union and the Current Refugee Crisis" (paper presented at the Center for Intercultural Studies, Saint Louis University, Saint Louis, Missouri, February 5, 2016).

57. Carol Strenger, "Brexit Reflects EU's Failure to Create a European Identity – Isreal Should Take Heed," *Haaretz*, June 24, 2016, accessed August 22, 2016, http://www.haaretz.com/world-news/europe/.premium-1.726906.

58. Paul Whiteley and Harold D. Clarke, "Why did Older Voters Choose Brexit? It's a Matter of Identity," *The Conversation*, June 25, 2016, accessed August 22,

2016, http://theconversation.com/why-did-older-voters-choose-brexit-its-a-matter-of-identity-61636.

59. Donald J. Trump, Republican National Convention speech, July 21, 2016, accessed August 22, 2016, http://www.politico.com/story/2016/07/full-transcript-donald-trump-nomination-acceptance-speech-at-rnc-225974#ixzz4FiNnOL3l.

60. Jonathan Rothwell, "Explaining Nationalist Political Views: The Case of Donald Trump" (Draft Working Paper, August 1, 2016).

Chapter 7

Politics, Religion, and Debt

Translating Lives into Normative Frameworks for Asylum Seekers in Italy

Tommaso Sbriccoli

At present, Europe and the United States are both closing their borders, curbing access to their territory and to rights for noncitizens. This trend, rapidly increasing and coextensive with the actual or planned construction of walls and the externalization of frontiers, acts on two levels. On the one hand, it blocks, much more than in the past, the very possibility of people to move. Freedom of movement in general is challenged, by introducing increasingly restricting norms, obstacles, and forms of control. On the other hand, more and more, the right to enter Western countries is detached from the personal stories and trajectories of persons. Even the most important exception in international law to the possibility of preventing foreigners from entering another state, that is the right granted to people to seek asylum, is now under attack both in the EU and in the United States.[1] People moving from "non-Western" to "Western" countries, be they refugees, migrants, tourists, or even businessmen, must go through increasingly tougher procedures and are seen more and more as a frightening, homogenous mass, rather than as individuals, each bearer of one's own reasons and circumstances. Thus, freedom of movement in general and the individual right to escape one's country and seek refuge elsewhere are both at the center of restricting policies and discourses. In this context, why people want or need to move, and the story behind their (blocked) journeys, lose importance; the very act of attempting to cross a border acquires salience, disqualifying the search for the reasons behind it.

"Translation" into another culture thus appears to be impeded in its twofold meaning: the possibility to take (something) from one place to another (its original Latin etymology), and the attempt of transposing sense across languages and worldviews. What gets lost in this movement is the specific materiality of people's rights, built as it is into the relational and intersubjective construction of a shared understanding of what is just and what is not. Rights, and human rights specifically, remain trapped in their virtual, transcendental aspect. They work only as general legal frames, excluding or including subjects according to the freer or stricter interpretation embraced by politics in a given moment in time. But what if we try instead to understand human rights as an horizon of translatability, across and along which instances coming from below can meet and negotiate meaning? What if human rights were the product of intercultural translations, rather than the mere translation of cultural products, as they are often accused of being?[2]

In what follows, I do not intend to put forward a predetermined view of what human rights are or ought to be. Human rights, in fact, apart from being legal principles recognized in international treaties and national legislations, are also, and maybe mainly, a discursive field, shaped by institutions and disciplines, and made up of overlapping, and often competing, views.[3] As Sally Engle Merry has rightly pointed out, human rights are often characterized by a double movement, translating frames from international institutions to local settings, and reframing local grievances in a global legal idiom. In the process, much is at stake, and human rights' translations in both directions entail complex dynamics connected with political and economic fields of forces. According to Merry, "intermediaries such as community leaders, nongovernmental organization participants, and social movement activists play a critical role in translating ideas from the global arena down and from local arenas up."[4] Such figures, whom she calls "human rights translators," negotiate meaning in the middle of the two poles constituting the discursive field of human rights. Though embedded as they are in both extremes, their capacity to translate is strongly compromised by the constraints each of the two fields produces.

In this chapter, drawing on my long-term experience as anthropological consultant in cases of asylum claims, I will show how an anthropologist can act as a "translator" in Merry's sense, although in a slightly different way. First of all, the translation I will discuss occurs only in formal legal settings, at one or more of the steps foreseen by the asylum procedure.[5] Consequently, it immediately confronts the already given normative frameworks, and the room for negotiating meaning is relatively small. Second, the anthropologist in this context often works with people whose understanding of the legal field into which they are inserted (its logic, its idiom, even its cognitive basis) is extremely poor, if not totally absent. Yet, this "givenness" and the obscurity of the legal and normative contexts paradoxically allow a shared reconfiguration of people's understanding of their own existential trajectory, and, in turn, (sometimes), a peculiar bending of the normative framework so as to partly redefine—from below—the reach of human rights. Anthropological expertise in this field, when coupled with juridical competence, may produce a space of intercultural redefinition of meaning that makes human rights work in terms of translatability rather than as an already given and almost immutable set of rules. In this process, narratives acquire central importance, as they are the fulcrum around which sense can be negotiated between the actors involved.

NARRATIVES AS FIELDS OF
NEGOTIATION OF MEANING

Narratives and narration are significant at all steps in the unfolding of most legal procedures. Both facts and their legal relevance are constructed and assessed to a large extent through narratives. At the same time, the collecting of life stories has been a very important method in many social sciences like anthropology, sociology, and oral history. Story telling is indeed one of the most important features of the way human beings convey meaning and understand the world. As such, the analysis of how narratives and life stories are assessed, the procedures they are submitted to, and the conditions of their interpretation in relation to different contexts should acquire central importance if we are to grasp the epistemic ground of the knowledge processes.

Narratives and life stories as they are elicited in courts, legal forums, or the social scientist' fieldwork, in fact, do not exist in a supposed "objective purity." They rather acquire their internal coherence and overall sense only in relation to the instances that trigger and provoke their emergence.[6] When dealing with the process of asylum claiming, such premises become even more cogent. The life story of a person claiming asylum is often the only thing she has at her disposal to prove she is entitled to international protection. Consequently, the elicitation of the story itself, its production so to say, becomes the field within which various epistemic instances—from that of the asylum seeker himself to the Commissioner, from the lawyer to the judge, and sometimes also to that of different experts, including the anthropologist—confront each other, each by utilizing its categories, its sets of values, and even its political attitude.[7] By addressing asylum seekers' narratives as objects of knowledge, and utilizing the analytical tools of anthropology and legal analysis, I thus hope to show how they can become the field for identifying new, trans-local and transcultural common grounds for the recognition of rights.

In fact, the opening, or unpacking, of asylum seekers' narratives in order to understand the conditions of their translatability can bring to extremely fruitful results. It can allow for the establishment of a horizon of commensurability between practices, facts, and interpretations that might otherwise be compared and matched only with great difficulty. This activity, if enacted with an anthropological sensibility and expertise, can reorganize the discourse on human rights through the practices of inter-spatial and intercultural translation, rather than through the already existing givens according to which individual stories can, or cannot, be granted recognition.

In this way, personal narratives become fields where meaning can be negotiated, and new, shared interpretations of the world can take place. On one hand, making explicit to asylum seekers the logic according to which their stories will be assessed in legal settings allows them to autonomously reconfigure their own understanding of their life trajectories. As it will appear clearly in what follows below, this does not mean at all "creating" or "inventing" stories fitting the normative framework of asylum, but it rather entails a redefinition of one's subjectivity within the legal discourse. On the other hand, by reasoning together about the details of a life story, and about the ethical or moral considerations it triggers (about what is right and wrong, just and unjust, fair and unfair, etc.), the asylum seeker, the anthropologist, and the legal expert can identify particular situations that are significant in terms of rights' violation, widening in this manner the reach of human rights through a bottom-up process.

This twofold aspect characterizing the reconfiguration of personal narratives toward the production of new subjectivities, and the identification of new configurations of rights infringement will be considered by presenting two sets of cases concerning asylum seekers of Bangladeshi origin. The first relates to Hindu Bangladeshis persecuted for their religious affiliation. The second gathers cases about debt migrants make to leave their country. As the cases presented will show, in Bangladeshi asylum seekers' narratives' themes like religion, politics, risk, persecution, debt, and dependence overlap in ways that challenge asylum law's precise categorial divisions, making it often difficult to match the logic informing applicants' stories with the logic required by the human rights' discourse in asylum cases. Such apparent incommensurability often disqualifies asylum seekers' applications, as commissions and courts fail to acknowledge continuities and translatability at a deeper level between the narratives they are presented with and the norms and principles they are supposed to apply.[8]

These cases originate from my long-term experiences as a legal and anthropological consultant for many associations working with asylum seekers in Italy. As an anthropologist of South Asia, speaking Urdu and Hindi, I have in fact had the chance to directly support and help many South Asian asylum seekers with their applications. My anthropological and historical knowledge of their countries of origin has allowed me, or so I hope, to work at the intersection between individual experiences, with their own logic, and the Italian/Western legal framework, with its normative constraints. In the next two sections, I will present the cases and analyze the work of inter-translation and interpretation that has occurred at the crossing between the different world-views involved in this process.

TRANSLATING LOGICAL FRAMEWORKS

Alamin's[9] story was first collected by an operator in a center for asylum seekers in Italy. When I set myself to work on the preparation of its file for the Florence Territorial Commission, the operator told me: "Don't spend too much time on him, he is surely an economic migrant." The distinction between economic migrant and refugee, although not legally significant, has acquired nonetheless in Italian (and European) public discourse a particular strength, and it informs the mindset of people working with asylum seekers, making it particularly difficult to address properly and without biases the cases of each of the persons applying for asylum. The story read, in short: "Alamin lived in a rural village. While working in a construction site he killed by accident the contractor and eventually ran away to Dhaka, from where he fled to Libya." Raju's story, in turn, when first collected ran as follows: "Being an activist for the Awami League party, he was attacked by some members of the opposite party on many occasions. He was severely beaten on one occasion and eventually decided to leave the country." When Raju arrived in Italy, his party had just recently won the election.

Both these stories would barely qualify the applicants for the right to be granted international or humanitarian protection. One is a case of negligent homicide, while the other is about pre-electoral political fights. But once we increase the ethnographic resolution, many new details appear which modify the overall sense of these stories. Both applicants were in fact Hindus living in Bangladesh, a country that is notorious for events of persecution directed at Hindu citizens. When keeping this fact in mind, their stories acquire a very different internal logic.

Alamin was working for an important Muslim contractor in his village, as his father used to do before him. One day, a wooden board he was lifting fell down, right on the head of his boss. A man working with him persuaded him to run home. When Alamin told his family what had happened, they immediately gave him some money and sent him to Dhaka to his brother's place. In the evening, the news of the death of the contractor arrived, and his father and mother also opted to leave the village. In Dhaka, the family decided to use all their savings to send Alamin out of the country, fearing for his life as both police and the villagers were looking for him, the former to arrest him and the latter for revenge.

Raju, on the other hand, lived in a rural village and was interested in politics. A supporter of the Awami League, he joined demonstrations and volunteered for his party. During the election campaign, he was personally attacked by members of an Islamist political party, the Jamaat-e-Islami, who contested his rights, as a Hindu, to participate in the country's political life. The same people also attacked the Hindu temple which he used to attend for prayers, and finally seriously injured him while he was buying food in a shop in his neighborhood.

Both Alamin and Raju, while telling their stories, showed genuine fear at the idea of being sent back to Bangladesh, but they identified the causes of their escape and of this fear not in their being Hindu, but in more vague terms referring to the general situation in their country of origin. For Alamin, it was the renowned unfairness of Bangladesh police and judicial system, while for Raju it was the increasing violence of his country's politics. For both of them, immersed as they were in situations of structural violence and "naturalized" inequality[10], it was almost impossible to articulate autonomously their experiences in a story whose internal logic could fit the standards required by asylum law. Yet, their stories and their understanding of the causes of their problems can tell us a lot about how asylum law's clear-cut separation between the political and the religious, as well as other kinds of reasons of persecution, do not correspond to the way in which people actually conceive and conceptualize their situation. While for Alamin the main reason for leaving his country was the unfairness of police and judges, and so the impossibility of enjoying a fair trial, for Raju it was the fact that he could not participate in the political life of his country due to the persecution enacted by his political adversaries. While working with them, I made explicit reference to the possibility that their problems could also be due to their being Hindu. Raju and Alamin almost immediately started reconsidering their experience in the light of this fact. What they realized, or managed to focus on, was that their specific problems, general and widespread as they were in Bangladesh, could have been made harder and more difficult to solve because of they being Hindu. Such understanding provoked a shift in their subjectivity, that is, in the way they thought of themselves in relation to what happened and how they framed their representations of themselves. So much so that Alamin, during the interview with the Territorial Commission, reported to the interviewer a fact that he had not recounted during our conversations: that when living in Libya he was once attacked because of his religion, as some men beat him up during the Ramadan because he was eating during the holiday.

The significance of this process does not lie in the fact of explaining to the "ignorant" Other the real meaning and logic of her own life. Rather, it lies in the shared elaboration of a new area of reciprocal understanding. In this space, individual experience can be understood in its proper terms, and it is reorganized in a way that allows for its translation by means of external

categories: a process of real adaptation between the two systems.[11] Consequently, the subjectivity of the person is shaped so as to maintain the original
logic of her story intact. This, in turn, forces the two systems to find a space
of inter-translatability which can produce a new angle of view, and eventually
act as a point of departure for detecting further fields of commensurability.
This process becomes even more transparent when we move to the second set
of cases, those concerning debt.

DEBTS AND HUMAN RIGHTS

Many Bangladeshis now living in Italy have spent months, or even years,
working in Libya.[12] Libya was often the definitive (although probably temporary) destination of their migration, as salaries were good in comparison to
Bangladesh, and jobs were easy to find. In order to leave Bangladesh, though,
many had to incur significant debts with usurers and moneylenders. These
debts, besides interest rates ranging from 30 percent to 100 percent per year,
also involved guarantees in the form of the debtor's land and/or house. This
guarantee, however, was not based on the real and assessed value of the asset.
When signing loan contracts, asylum seekers were actually ceding property
in their house or land to the usurer. The latter could eventually, in the case of
debtor's default, register it in his name and take possession of the real estate,
no matter if its value corresponded to or exceeded the owed amount.

Debt is in itself considered mainly an economic category, one that seldom
is connected to the field of human rights. Actually, in the opinion of many
scholars, we nowadays live in a "society of debt," with the latter shaping
our relation to the State and the market, in some ways even configuring the
way we constitute ourselves as subjects.[13] Usury, it is true, is seen as an
illegal practice, and protection from usurers is still on the agenda of many
governments. A person taking on debts to emigrate is usually considered, in
the general understanding, as an economic migrant, a sort of entrepreneur
who borrows his initial capital in order to set up his own business in another
country. But if we look more closely at the lives and the background of these
Bangladeshi asylum seekers, what emerges seems much more connected to
practices of exploitation and violence than at first would appear.

Debts incurred by Bangladeshi asylum seekers are often properly understandable only when considered in the context of the local networks of structural
dependence, inequality, and power. Indebtedness and migration thus appear
as practices deeply linked to individual, family, and social environments
in which they play a twofold, contradictory role. On the one hand, they
are attempts at emancipation from those very networks of dependence and
inequality. But, on the other hand, they often end up simply reproducing and

reinforcing the very conditions of inequality and dependence from which they have emerged in the first place.

Furthermore, the features of these debts point to a noteworthy aspect that especially concerns us here. Providing real estate as guarantee for a debt (without an assessment of its actual value) relates in the Italian law to what is known as *Patto Commissorio*, forbidden in the country's legislation by articles number 2744 and 1963 of the Civil Code.[14] The rationale of such legislation goes back very far in time, to the Roman Emperor Constantine, and was originally socio-ethical in intent, aiming to avoid a situation when a person in need of incurring debt would be forced to renounce his means of subsistence because of such need or due to high interests. Interestingly, what the Roman legislator appears to have understood was the enormous potential of the *Patto Commissorio* to establish and reproduce at the local level situations of significant economic and social injustice. This kind of practice, if authorized, could, in fact, eventually lead to the massive concentration of economic and political power in local, private hands, which could in turn act as competitor to the state, and turn citizens into servants. This is exactly what the debt practices found in Bangladesh seem to potentially imply.[15]

By establishing a level of comparison and commensurability between debt practices in Bangladesh and the *Patto Commissorio*, and by charging this connection with the ethical rationale originally underlying the latter's prohibition, we can open individual, localized narratives toward a wider horizon of rights recognition. The prohibition of *Patto Commissorio* in Italy can be thus mobilized in order to ask for the recognition of a humanitarian protection for Bangladeshi asylum seekers who hold such kinds of debts, as their return to their country of origin would imply the possible loss of their means of subsistence and carry an effective risk to their and their family's dignity and integrity.

In this way, the cultural history of the *Patto Commissorio* can shed a different light, so to speak, on the kinds of applications it can be utilized for within international and supranational provisions in the field of human rights.

However, its humanitarian value can be rediscovered—even within the Italian normative code—only thanks to the interterritorial and semiotic implications of asylum claiming, as well as to the very presence of Bangladeshi debtors on Italian territory. It is only their migration and their need for protection that generate an otherwise unexpected spatial and semantic proximity, and an unprecedented cultural twist—between Italy and Bangladesh, and between the normative and cultural codes of the two countries. These, in turn, can make the prohibition of the *Patto Commissorio* acquire humanitarian relevance.

These cases are thus a site for potentially developing a creative inter-translation between individual stories, local and global contexts, and Italian asylum (and human rights) legislation, in order to identify, through a bottom-up approach, new trajectories for the delineation and protection of human rights and dignity. Such a process can only take place through an intense interdisciplinary work that has as its starting point a careful, anthropological unpacking of the subjects' life stories, with the aim of reconstructing their internal logic and the sociocultural context within which they can be properly understood.

This work, at the crossroads of anthropology, semiotics, and law, is not quite as predictable as might appear at the first glance. It is important to note that when those less ready and able to investigate the internal logic of such experiences elicit the life stories of these asylum seekers, the results are often deeply discouraging. Territorial Commissions, for instance, almost always fail to acknowledge the tragic situation of these persons and the implications of such debts for their lives, treating them as simple borrowers with no rights to be protected. Let's take an example from the transcription of the interview of one of these Bangladeshi asylum seekers at the Rome Territorial Commission.[16]

Commissioner: How do you think you will give back the money you borrowed?
AS: I am fine here. I am safe. I will work and send back money to pay the debt. But even if I won't, at least here in Italy my life won't be at risk.
Commissioner: And what about your family?
AS: My family is being harassed by the usurers. They threat them. But they want me. If I don't go back, they will keep threatening my family until the debt is paid, but if I go back they could kill me.
Commissioner: Why should they kill you? Couldn't they just take your house and land, and maybe send you to prison?
AS: If I go back they will come and ask for money, and if I have not it I cannot allow them to take my land and house, it is everything I have to live on. This is why they would kill me.
Commissioner: You showed to me a contract in which it is written that if you don't give the loan back they are entitled to take your land and house. How could you not give them to the creditors?
AS: It is not that I don't want to give them my land, but it is the only thing from which I can sustain myself and my family. How can I give it to them? This is why they would kill me to get my land.

It appears clearly from this extract how the commissioner does not seem to understand how a contract could not be but honored, even though the deal would not be legal in Italy. In his mind, a contract is stronger than anything else, a conception that betrays the economistic view that is often found at the basis of the legal operators' assessing models in this field. This view, though, completely ignores both the actual context behind the asylum seekers' stories, and the potential way in which it can be made to resonate with Italian normative framework and the international provisions on human rights. Also, lawyers are often skeptical in putting forward such complex work of inter-translation, as it would require much more work than usual, as well as the help of experts. Yet, it is only thanks to this kind of effort, interdisciplinary in its nature, that asylum seekers' narratives can become the field upon which developing translations of personal life trajectories into interculturally shared and innovative interpretations of human rights.

CONCLUSION

People have always moved and will keep moving, notwithstanding attempts at blocking borders and preventing migration. When leaving one place for another, the only thing a person will surely never leave behind is a story. Along with it, though, she will also take with her the cognitive and symbolic tools with which she gives meaning to it, and to whatever else may befall her. Worldviews move with people, and in turn they change with movements and intersubjective interactions.

When confronted with instances external to the logic informing their "owner's" understanding of the world or of its particular situation, stories become a field for negotiation of meaning and a means for potential reconfiguration of subjectivities. In this process, there is room for establishing a space for sharing different views about events, and eventually elaborating a common ground for interpretation.

As the cases discussed here show, the process of asylum claiming can be very fruitful in uncovering and analyzing such dynamics. The collaboration with asylum seekers on their life stories by adopting anthropological methods and expertise allows us to highlight the complex character of narratives in the legal context, as well as to realize the importance of paying attention to the ways they are elicited and interpreted. When carried out thoughtfully, with the involvement of experts like jurists, lawyers, and even semioticians, such efforts are capable of producing new trans-local (and, in a sense, even transhistorical) interpretations of rights, a result that could have important implications even for the recognition of rights locally in Western countries. As such, the above examples can, hopefully, be viewed as instances of how cognitive spaces can be opened up for a critique of the supposedly universal validity of human rights, and for a redefinition of their emancipatory potential in serving justice.

NOTES

1. Jacqueline Bhaba, "Internationalist Gatekeepers? The Tension between Asylum Advocacy and Human Rights," *Harvard Human Rights Journal* 15 (2002): 155–182. She sees asylum as "the process that keeps migration exclusion morally defensible while protecting the global gatekeeping operation as a whole" (ibid., 161). The dialectic between "normal" migration and asylum is certainly complex and needs problematization. When asylum also comes under attack, however, there is apparently a new need to reflect on the morality of exclusion.

2. Didier Fassin, *Humanitarian Reason. A Moral History of the Present* (Berkeley and Los Angeles: University of California Press, 2012). Fassin's work analyses Western humanitarianism as a particular form of government, and lucidly shows the contradictions underlying it.

3. Nicola Perugini and Gordon Neve, *The Human Right to Dominate* (Oxford: Oxford University Press, 2015). The authors show how the discourse on human rights can be subverted to the point of being deployed to further subjugate the weak and legitimize domination.

4. Sally E. Merry, "Transnational Human Rights and Local Activism: Mapping the Middle," *American Anthropologist* 108, no. 1 (2006): 38.

5. For anthropological expertise in courts and other legal settings, see Livia S. Holden, ed., *Cultural Expertise and Litigation: Patterns, Conflicts, Narratives* (London: Routledge, 2011); and Anthony Good, *Anthropology and Expertise in the Asylum Courts* (London: Routledge, 2007).

6. The work of Conley and O'Barr on litigants' ways to formulate their problems in US courts provides a perfect example of how important is the way narratives are framed, their reliance on different cultural models, and how all this affects their efficacy: John M. Conley and William M. O'Barr, *Rules versus Relationships: The Ethnography of Legal Discourse* (Chicago: University of Chicago Press, 1990). For a comparison of Indian style of talk in traditional legal settings to that occurring in Western formal courts, showing how the contextual task of the legal context may allow for different ways of ordering speech and producing narratives, see Robert M. Hayden, "Turn-Taking, Overlap, and the Task at Hand: Ordering Speaking Turns in Legal Settings," *American Ethnologist* 14, no. 2 (1987): 251–270.

For analyses of the epistemic and moral processes in narratives by female victims of abuse in the Italian legal context, see Alessandra Gribaldo, "The Paradoxical Victim: Intimate Violence Narratives on Trial in Italy," *American Ethnologist* 41, no. 4 (2014): 743–756.

7. For a study that analyses in detail the way asylum seekers' narratives are produced and assessed by different epistemic instances, see Tommaso Sbriccoli and Stefano Jacoviello, "The Voice in C. The Creole Attitude of a Bangladeshi Refugee in Italy," in *Shifting Borders. European Perspectives on Creolisation*, eds. Tommaso Sbriccoli and Stefano Jacoviello (Newcastle upon Tyne: Cambridge Scholars Publishing, 2012), 83–109.

8. In Italy, Territorial Commissions (TCs) are the first judicial step for asylum cases. They are administrative bodies chaired by an officer of prefecture, and consist of a police officer, a representative of territorial institutions (municipality or

State-Cities Conference) and a representative of UNHCR. TCs should interview asylum claimers as soon as possible, even though usually applicants have to wait between six and twelve months and sometimes even longer before being heard. In the meantime, applicants without documents or who enter Italy illegally have to stay inside appropriate structures and centers financed by the Italian Government. While decisions about the granting of a form of protection should be made by all the members of the TC together, interviews of applicants can be carried out by only one member of the TC, in order to speed up the procedure. Idiosyncrasies of individual officials are thus amplified. Furthermore, the risk of the individual officers applying different standards while gathering information, and judging the case occurs more often owing to the interviewers' diverse backgrounds. The risk of this happening increases if we consider that applicants almost never have the chance to hire a legal representative to support them in this context. If refugee status is rejected by the TC, applicants can appeal in the civil courts, which act with a single presiding judge, within 30 days from the date of rejection. In the case of a further refusal, it is still possible for applicants to appeal to the Appeal Courts.

9. Names of places and persons have been changed so as to respect people's privacy.

10. The concept of structural violence, firstly proposed by Johan Galtung in, "Violence, Peace, and Peace Research," *Journal of Peace Research* 6 (1969): 167–191; has been later productively elaborated by Paul Farmer in, "An Anthropology of Structural Violence," *Current Anthropology* 45, no. 3 (2004): 305–325.

11. For a definition of the capacity of reorganizing multiple subjectivities along different planes of pertinence, or to transferring them (that is, translating them) from one plane to another, as "creole attitude," see Sbriccoli and Jacoviello, "The Voice in C. The Creole Attitude of a Bangladeshi Refugee in Italy."

12. The cases dealt with in this section are discussed in detail in Tommaso Sbriccoli and Mario Ricca, "Shylock del Bengala. Debiti migratori, vite in ostaggio e diritto d'asilo. (Un approccio corologico alle implicazioni anti-umanitarie del patto commissorio)," *Calumet, Intercultural Law and Humanities Review* 2 (2016).

13. See, for instance, Zygmunt Bauman and Citlali Rovirosa-Madrazo, *Living on Borrowed Time: Conversations with Citlali Rovirosa-Madrazo* (Cambridge: Polity Press, 2007).

14. Common law does not foresee a specific prohibition for such practices. The usual English translation of *Patto Commissorio* is "agreement of forfeiture." See Giovanni. Valcavi, "Intorno al divieto di patto commissorio, alla vendita simulata a scopo di garanzia ed al negozio fiduciario," *Il Foro* 1 (1990). [An English translation, "On the prohibition of the agreement of forfeiture, the simulated sale for the purpose of guarantee and the trust agreement," is available at the following link: http://www. fondazionegiovannivalcavi.it/english/writings-on-civil-law/14_On-the-prohibition-of-the-agreement-of-forfeiture.pdf]. Sometimes, one can find the term "security" or "collateral" used to define the asset given in guarantee. See, for instance, Amit Bahaduri, "On the Formation of Usurious Interest Rates in Backward Agriculture," *Cambridge Journal of Economics* 1, no. 4 (1977): 341–352; and Kaushik Basu, "Implicit Interest Rates, Usury and Isolation in Backward Agriculture," *Cambridge Journal of Economics* 8, no. 2 (1984): 145–159.

15. See Tommaso Sbriccoli and Mario Ricca, "Shylock del Bengala. Debiti migratori, vite in ostaggio e diritto d'asilo," for a description of the socio-political logic behind such debts, and Bahaduri, "On the Formation of Usurious Interest Rates in Backward Agriculture," and Basu, "Implicit Interest Rates, Usury and Isolation in Backward Agriculture," for the economic logic informing them.

16. An extract from the transcript of an interview of a Bangladesh asylum seeker at the Rome Territorial Commission.

Chapter 8

The Role of Human Rights Frameworks in Refugee Host State Integration

Rachel Santon

By the end of 2015, the United Nations High Commissioner for Refugees (UNHCR) had identified 21.3 million refugees globally, with developing countries hosting over 80 percent of them.[1] The growth of the refugee population is an increasing concern that affects countries of origin, host countries, international aid organizations, and, most importantly, refugees themselves. The tendency of governments, nongovernmental organizations (NGOs), aid agencies, and policymakers to conceptualize the human rights of refugees through security and victimization frameworks prevents refugees from making valuable economic and social contributions. This analysis argues that these frameworks inhibit refugees from enacting their agency and achieving their ultimate capacity as human beings.

The chapter will evaluate the extent to which particular human rights interpretations and consequent policies in different countries prevent or enable refugees to assume agency and to socially and economically contribute in the world. Such human rights policies include the right to employment, freedom of movement, freedom of religion, and freedom to participate in the cultural life of the community. The study will qualitatively investigate common human rights standards related to the legal, economic, and social integration of refugees into their host societies. This analysis will explore how policies differ among various host countries, the human rights norms implicit in the differing policies, and the impact those differences have on refugees' lives in new environments. This study recommends a conceptual shift in the refugee aid industry to view refugees as a human rights issue rather than as burdens and security threats. Although cultural differences among countries complicate the attainment of a universal consensus on refugee human rights, it is still worth striving for a more unified response. Acknowledging the different human rights standards in various countries will illuminate both the challenges of upholding a universal set of human rights for refugees and the importance of seeking a global consensus on human rights for refugees.

After defining key terms, I will review international refugee law, describe the current refugee crisis, and outline the reasons refugee issues should be considered human rights issues. I will follow with an overview of the different frameworks used to understand refugee human rights, and an examination of practical applications of those frameworks in legal, social, and economic integration of refugees in host states. This analysis will conclude with arguments for considering refugee human rights as universal rights, and the implications of promoting a unified framework for addressing refugee human rights issues.

DEFINITIONS OF KEY TERMS

Given the multitude of interpretations for who qualifies as a refugee, it is necessary to define what the term refugee means in relation to the argument of this chapter. The UNHCR defines a refugee as someone who "owing to a well-founded fear of being persecuted for reasons of race, religion, nationality, membership of a particular social group or political opinion, is outside the country of his nationality, and is unable to, or owing to such fear, is unwilling to avail himself of the protection of that country."[2] This definition would also include people fleeing due to conflict or war. It is important to note that the UNHCR definition excludes economic migrants who are leaving their homeland due to crippling, and often, life-threatening poverty. Loescher points out that the close relationship between political conflict and social and economic challenges often creates difficulty in distinguishing between refugees and migrants.[3] While economic migrants choose to leave their home countries for the promise of a better financial future in a different country, refugees are forced to leave their home countries due to direct threat to their lives from their own governments or hostile groups within the country. As almost all states accept the UNHCR definition of refugee, to understand human rights issues relating to refugees and their resulting capacity or incapacity to provide valuable contributions, it is necessary to work within this framework. Therefore, this analysis accepts the UNHCR definition of a refugee and considers refugees as people who fall under that definition.

In addition to this understanding, it is also important to briefly define what this analysis means, in regard to refugees, by the term "actor." Traditional international relations theories of realism and liberalism view the state as the most important actor in world politics.[4] This perspective tends to marginalize the political contributions or significance of people within the state. While states are certainly powerful actors that have a significant amount of influence over the global political sphere, they are not the sole entities with political influence. Therefore, to attain a more complete view of international interactions, it is impossible to leave out intergovernmental organizations (IOs), NGOs, multinational corporations (MNCs), and, especially, individuals from the category of "actor." Given this broad recognition of the complexities of interactions within the international political world, this chapter defines the term "actor" as an individual or entity that has the power and autonomy to influence political, economic, and social outcomes for themselves and the world around them. With that definition in mind, this chapter will primarily be focusing on the capacity of refugees to engage in the society of their host states as self-sufficient, individual actors.

INTERNATIONAL REFUGEE LAW

To provide a complete picture of the human rights challenges refugees face concerning their different forms of integration into the society of a host state, this section will outline the basic premises and history of international refugee law. Although not all states have signed the United Nations conventions that define refugee rights, customary international refugee law encompasses a set of standards that applies to all states. Therefore, the norms related to refugee treatment that have evolved into universal international regulations truly affect all states within the international community. The ways in which states have interpreted these norms and developed subsequent policies to address refugee issues, however, are not universal.

From the beginning of history, political persecution has caused people to flee their homelands in search of greater security and the opportunity for a better future. Although refugees have always existed, an awareness and widespread practical acceptance of "the responsibility of the international community to provide protection and find solutions for them dates only from the time of the League of Nations and the election of Dr. Fridtjof Nansen as the first High Commissioner for Russian refugees in 1921."[5] The international refugee regime emerged in response to the multiple crises that arose throughout Europe during the beginning of the twentieth century. Post–World War I upheavals in Europe rendered many former citizens stateless with little recourse but to continually enter countries illegally, be expelled, and re-enter illegally once more.[6] Without documents that prove citizenship, individuals lack the right to legally exist in any country.

Arendt argues that statelessness is a fundamental deprivation of human rights that is "manifested first and above all in the deprivation of a place in the world which makes opinions significant and actions effective."[7] Without possessing citizenship of a state, individuals lack the basic capacity to claim rights. Given this reality, the early twentieth century crises throughout Europe spurred the establishment of an international refugee regime that sought to enable stateless people to claim basic rights and reside legally in a host state. While refugee status was originally only given to denationalized Russians, continuing crises and the development of "Nansen passports" to facilitate the identification and exchange of refugees quickly enabled other groups of Europeans to claim refugee status.[8] Still, while governments generally accepted the legal status of refugees to reside in their countries, until 1933, refugees had no other formal rights.

In 1933, a convention was produced in which efforts were made to secure basic rights for Russian and Armenian refugees. However, very few countries signed the convention, and only those two nationalities were provided with the chance to claim rights. After increasing movement of refugees as a result of fascism and a growing uncertainty and confusion regarding refugee status and rights, the UNHCR was established in 1950 and it quickly developed the 1951 Refugee Convention.[9] It outlines who qualifies as a refugee, establishes the principles of non-refoulement, meaning that states have no right to forcibly return refugees to a country in which they suffer the threat of persecution, and extends to them the rights to identification documents, administrative assistance, and a minimum standard of treatment accorded to aliens generally.[10] While still highly controversial, this legal document at least nominally grants refugees social and economic rights, including the right to wage-earning employment, in their host countries. The 1967 Protocol Relating to the Status of Refugees revised the 1951 Refugee Convention definition of refugees to include refugees seeking asylum due to events occurring after 1951 and removed any remaining geographical limitations to claiming refugee status.[11] These documents firmly and legally established status eligibility as well as basic refugee rights and protections.

The provisions afforded to refugees by the UNHCR legal framework are only intended to be temporary. The UNHCR is itself dependent on voluntary contributions and this often "forces it to adopt policies that reflect the interests and priorities of the major donor countries."[12] States often seek solutions to the refugee problem that are short-term and lack the sustainability to enable refugee self-sufficiency. The body of international law's lack of clearly laid out long-term solutions to refugees has prompted each country to devise its own, unique refugee policies. States develop these policies as an extension of their cultural views on refugee human rights. The different frameworks that have evolved from varying cultural perceptions of human rights will be outlined later in this chapter.

THE CURRENT REFUGEE CRISIS

In recent years, the refugee crisis has escalated to being the worst since World War II. In large part, due to the conflict in Syria, by the end of 2015 there were an estimated 21.3 million refugees worldwide.[13] Annual statistics continue to exceed all previous records for global forced displacement. Notably, over half of the world's refugees are under the age of 18.[14] The UNHCR estimates that 1 out of every 122 humans is either a refugee, internally displaced, or seeking asylum.[15] To put this in perspective, if this population were its own country, it would be the world's 24th biggest. Syria is the world's biggest producer of both internally displaced people (7.6 million) and refugees (3.88 million at the end of 2014). Afghanistan (2.59 million) and Somalia (1.1 million) are the next biggest refugee source countries.[16] In 2014, Turkey became the world's top refugee-hosting nation with 1.59 million Syrian refugees.[17] Developing countries host approximately 86 percent of the world's refugee population.[18] With numbers this high, refugees are spilling into Europe in the hundreds of thousands, and long-term plans are necessary to maintain order and stability in the wake of massive population increases. The scale of this growing phenomenon is worth noting to understand the volume of people whose human rights are being directly impacted by the frameworks policymakers are employing to respond to the crisis.

WHY ARE REFUGEES A HUMAN RIGHTS ISSUE?

Given the overwhelming scale of this global displacement, why is it important to view "refugeeism" as a human rights issue? Primarily, the 1948 Universal Declaration of Human Rights outlines several basic human rights principles afforded to everyone that are also extremely relevant to refugees. Although the following articles are not comprehensive of the Universal Declaration's protections of refugee rights, as additional articles could certainly apply to refugees, these articles outline significant, fundamental rights considerations related to "refugeeism."

Article 3 states that "everyone has the right to life, liberty, and security of person."[19] The very reason refugees flee their homelands is due to a threat to their life, liberty, and security. They often seek asylum to prevent persecution and death in their countries of origin. Article 6 states that "everyone has the right to recognition everywhere as a person before the law."[20] Refugees, often lacking identification documentation, struggle to gain recognition before the law. This article should help to protect the rights of refugees; however, their displacement and often "statelessness" frequently puts them in a limbo in which laws do not consistently recognize their rights.

More directly, Article 13 specifies that "everyone has the right to leave any country, including his own, and to return to his country."[21] Refugees have the legal right to leave their dangerous origin countries and to return to them once they are safe again. Article 14 states that "everyone has the right to seek and to enjoy in other countries asylum from persecution."[22] Persecution can encompass many forms, and, as previously stated, the 1951 Refugee Convention defines a refugee as someone who "owing to a well-founded fear of being persecuted for reasons of race, religion, nationality, membership of a particular social group or political opinion, is outside the country of his nationality, and is unable to, or owing to such fear, is unwilling to avail himself of the protection of that country."[23] Article 23 specifies that "everyone has the right to work, to free choice of employment, to just and favourable conditions of work and to protection against unemployment."[24] This assertion is significant for refugees as, due to legal or social restrictions, many are prevented from working in their host state. Finally, Article 27 states that "everyone has the right freely to participate in the cultural life of the community, to enjoy the arts and to share in scientific advancement and its benefits."[25] Refugees are often forced to reside in closed-off camps for months or even years at a time, during which they have little or no opportunity to participate in the cultural life of their surrounding community. The Universal Declaration of Human Rights is an appropriate starting point for understanding why refugee issues are human rights issues. After all, refugees flee their home countries to reclaim the rights outlined in the declaration that they have been denied.

VARYING HUMAN RIGHTS
FRAMEWORKS FOR REFUGEES

Although no concrete frameworks for dealing with refugees have been laid out, aside from the aforementioned rights outlined in the Universal Declaration of Human Rights, the literature and implemented policies suggest that states, NGOs, and other relevant parties are using particular frameworks to address refugee issues. These can be viewed both as policy frameworks and as human rights frameworks as they are influenced by how actors perceive refugee human rights and also have a direct bearing on the fulfillment of refugee human rights. I have identified these frameworks as the victimization/aid paradigm, the security framework, and the capabilities approach.

Although there exists no explicit "theory of refugees" and "little systematic research has been done to promote the understanding of refugeeism as a global problem," when conceptualizing refugees' human rights, scholars, NGOs, and states are commonly working from a particular theoretical framework.[26] I understand this framework as a victimization/aid paradigm. This model stems from a cultural norm of humanitarianism and goodwill toward other humans. This particular model for relating with refugees emphasizes the short-term provision of food aid and other subsistence resources. It does so through the lens of victimization of passive refugees who depend on these programs for survival. This theory stresses external assistance from above with little to no attention afforded to refugee interests or human empowerment.[27] The victimization model prescribes external, temporary solutions that are unsustainable and prone to the ultimate re-victimization of the refugees they aim to help. This framework views human rights through a sort of savior/victim ideology. With this mentality, the "saviors" (host states, NGOs, aid workers, etc.) place their vision of refugees' needs and rights onto refugees. This act discounts refugees' unique needs and fulfillment as actors in their own lives, and ultimately prioritizes certain human rights over others. For example, this framework would emphasize refugee rights to asylum, freedom from persecution, life, food, and shelter, but would minimize or completely disregard the necessity of rights such as employment, development of personality, and participation in the cultural life of the community. This model, well-intentioned or not, produces increased victimization of refugees, fails to view them as capable actors, hinders their integration or repatriation, and prevents them from making valuable social and economic contributions to their host states.

The security approach to human rights views refugees as direct threats to the safety of the host state. This model stems from a cultural view of human rights as less important than power and national security. Though it perceives refugees as strong actors, it does so with an emphasis on fear and national security rather than human empowerment. This approach often results in denial of refugee status and varying methods of preventing refugee integration. The security framework ultimately views refugees as dangerous liabilities with the power to damage national security and stability. In doing so, it promotes a view of human rights that prioritizes the security rights of host states' citizens over the security rights of refugees. This conceptualization ultimately suggests that the human rights of people living in host states are inherently of more value than the human rights of refugees.

Alternatively, policymakers sometimes employ the human capabilities model to understand the rights of refugees as well as their ability to make strong contributions to their host states. This model stems from a cultural view that prioritizes human rights as an essential element of fulfilling the human experience. The capabilities approach focuses primarily on the type of life that humans are able to achieve, and emphasizes choice in relation to what people are actually able to be and to do.[28] The capabilities model views humans as active rather than passive victims and focuses on the human's ability to achieve Amartya Sen's notion of functionings, such as being adequately nourished, achieving self-respect, and taking part in the life of the community.[29] Through this human rights framework, refugees transform from victims into significant actors that have their own interests and motivations, and possess the capacity to enact political, social, and economic change. Unlike the victimization model, the human capabilities model is an approach that views refugees as dignified humans with the right to shape their own destiny. The model inherently focuses on long-term, sustainable programs rather than temporary solutions to refugee crises.

LEGAL INTEGRATION

When refugees flee their home states in search of refuge in host states, they are met with differing forms of legal regulations and restrictions. Some countries have strict rules that compel refugees to become permanent residents quickly after arriving in the host state, while others impose restrictions that prevent them from becoming permanent residents for a long period of time or perhaps not at all. Moreover, some states actively engage in the forced deportation of refugees either immediately upon their arrival or after many years of living in the host state. These legal frameworks stem from variations in the outlined human rights frameworks, and these frameworks directly impact refugee capacity to integrate into their host state. The remainder of this section will outline the different legal integration policies employed by policymakers working within the three distinct frameworks.

Victimization/Aid Paradigm

The victimization paradigm inhibits refugees' legal integration. Some countries mandate that refugees must fulfill certain requirements before being granted permanent resident status. Norway, for example, requires that refugees complete an introductory course integration program within three years of being granted refugee status in Norway in order to become permanent residents.[30] This introductory program is required for refugees between the ages of 18 and 55 and consists of 550 hours of language training and 50 hours of social and cultural studies.[31] Notably, the introductory program is a full time requirement that inhibits refugees from seeking full time employment until its completion. Although such a program is certainly helpful in facilitating refugee adaptation to their host state, in the medium term, it prevents refugees from getting back on their feet.

Additionally, some countries mandate that refugees participate in social welfare programs. For example, Norway currently mandates that refugees, in equality with its citizens, register for social security benefits.[32] The Norwegian government is currently considering a proposal to restrict social security benefits for refugees to encourage integration, but this policy will likely not come into effect for sometime.[33] Social benefits in and of themselves can be extremely helpful for refugees as they try to set up their lives in a new country. However, when participation in welfare systems is a requirement, this removes the onus from refugees and, instead, makes them dependent on the host state government for survival. As previously referenced, these types of requirements suggest a validation of certain refugee human rights, such as rights to life, liberty, and shelter, while invalidating others, such as participation in the cultural life of the community and employment. They do so by enforcing an environment in which refugees become isolated and rely on the government rather than their own initiative and skills for needs fulfillment.

Security Framework

An emphasis on restricting refugee human rights to diminish security threats often leads to the legal prevention of refugee attainment of permanent resident status, failure to acknowledge refugee status, and forced repatriation. Due to a failure to acknowledge refugee status, Gulf countries display a strong reluctance to extend permanent residence rights to any non-nationals. In Saudi Arabia, for example, refugees are allowed into the country on work permits which are temporary and can be canceled at any time.[34] In most Gulf states, there is no opportunity for refugees to remain permanently without work, and once their work contracts have expired, these "migrant workers" must return to their home countries.[35] The Gulf states' unwillingness to acknowledge the legal status of refugees as well as their strong restrictions of refugees' ability to reside permanently within their borders conveys an implicit fear of refugees and a lack of acknowledgement of their human rights.

Forced repatriation is another outcome of a security view of refugee human rights. Norway has recently been in talks with the Eritrean government regarding a proposal to repatriate approximately 500 refugees currently residing in Norway.[36] In 2010, the UNHCR expressed concern regarding Sweden's forced deportation and repatriation of Iraqi asylum seekers.[37] Hmong refugees in Thailand have recently been forced to repatriate back to Laos.[38] Additionally, China has recently faced international scrutiny due to its forced repatriation of North Korean refugees over the past two decades.[39] China has justified these deportations by failing to acknowledge refugee status and instead defining these populations as economic migrants.[40] The policies and practices of forced repatriation of these countries and many others directly violate the principle of non-refoulement in the 1951 Convention. These practices prevent refugees from finding safety and, ultimately, from reclaiming their human rights.

Human Capabilities Approach

Finally, countries employing the capabilities approach provide refugees access to legal integration through permanent resident status. For example, the United States legally requires refugees to apply for Lawful Permanent Resident (LPR) status within one year of physical presence in the country. This status enables refugees to "own property, attend public schools, join certain branches of the US Armed Forces, travel internationally without a visa, and, if certain requirements are met, apply for US citizenship."[41] Accruement of LPR status enables refugees in the United States to move freely within their host state and to seek most forms of economic advancement available to US citizens. This policy is somewhat controversial as it forces refugees to obtain permanent residence status rather than giving them the choice. Although making permanent residency a requirement could be problematic for some refugees who do not possess a certain level of English competency and other employment skills, it certainly suggests a human rights framework that views refugees as capable of self-sufficiency. Furthermore, the cessation of financial and healthcare assistance for refugees, except in extraordinary circumstances, after eight months, provides an impetus for refugees to learn English and gain employment quickly.

Though not a requirement, Canada also allows refugees to apply for permanent resident status.[42] Sweden has recently begun offering permanent resident permits to Syrian refugees almost immediately upon being granted refugee status. Similar to Canada, this legal provision is different from that of the United States in that the permanent resident permits are offered and not required. In describing Sweden's regulation, Pya Prytz Phiri, head of the UNHCR's regional representation for Northern Europe, has emphasized that "from a humanitarian aspect it is the right thing to do, but also we believe it is a very good thing for Sweden to do in its own interest, because with the refugees integrating quickly then they are also quickly able to contribute."[43] Whether required or offered, providing access to permanent resident status demonstrates a clear human rights view of refugees as capable actors who possess the personal fortitude to take the first steps to integrate into their host state societies to begin building new lives for themselves.

SOCIAL INTEGRATION

The elements that impact the social integration of refugees in their host states, such as NGO policies and the social environment toward refugees play a crucial role in the capacity of refugees to realize the full extent of their human rights. The ways in which organizations and individuals within host states conceptualize refugee rights, whether through victimization, security, or human capabilities paradigms, impact refugees' capacity to play a vital role in the social life of that state.

Victimization/Aid Paradigm

The victimization human rights framework promotes the provision of emergency-level services which can produce aid dependency. For example, in the last decade, Burmese refugees in Thailand have become almost completely dependent on aid from NGOs.[44] The NGOs commonly view refugees as having immediate emergency needs and focus on those needs rather than their needs of sustainability and self-sufficiency. This, again, stems from a human rights focus that emphasizes basic survival rather than dignity. A study which conducted interviews of refugee-related NGOs in Lebanon discovered that "respondents were convinced UN relief aid was too short-term and relief-focused, which disempowers the refugee communities by generating dependency on relief distributions."[45]

One major issue that is common among refugee host countries is the way refugee camps are envisioned and run. In providing aid to long-term refugees typically residing in camps, the policy of the UNHCR and other NGOs has been one of "care and maintenance."[46] A recent Migration Policy Institute policy brief argues that refugee camp assistance produces dependence, and that this "long-term dependency for forced migrants, coupled with a lack of membership in a state, denies millions of persons a present and a future."[47] This reality, resulting from a human rights framework that prioritizes aid over self-sufficiency, can be viewed in refugee camps across the world. In the Dadaab Camp in Kenya, refugees are "frozen in time," as they are not allowed to leave the camp, and though the camp was built in 1991, no permanent structures for water or food provision have ever been built.[48] In Tanzania's Nyarugusu Camp, refugees are prohibited from traveling more than 4 kilometers from the camp boundaries.[49] When they do venture further to buy groceries to supplement their food aid or to work illegally, if stopped by police, they are forced to pay large bribes or be arrested.[50]

In countries where short-term assistance and refugee camps are the primary methods of addressing refugee needs, refugees become re-victimized and left with little hope for a sustainable future. It is the short-term nature of the victimization/aid human rights framework that produces this day-to-day type of living and constant uncertainty.

Security Framework

The security human rights framework tends to facilitate xenophobic environments that greatly inhibit refugees from socially integrating. For example, the recent arrival of Syrian refugees in Turkey has sparked security fears and violent xenophobic attacks. In 2013, a car bomb aimed at Syrian refugees coupled with numerous violent acts against individual refugees caused many of them to flee violent discrimination in Turkey to return to their unsafe homes in Syria.[51] Even Germany, a country that has welcomed hundreds of thousands of refugees since the beginning of the crisis, has seen a drastic uptick in xenophobic attacks against refugees. In 2015, at least 222 serious incidents of arson, violent attacks, and hate crimes were committed against refugees seeking shelter in Germany.[52] In the United States, incidents against Muslims have also risen in 2015–2016, additionally fueled by the presidential campaign.[53] As the vast majority of Syrian refugees are Muslim, these xenophobic sentiments and attacks have also been directed toward refugees.

The security framework, in which the rights and safety of citizens are prioritized above all other humans, has produced an atmosphere in many countries that inhibits refugees from socially integrating. The discrimination they face isolates them from their surrounding communities and prevents them from enjoying their human right to be a part of community life. Instead, these refugee groups are often forced to build a sense of community within their own groups, and become unable to access the connections and benefits of the wider outside society.

HUMAN CAPABILITIES APPROACH

In contrast, the capabilities view of refugee human rights emphasizes a collaborative effort to assist refugees in integrating and reaffirming their human rights. At a time when Sierra Leone hosted close to 100,000 refugees, an NGO called The Foundation for International Dignity "conducted mediation workshops between refugees and host communities in camps in Sierra Leone."[54] Such programs have helped to mitigate the tension between refugees and their host communities and, as such, have assisted in greater ease of refugee integration into Sierra Leonean society. Similarly, in Jordan, an NGO known as JEN has worked to provide hygiene and sanitation education, mental health services, and skills building for refugees.[55]

In Germany, individual volunteers have gathered in groups around refugee camps and housing "to offer language classes and assistance in dealing with authorities or medical services."[56] Volunteers offering language classes and informal lessons to refugees has also become increasingly common in the United States, the United Kingdom, Sweden, and other countries.[57] These organizations and individuals are working within a human rights framework that seeks to empower refugees to achieve their full potential and fulfill their human capabilities through social integration in their host states. Language is an essential skill that enables refugees to become a part of and contribute to their new societies.

ECONOMIC INTEGRATION

In addition to host states' legal regulations and social integration norms, their facilitation or inhibition of economic self-sufficiency demonstrates a clear view of refugee human rights through victimization, security, or human capabilities frameworks. Significantly, the employment laws, welfare regulations and provisions, and business policies related to refugees determine their capacity to economically contribute to their host societies. When these policies are prohibitive of refugee employment and economic integration, refugees can instead serve as an economic drain on their host countries. The refugee employment policies of host states also affect refugees' capacity to develop skills, and, therefore, impact their future ability to reintegrate into the economic life of their home state upon potential future repatriation.

Victimization/Aid Paradigm

The victimization approach often requires refugees to fulfill certain requirements before working, and often produces aid dependency. In Norway, refugees receive full welfare benefits as long as they participate full time in the introductory program.[58] As previously mentioned, participation in this program precludes full-time work. Although the opportunity to learn the language and culture of Norway before seeking employment, along with the accompanying welfare benefits, is certainly a helpful means of easing refugees into Norwegian society, it simultaneously prevents refugees from building their own livelihoods. In fact, refugees in Norway become economically stationary as they live out the 2–3 year introductory period, waiting for the opportunity to become self-sufficient and productive members of society. Similarly, as refugees in the United Kingdom typically do not have the right to work, they are reliant on government assistance. Healthcare is free, housing is provided, and cash support of £5.28 a day is given.[59] Welfare provisions, though beneficial in that they enable refugee survival, can easily produce aid reliance and prevent refugees from carving out meaningful livelihoods for themselves in their host societies. When these provisions are required or so substantial that refugees see little purpose in finding their own means of income, they promote a human rights framework that treats refugees as victims to be coddled and inhibited from forging their own paths in their new societies.

Security Framework

As a cultural extension of viewing refugee human rights in terms of internal security, some countries greatly restrict refugee access to employment. In addition to physical security concerns, Gulf states are also focused on employment security for their own citizens and have cited worries that Syrians might eventually compete for jobs as a reason for not admitting Syrian refugees.[60] Besides greatly restricting refugee access into these countries, implementation of this framework has produced immense work restrictions for those refugees who do manage to gain entry. For example, Saudi Arabia requires refugees to obtain residence permits and employer sponsorship in order to live outside refugee camps and gain employment. Given the aforementioned xenophobic environment in Gulf states, employers are unlikely to provide this necessary sponsorship. Similarly, in Turkey, while skilled refugees are able to work within camps, work permits are not granted to refugees for employment within the outside Turkish community.[61] Such employment restrictions for refugees display a human rights framework that prioritizes both the physical and monetary security of host states' citizens over that of refugees. This framework ultimately prevents refugees from economically integrating into the host state.

Human Capabilities Approach

Finally, a capabilities view of refugee human rights results in refugees' almost immediate access to employment rights. As an example of the capabilities framework, in the United States, refugees have the right to work immediately upon arrival, and must merely show their refugee admission stamp to employers as proof of employment eligibility.[62] This policy enables refugees to begin searching for employment immediately after arriving in the host country. As such, it demonstrates a view of refugees as capable actors who have the capacity to make valuable economic contributions. More importantly, it enables them to actually make such contributions and, in theory, to quickly achieve self-sufficiency. Remarkably, the USCIS asserts that "by all accounts refugees are mostly 'self-sufficient' within 8 months."[63] Similarly, in Germany, refugees can begin working after residing in the country for three months, but must obtain approval from the municipal immigration office before accepting the job.[64] It is worth acknowledging that these employment policies that encourage refugees to rapidly achieve employment are not on their own perfect and can lead to issues such as difficulty gaining fulfilling employment, due to language deficiencies, and abuse through sub-standard payment. Though such issues require the implementation of additional policies to correct them, the human capabilities framework facilitates an employment platform for refugees that is an excellent starting point for reclaiming dignity and achieving self-sufficiency and ownership over their future.

WHY REFUGEE HUMAN RIGHTS SHOULD BE CONSIDERED UNIVERSAL

Given this evaluation of the effects of differing human rights frameworks on the capacity of refugees to integrate and enjoy all of their human rights in their host societies, I argue that refugee human rights should be considered universal. External displacement is a global issue with spillover effects in nearly every country. As this issue continues to grow, a global, unified response is needed to appropriately address refugee issues and needs. As has been highlighted throughout this chapter, human rights conceptions that deviate from the Universal Declaration of Human Rights have produced negative consequences. When countries fail to provide security and other rights, such as employment and cultural participation, refugee populations become alienated from their host communities. This is especially true when freedom of movement is restricted and refugees are forced to live long-term in isolated camps. Separating refugees from their host community populations and preventing them from integrating can also create an atmosphere of fear. This fear often plays out in xenophobic or violent actions against refugees. Additionally, feeling unsafe in their new host states, refugees often try to leave the dangerous environment by reinitiating the asylum seeking process in a different country. In their struggle to find safety, many also find themselves internally displaced within the host country. These outcomes are negative and damaging for refugees as well as host states and origin states.

From this overview, it should be clearer that giving refugees the legal, social, and economic means to integrate into the society of their host states enables them to act with agency and dignity and to develop skills that will aid them in maintaining self-sufficiency in their host states and upon possible repatriation. However, conceptualizing refugees as more than just helpless victims in need of handouts also yields extensive benefits to host states and home states. Some of the benefits host states glean when viewing refugee human rights through the capabilities framework include increases in workforce productivity, a much-needed provision of labor for countries with ageing populations, and an increase in economic growth.[65]

CONCLUSION

Different countries view refugee human rights through different lenses. The same country may also simultaneously hold multiple human rights views of refugees. Although culture plays a large role in constructing the understandings of human rights, the global nature of the refugee phenomenon necessitates as global a framework as possible. Though this framework may look and function with variations from country to country, based on that country's culture, the goal of every state should be to promote refugee human rights so that refugees can fulfill their human capabilities. Ultimately, understanding refugee human rights through the human capabilities framework facilitates a view of refugees as self-sufficient actors rather than passive victims. This conceptualization makes possible the development of policies that enable refugees to transcend the savior/victim and security threat paradigms to make significant contributions in their host states. An engaged understanding of refugees as dignified actors can mitigate tensions between refugees and their host communities, and enable refugees to become economically independent and constructive members of their host societies.

NOTES

1. "Figures at a Glance," UNHCR, accessed July 28, 2016, http://www.unhcr.org/en-us/figures-at-a-glance.html.

2. "Refugees," UNHCR, accessed February 1, 2016, http://www.unhcr.org/pages/49c3646c125.html.

3. Gil Loescher, *Beyond Charity: International Cooperation and the Global Refugee Crisis* (New York: Oxford University Press, 1993), 6.

4. Jack Donnelly, *Realism and International Relations* (New York: Cambridge University Press, 2000), 7.

5. Erika Feller, "The Evolution of the International Refugee Protection Regime," *Journal of Law & Policy* 5, no. 129 (2001): 130, accessed October 20, 2015, http://openscholarship.wustl.edu/law_journal_law_policy/vol5/iss1/11.

6. Loescher, *Beyond Charity*, 36.

7. Hannah Arendt, *The Origins of Totalitarianism* (London: Allen & Unwin, 1961), 296.

8. Loescher, *Beyond Charity*, 37.

9. "Resources for Speakers on Global Issues," United Nations, accessed February 1, 2016, http://www.un.org/en/globalissues/briefingpapers/refugees/aboutUNHCR.html.

10. Guy Goodwin-Gil, "Convention Relating to the Status of Refuges," United Nations Audiovisual Library of International Law, accessed February 1, 2016, http://legal.un.org/avl/ha/prsr/prsr.html.

11. UN General Assembly, "Protocol Relating to the Status of Refugees," *United Nations, Treaty Series*, no. 606: 268–276, accessed October 21, 2015, https://treaties.un.org/pages/ViewDetails.aspx?src=TREATY&mtdsg_no=V-5&chapter=5&lang=en.

12. Loescher, *Beyond Charity*, 137.

13. "Figures at a Glance."

14. Ibid.

15. "Refugees."

16. Ibid.

17. Ibid.

18. Ibid.

19. "The Universal Declaration of Human Rights," United Nations, accessed June 15, 2016, http://www.un.org/en/universal-declaration-human-rights/.

20. Ibid.

21. Ibid.

22. Ibid.

23. "Refugees."

24. "The Universal Declaration of Human Rights."

25. Ibid.

26. Harto Hakovirta, "The Global Refugee Problem: A Model and Its Application," *International Political Science Review* 14, no. 1 (1993): 36, accessed October 20, 2015, http://www.jstor.org/stable/1601374.

27. Glenn Ashton, "Helping Africa to Help Itself: The Ideology of Food," The South African Civil Society Information Service, accessed October 20, 2015, http://sacsis.org.za/site/article/1744.

28. Thomas Wells, "Sen's Capability Approach," Internet Encyclopedia of Philosophy, accessed February 2, 2016, http://www.iep.utm.edu/sen-cap/#SH3a.

29. Amartya Sen, "Development as Capability Expansion," *Journal of Development Planning* 19 (1989): 44, accessed October 20, 2015. http://morgana.unimo re.it/Picchio_Antonella/Sviluppo%20umano/svilupp%20umano/Sen%20develop ment.pdf.

30. "Norway," European Resettlement Network, accessed October 21, 2015, http://www.resettlement.eu/country/norway.

31. Ibid.

32. "Norway to Limit Social Security Benefits for Refugees," The Nordic Page, accessed August 3, 2016, http://www.tnp.no/norway/politics/5330-norway-to-limit-social-security-benefits-for-refugees.

33. Ibid.

34. Deborah Amos, "Gulf Countries Face Criticism for Refusing to Resettle Syrian Refugees," *NPR*, October 6, 2015, accessed October 21, 2015, http://www.npr.org/2015/09/22/442582465/gulf-countries-face-criticism-for-refusing-to-resettle-syrian-refugees.

35. Michael Stephenes, "Migrant Crisis: Why the Gulf States are not Letting Syrians in," *BBC*, September 7, 2015, accessed October 21, 2015, http://www.bbc.com/news/world-middle-east-34173139.

36. Mark Anderson, "Norway Minister Threatens to Deport Eritrean Migrants," *The Guardian*, June 27, 2014, accessed October 21, 2015, http://www.theguardian.com/global-development/2014/jun/27/norway-deport-eritrean-migrants-asylum-seekers-immigration.

37. "UNHCR Dismayed at Forced Repatriation of Iraqis; Reports Increase in Flight of Iraqi Christians," *UNHCR*, December 17, 2010, accessed October 22, 2015, http://www.unhcr.org/4d0b45476.html.

38. "Thailand: Forced Repatriation of Hmong Refugees to Laos Denounced," *Doctors Without Borders*, May 20, 2009, accessed October 22, 2015, http://www.doctorswithoutborders.org/news-stories/press-release/thailand-forced-repatriation-hmong-refugees-laos-denounced.

39. Roberta Cohen, "China's Forced Repatriation of North Korean Refugees Incurs United Nations Censure," *Brookings*, July 7, 2014, accessed July 20, 2016, https://www.brookings.edu/opinions/chinas-forced-repatriation-of-north-korean-refugees-incurs-united-nations-censure/.

40. Ibid.

41. Jie Zong and Jeanne Batalova, "Refugees and Asylees in the United States," Migration Information Source, accessed February 5, 2015, http://www.migrationinformation.org/feature/display.cfm?ID=907.

42. "Understand Permanent Resident Status," Government of Canada, accessed July 15, 2016, http://www.cic.gc.ca/english/newcomers/about-pr.asp.

43. Yermi Brenner, "Sweden's Refugee Policy Sets High Standard," *Al Jazeera*, November 24, 2013, accessed October 21, 2015, http://www.aljazeera.com/indepth/features/2013/11/sweden-refugee-policy-sets-high-standard-2013112485613526863.html.

44. Marie T. Benner, Aree Muangsookjarouen, Egbert Sondorp, and Joy Townsend, "Neglect of Refugee Participation," *Forced Migration Review* 30 (2008): 25, accessed October 22, 2015, http://www.fmreview.org/FMRpdfs/FMR30/25.pdf.

45. Leila Zakharia and Sonya Knox, "The International Aid Community and Local Actors: Experiences and Testimonies from the Ground," Civil Society Knowledge Center, accessed October 22, 2015, http://cskc.daleel-madani.org/paper/international-aid-community-and-local-actors.

46. Alexander T. Aleinikoff, "From Dependence to Self-Reliance: Changing the Paradigm in Protracted Refugee Situations," Transatlantic Council on Migration, accessed July 15, 2016, http://www.migrationpolicy.org/research/dependence-self-reliance-changing-paradigm-protracted-refugee-situations.

47. Ibid.

48. Aamna Mohdin, "When Refugees Camps Last Three Generations, We Must Accept they're not Going Anywhere," *Quartz*, November 30, 2015, accessed July 15, 2016, http://qz.com/560768/when-refugees-camps-last-three-generations-we-must-accept-theyre-not-going-anywhere/.

49. Elizabeth Cullen Dunn, "The Failure of Refugee Camps," *Boston Review*, September 28, 2015, accessed July 16, 2016, https://bostonreview.net/editors-picks-world/elizabeth-dunn-failure-refugee-camps.

50. "United Republic of Tanzania," UNHCR, accessed July 16, 2016, http://www.unhcr.org/50a9f81f16.pdf; Dunn, "The Failure of Refugee Camps."

51. Jonathan Krohn, "Amid Ethnic Tension in Turkey, Some Syrian Refugees Return to a War Zone," *The Atlantic*, May 17, 2013, accessed October 30, 2013, http://www.theatlantic.com/international/archive/2013/05/amid-ethnic-tension-in-turkey-some-syrian-refugees-return-to-a-war-zone/275966/.

52. Al Jazeera, "Germany Sees Rise in Crimes Against Refugees," *Al Jazeera*, December 7, 2015, accessed July 16, 2016, http://america.aljazeera.com/articles/2015/12/7/germany-sees-rise-in-crimes-against-refugees.html.

53. Murtaza Hussain, "Hate Crimes Rise Along with Donald Trump's Anti-Muslim Rhetoric," *The Intercept*, May 5, 2016, accessed July 16, 2016, https://theintercept.com/2016/05/05/hate-crimes-rise-along-with-donald-trumps-anti-muslim-rhetoric/.

54. Jeremy Konyndyk, "Towards a New Model for Post-Emergency Refugee Assistance," *Humanitarian Exchange Magazine* 31 (2005), accessed November 1, 2013, http://www.odihpn.org/humanitarian-exchange-magazine/issue-31/towards-a-new-model-for-post-emergency-refugee-assistance.

55. "JEN Recognizes the Needs in the Fields and Builds and Maintains Self-Reliance," JEN, accessed October 22, 2015, http://www.jen-npo.org/en/project/project_jordan.php.

56. Leonid Bershidsky, "Why Germany Welcomes Refugees," *Bloomberg View*, September 9, 2015, accessed October 22, 2015, http://www.bloombergview.com/articles/2015-09-09/why-germany-welcomes-refugees.

57. Kristina Robertson and Lydia Breiseth, "How to Support Refugee Students in the ELL Classroom," Colorin Colorado, accessed July 17, 2016, http://www.colorincolorado.org/article/how-support-refugee-students-ell-classroom. "Volunteering Project," North of England Refugee Service, accessed July 17, 2016, http://www.refugee.org.uk/volunteering. Rachel Obordo, "Teaching Refugees Languages: 'No Specific Skills Required, Just a Desire to Help and a Friendly Smile,'" *The Guardian*, September 11, 2015, accessed July 17, 2016, https://www.theguardian.com/world/2015/sep/11/teaching-refugees-languages-no-specific-skills-required-just-a-desire-to-help-and-a-friendly-smile.

58. Anniken Hagelund and Hanne Kavli, "If Work is Out of Sight. Activation and Citizenship for New Refugees," accessed October 26, 2015, http://fafo.no/~fafo/media/com_netsukii/Hagelund_Kavli.pdf.

59. "Asylum in the UK," UNHCR, accessed July 17, 2016, http://www.unhcr.org/en-us/asylum-in-the-uk.html.

60. Barbara Boland, "Why the Islamic Gulf States Aren't Taking Syrian Refugees," *Washington Examiner,* September 4, 2015, accessed July 17, 2016, http://www.washingtonexaminer.com/why-the-islamic-gulf-states-arent-taking-syrian-refugees/article/2571469.

61. Dasha Afanasieva, "Turkey Will Not Give Syrian Refugees Right to Work – Labour Minister," *Reuters,* August 7, 2015, accessed October 26, 2015, http://uk.reuters.com/article/uk-turkey-syria-refugees-workers-idUKKCN0QC1UH20150807.

62. "Refugees," USCIS, accessed July 17, 2016, http://www.uscis.gov/humanitarian/refugees-asylum/refugees.

63. Don Barnett, "The Progress of Refugees: How Are We Doing?" Center for Immigration Studies, accessed November 6, 2013, http://www.cis.org/Barnett/Ref ugees-Self-Sufficient.

64. Greta Hamann, *DW*, January 10, 2015, accessed October 24, 2015, http://www. dw.com/en/when-refugees-want-to-work-in-germany/a-18737104.

65. Andrew Soergel, "Refugees: Economic Boon or Burden?" *U.S. News*, September 15, 2015, accessed October 21, 2015, http://www.usnews.com/news/blogs/da ta-mine/2015/09/15/would-syrian-refugees-be-an-economic-boon-or-burden; Doug Saunders, "Germany: Where the Refugee Flood is a Solution, not a Problem," *The Globe and Mail*, May 23, 2015, accessed October 21, 2015, http://www.theglobea ndmail.com/globe-debate/germany-where-the-refugee-flood-is-a-solution-not-a-prob lem/article24565583/; Jon Stone, "Germany's Economy will Grow Faster because of the Million Refugees it is Helping, Study Finds," *The Independent*, October 5, 2015, accessed October 21, 2015, http://www.independent.co.uk/news/uk/politics/ germanys-economy-will-grow-faster-because-of-the-million-refugees-it-is-helping-study-finds-10505647.html.

Part IV

RIGHTS AND CULTURAL DIFFERENCE

Chapter 9

Defending Liberty from Tyranny in Dostoevsky's Siberia

The Impact of Captivity on an Intercultural Consensus Regarding Human Rights

Elizabeth Blake

In looking to Russia, both past and present, the concepts of *universal* human rights and an inalienable right to liberty seem peripheral to public discourse, and may be associated more with dissidents and the marginalized than with those in the center of the political spectrum.[1] A recent study of these movements by a political scientist at the University of Rennes, Cécile Vaissié, attests to their lasting significance by recalling a slogan, "For your Freedom and Ours," brought by dissidents to Red Square on August 25, 1968, in protest against the Soviet invasion of Czechoslovakia. With a nod to the slogan's roots in nineteenth-century Polish liberation movements, Vaissié clarifies that the twentieth-century "Russian democrats" here recognize that "the struggle for freedom of one nation extends the freedom of all other nations."[2] While Vaissié characterizes the movement for freedom for both one's own and another's nation as "one of the most noble humane acts of the twentieth century," she does not reflect upon the human atrocities in this same century in labor, prison, and concentration camps in Poland and Russia that attest to traditions of nationalisms and exceptionalisms rooted in nineteenth-century histories that, when infused with twentieth-century Realpolitik (bolstered by technological advances), at the very least threatened the universality of human rights, and at their worst sanctioned genocides.[3] The recent discovery of lost pages from the diary of Heinrich Himmler (head of the SS in Nazi Germany) in a Russian military archive and its publication in a German newspaper underscore both the international cooperation frequently required to violate human rights on a mass scale as well as the multinational effort to expose the abuse of such rights. At the same time, the tenacity of certain slogans demanding human rights (not only "Za naszą i waszą wolność [For your freedom and ours]" but also "Liberté, Egalité, Fraternité!") appeal to multiple generations across a multicultural socio-economic spectrum thereby suggesting that some common thirst for liberty that transcends ages and continents may be found among dissenters on the margin, and among those whose voices they represent.

The international community recognized its shared failure to provide even minimal human rights protections in the wake of World War II when the European Convention on Human Rights was formed and the United Nations General Assembly voted in 1948 to safeguard the fundamental dignity and equal rights of each person with the Universal Declaration of Human Rights (UDHR). Nevertheless, freedom of movement, a spirit of brotherhood, and freedom from arbitrary detention were not effectively protected by the United Nations; however, the Final Act (1975) of the Conference on Security and Cooperation in Europe in Helsinki did advance human rights even behind the Iron Curtain by outlining specific cooperative educational exchanges and economic initiatives on which the signatories resolved to collaborate to promote peace and security.[4] This experience suggests that the attempt to define the rights of the person may be less effective at supporting basic rights of individuals than a commitment to engage in intercultural endeavors that promote a shared protection of the well-being of citizens residing in a nation other than one's own. This concept of inalienable natural rights that transcend national borders emboldened those within the nineteenth-century Russian Empire who preferred France's revolutionary *Declaration of the Rights of Man and of the Citizen* (*Déclaration des droits de l'homme et du citoyen*, 1789) and *Code Napoléon* (1804) to the arbitrary will of the sovereign that governed the tsar's realm. At the same time, more conservative Russian intellectuals, especially those with Slavophile tendencies, expressed skepticism about the language of rights transcending national borders, as is evident in the ironic appeals to an individual's welfare [*blago cheloveka*] or the common good [*blago*]—invoked by Lev Tolstoy in *War and Peace* (*Voina i mir*)—which were the sentiments that motivated the parvenu Napoleon Bonaparte's bloody invasion of Russia.

Ardent nationalism espoused by many Russian nineteenth-century intellectuals of various political views impeded the recognition of universal rights. For example, according to Vissarion Belinsky (and later Fyodor Dostoevsky), the Russian nationality would create "a pan-human world culture" instead of the cosmopolitanism lacking in national character.[5] With European culture decisively distinct from Asia and with Pan-Slavism on the rise, the Russian press encouraged intercultural dialogue but displayed less enthusiasm for universalist concepts. Such Russocentrism marginalized underrepresented ethnic groups in the Empire, for example, Poles,

Lithuanians, Belarusians, Ukrainians, Karbadians, and Circassians, whose subversive activities could earn them a sentence to Siberian penal servitude or exile. In the 1840s and 1850s, several uprisings and conspiracies in historically Polish lands resulted in the imprisonment and exile of Polish, Lithuanian, Belarusian, and Ukrainian intellectuals into the Russian wilderness of Siberia or the forts on the Orenburg line, where they shared prison fortresses and military duties with members of the Russian army and with Russian political prisoners, such as the Petrashevsky conspirators, including Dostoevsky and Aleksei Pleshcheev. Many of the writers of Polish, Ukrainian, and Russian from this generation, who shared exile in Western Siberia or the forts on the Orenburg line, collaborated when advocating for basic human rights after their Siberian captivity, thereby reflecting a transnational dedication to these rights.

DEPRIVATION OF RIGHTS

In the middle of the century (1830–1860), Poles and Lithuanians supporting liberation from occupation by Prussia, Austria, and Russia understood that if the rights of men [*les droits de l'homme*], were to be extended to them, nationalists in Poland would have to convince those in the West to support their cause of independence against the interests of the Russian tsar. The expectation that a Napoleonic dynasty that had once established the Duchy of Warsaw could effectively champion human rights is expressed in Bolesław Prus's novel *The Doll* (*Lalka*, 1890), in which the dynasty is depicted as God's agent of justice: "Remember that God sent the Bonapartes to put the world to rights, and as long as there is no order and no justice in the world, then the Emperor's last testament will not have been carried out."[6] Although Alexander II's general amnesty (1856) restoring to Polish, Lithuanian, and Russian political prisoners some rights (but not necessarily property) allowed many former exiles to return, most prisoners, unlike Fyodor Dostoevsky, arrived home without support for the absolute authority of the Russian tsar. Many of these exiles who authored texts advocated for greater freedoms not only for their compatriots but for a range of nationalities represented in the Russian Empire (e.g., Ukrainian, Lithuanian, Polish, Belorussian, or Russian). Dostoevsky's comrade in Omsk, Józef Bogusławski, recalls an instinctive mutual sympathy arising between the Poles and their fellow Karbadian and Circassian inmates, despite their difficulty communicating, because the latter understood that "we are sons, like they, of an oppressed people."[7] In addition, the Russian anarchist in London, Mikhail Bakunin, and Polish exile in Paris, Bronisław Zaleski—both of whom experienced imprisonment and exile in Nicholas I's Russia—recognized the importance of common freedoms. At the same time, some national particularities are preserved as is evident when Zaleski reminds Bakunin in *Mikhail Bakunin and His Appeal to Polish and Russian Friends* (*Michał Bakunin i odezwa jego do przyaciół rossyjskich i polskich*) that although liberty is dear to multiple cultures, it was Polish nationalists who recognized the interdependency of freedom by writing on their banners, "for your freedom and ours."[8]

Poles were in the unique position of having their native land partitioned among three empires which cooperated closely with one another to monitor and arrest conspirators who crossed borders in order to engage in armed conflict and to flee from authorities. For example, two of the inmates from Poland who shared Dostoevsky's prison camp in Omsk and left remembrances of the Russian author in the Dead House—Bogusławski and Szymon Tokarzewski were both implicated in cross-border flight to avoid tsarist authorities.[9] Of course, these cooperative agreements between nations also impacted Russian revolutionaries, as Russian journalist in exile Alexander Herzen protests when characterizing Bakunin's transfer from authorities in Saxony through Austria into the hands of Nicholas I as a multinational government conspiracy.[10] Therefore, the former political prisoners residing in the West (including Herzen, Bakunin, and Zaleski) understood that the defense of their liberties required an international recognition of fundamental rights, which would protect them from detention by security forces in multiple nations. In other words, Herzen's publication of many articles about the tsar's secret police and Siberian atrocities, including Rufin Piotrowski's vivid description of the flogging death of a priest in Omsk, in his famous journal *The Bell* (*Kolokol*) could be partially motivated by a desire to protect himself and his circle of émigrés from expulsion or deportation.[11]

Perhaps Polish exiled author and sketch artist Bronisław Zaleski, a co-conspirator of Bogusławski who was also arrested for his connection to Jan Röhr, best articulates the absence of rights in remote Russian regions, when demonstrating in his *Polish Exiles in Orenburg* (*Wygnańcy Polscy w Orenburgu*, 1866), that in Russia there existed "not the least idea and sense of law and duty," since "almost everything depends on the will of the individuals, on their caprice or various instincts."[12] As an example, Zaleski recalled that Ukrainian poet and painter Taras Shevchenko was forbidden "to write, to sing, and to draw," as a way of reminding the reader of how the unfortunate artist's sketches, tolerated by local authorities but not by Tsar Nicholas I, earned him a prolongment of his sentence and a relocation from Orenburg to the remote fortress of Novopetrovsk.[13] In Novopetrovsk, Shevchenko endured harsh treatment by a capricious officer in the same way that Dostoevsky and his comrades in Omsk suffered the abuse of the often drunk and petty Major Krivtsov. For this reason, after his release from prison, Dostoevsky fearfully writes his brother about concerns that in his weakened condition he will not survive military service: "It is possible to fear only one thing: people and tyranny. If you fall under a superior, who takes a disliking to you (there are such), he will pick on you, destroy you, or make service a misery, and I am so feeble" (*Pss*, 28.1:172).

Immediately after his return from exile to St. Petersburg, Dostoevsky subtly supported former Siberians, who more visibly advocated for human rights. In the early 1860s, Dostoevsky worked in the midst of former and future Russian, Ukrainian, and Polish exiles, and his appearance alongside the very popular poet Shevchenko at a benefit for Sunday school instruction for the masses advanced Dostoevsky's public reputation as an exile and martyr, thereby reminding the attendees of Nicholas I's repression.[14] Dostoevsky's subsequent presence at the well-attended funeral of Shevchenko in St. Petersburg gave him the opportunity to celebrate publicly the life of a beloved literary figure ruined by exile, whom Apollon Grigoriev soon thereafter celebrated as "the first great poet of the new great literature of the Slavonic world" in the April 1861 issue of the Dostoevsky brothers' journal *Time* (*Vremia*).[15] In attendance at the funeral were Shevchenko's co-conspirator the Ukrainian historian Nikolai Kostomarov and an Orenburg exile Paweł Kruniewicz as well as the soon-to-be arrested Mikhail Mikhailov. The 1861 arrest of Mikhailov for his involvement in the composition and circulation of the political pamphlet "To the Young Generation" ("K molodomu pokoleniiu") sent shockwaves through the progressive literary community, which submitted a petition protesting the arrest that included the signature of Dostoevsky's older brother and co-editor, Mikhail.[16] Fyodor Dostoevsky's participation alongside soon-to-be future progressive political martyr Nikolai Chernyshevsky in a March 1862 benefit performance for Mikhailov (then in Siberia) allowed Dostoevsky to warn the younger generation about the trials of Siberian exile by reading from the second part of *House of the Dead* (*Zapiski iz mërtvogo doma*) a story about a soldier named Mikhailov dying from consumption in the prison hospital. A recollection of the event demonstrates that Dostoevsky's reading enhanced his reputation among the student radicals viewing him primarily as a victim of a state repression and *House of the Dead* as a historical document: "Then the public, especially the young, looked at him only as at a former convict, as an ex-political prisoner [. . . .] *Dead House* appeared liked an unprecedented document of Russian hard labor [. . .] then Dostoevsky was still considered almost a revolutionary."[17]

Dostoevsky's contemporaries appreciated that the travails of *katorga* (penal servitude)—those that crippled Dostoevsky's co-conspirator in Omsk, Sergei Durov, and made manifest the effects of epilepsy on Dostoevsky's physique—were far more difficult to endure than Zaleski's, Pleshcheev's, and Shevchenko's sentences to Orenburg as soldiers.[18] Durov's ill health evoked the sympathy of fellow inmates, and later in 1857 necessitated his move to Southern Russia to live with fellow former Petrashevsky conspirator Alexander Palm. With his legs crippled by heavy labor and the weight of his prison chains, Durov continued to advocate for freedom and truth in his poetry: "How did we value rectitude?/ What pay did we give her?/ Indeed, all cried: death to Christ!/ Death to the seducer Socrates!"[19] Yet, exposure to the caprice of petty tyrants in Siberia encouraged Dostoevsky to seek solitude in the Omsk prison: "his antisocial behavior arose from a fear that some relations with people or illegal indulgences would be made known to a superior and would, as a consequence, aggravate his position."[20] Later this concern motivated the writer to appeal to authorities for a restoration of his rights. Indeed, Dostoevsky is ridiculed in fellow inmate Józef Bogusławski's memoirs for writing a "laudatory poem for Tsar Nicholas in which he [Dostoevsky] extols his [the tsar's] greatness and the power of his intellect."[21] The narrative of Dostoevsky's autobiographical novel *House of the Dead* suggests that he, even while deprived of his rights in Omsk, still defended privileges associated with the Russian nobility, as is evident in the recollections of a fellow inmate Szymon Tokarzewski:

"Nobility . . . Gentleman . . . Nobility, I am a gentleman . . . . We noblemen," he constantly repeated. Every time that he addressed us Poles saying "we noblemen," I always interrupted him. "Excuse me sir, I think that in this jail there are no noblemen; there are only people deprived of their rights [*są tylko ludzie praw pozbawieni*], there are convicts."[22]

Thus, although Dostoevsky displays empathy for fellow Siberians, he nevertheless emerges from Siberia with a desire to protect his noble privilege and a certain cynicism regarding the language of rights, which is associated with Western-leaning youth in his novels *Crime and Punishment* (*Prestuplenie i nakazanie*) and *The Idiot*. Perhaps his strongest advocate for individual (yet not universal) political rights is the murderous admirer of Napoleon, Rodion Raskolnikov, who maintains according to his extraordinary man theory that men like Sir Isaac Newton would have had the "right [*pravo*]" and even would have been obliged to destroy the lives of others if it had been necessary to bring their discoveries to humanity (*Pss*, 6:199). When Raskolnikov later admits that his murder of the pawnbroker was motivated not by the promotion rights but by his individual will, he eviscerates a foundational principle for Western Europe, which is mocked in *The Idiot* when Lizaveta Prokofievna censures the young men who claim to seek truth while demanding a share of the Prince's inheritance based not on a "juridical right [*pravo iuridicheskoe*]" but "a human right, a natural one, the right of common sense and of the voice of conscience [*pravo chelovecheskoe, natural'noe, pravo zdravogo smysla i golosa sovesti*]" (*Pss*, 8: 223, 238).

THE STRUGGLE FOR RIGHTS AFTER DEPORTATION

In the 1850s and 1860s, many former deportees understood that a greater recognition of shared rights was not the stuff of parlor talk but a means by which exiles might enjoy better protections from the caprice of Russian authority figures. These men, sentenced for subversive political activities to deportation as prisoners, soldiers, or settlers, keenly felt the deprivation of their rights, resulting in daily hardships that encouraged them to examine critically the systems of political authority and the ways in which they limit rights. After the 1856 amnesty, former deportees with a connection to the circle of exiles in Orenburg (including Pleshcheev, Shevchenko, Zaleski, Polish poet Edward Żeligowski, and Polish revolutionary Zygmunt Sierakowski), sought to advance by a variety of means the rights and protections of citizens within the empire. The inter-ethnic cooperation that helped sustain these exiles, many of whom were writers and artists, as they experienced deprivation and isolation while serving their sentences at Orenburg, Orsk, Ufa, Perovsky, or Ak-Mechet in the late 1840s and 1850s, is highlighted by Zaleski: "At that time the Moscow government sent to various provinces situated in the depths of Russia, an entire circle of people busying themselves with our literary production."[23] Although following the completion of their sentences, this mobile group of former exiles settled in Moscow, St. Petersburg, Warsaw, Vilnius, and Paris, they were united in their attempts to challenge various human rights abuses by addressing protection from corporal punishment, the right to life, and freedom of movement.

Pleshcheev, for example, helped Shevchenko with publishing connections in St. Petersburg, translated the poetry of fellow Ukrainian and Polish exiles from Orenburg (Shevchenko and Edward Żeligowski), and became friendly with influential Polish nationalist Sierakowski.[24] When Pleshcheev left for St. Petersburg in the spring of 1858, he re-established connections with several of these former political exiles (Shevchenko, Sierakowski, and Żeligowski) who were already residing in the capital city and further networked with liberal Russians like Chernyshevsky, Nikolai Nekrasov (editor of the progressive journal *The Contemporary* [*Sovremennik*]), and Mikhailov who knew them.[25] Pleshcheev's poem "The Decembrist" (1860) recalls the famous 1825 conspirators, many of whom shared the Siberian landscape with the Petrashevtsy, and connects their legacy to one of human rights:

Blessed the one, who old in years
Retains all the freshness of feeling [. . .]
Who is a friend not of slavery, but of freedom,
In whom a faith in truth [*istina*] lives
And who does not dispassionately gaze upon,

how the rights of humanity
The strong one arrogantly tramples.[26]

Pleshcheev invokes the phrase "rights of man [pravo cheloveka]" in his 1861
poem "To the Poet [Poétu]" when describing the desirable qualities in an artist whose song must remain strong even when his voice is silenced:

And be a dauntless fighter,
A fighter for the rights of man;
Do not let your soul fall
Into a shameful sleep, into the vice of ages.[27]

At the same time, Pleshcheev displays compassion for the poet broken in
Siberia in his poem "S. F. Durov," which Pleshcheev sent to their co-conspirator Alexander Palm upon the release of Durov to the "warm south" for
recovery, where Pleshcheev—his "colleague in exile"—hopes that Durov can
leave behind "malicious ailment" and "malicious grief."[28]

Zaleski's literary talents displayed in his reminiscences of servitude (especially
those of Shevchenko and Żeligowski), reminded his readership of the consequences resulting from the deprivation of rights in the tsar's realm. His political polemics with Russian anarchist Mikhail Bakunin, soon after the latter's
escape from Siberia enabled him to participate in the planning for the January
1863 Uprising in Warsaw, reminded the Russian anarchist that some Polish
nationalists were more cautious when using force to shape a new Europe.
Zaleski's sustained dedication to publishing about human rights violations
in the depths of Russia differs strikingly from Bakunin's grand displays of
armed resistance and perpetual revolutionary agitation. Zaleski maintains that
"everyone has the right to live [prawo żyć]" so that while he concedes "to
the Russian people the right to the sympathy of the civilized world" he still
demands in exchange "the never-expiring rights of freedom."[29] Zaleski argues
that violence, in the name of the tsar or the people, still brings death with
it but includes Bakunin when asserting that "we the buried for many years
but living" know "that eternally alive is justice, only."[30] In other words, in
defense of life Zaleski rejects the use of violent force in exchange for the realization of certain rights in keeping with criticisms of political systems raised
by Jean-Jacques Rousseau in *On the Social Contract or Principles of Political Right* (*Du contrat social ou Principes du droit politique*) when he demonstrates that even though the powerful transform force into right to ensure
their continued dominance "force does not bring about right [*force ne fait pas
droit*]."[31] For Zaleski, a sense of right is rooted in "duty, justice, and devo-
tion" to God and to fatherland, which had motivated him while in Orenburg
to arrange the relocation of his friend and national poet Edward Żeligowski

to this place of exile.[32] Shevchenko, who shared a few months of exile with Zaleski at the fort of Novopetrovsk in 1851 and thereafter exchanged letters with him, likewise reiterates in his late poetry the faith of the cross and "a holy free soul."[33] In the poem he dedicates to Zaleski, "In the Days When We Were Cossacks" ("Shche iak budi mi kozakami") Shevchenko romantically recalls the days when their nations lived freely as brothers before the arrival of the Catholic priests who sought to punish and burn. In this respect, both Zaleski and Shevchenko supported intercultural exchange that promoted freedom—not only from the Russian tsar but also from other historic forces threatening the liberty that they, having been deprived of their rights, now keenly cherished.

For Żeligowski, the development of an independent national literature depended upon Poland's political freedom, so in a letter to Zaleski in February 1863 he underscores liberty as the first goal of the January uprising and asserts the need for a political spectrum to arrive at this conclusion: "Remember my conversation with Herzen in London, whom I convinced [1] that political figures in Poland must allow all parties, since each has its force and influence on the country, and we are mainly interested in this force, and [2] that we have no time today to play with theory and to think about absolute progress."[34] Like Zaleski, Żeligowski feared the more radical elements among the Russian exiles, even though they represented the best hope for Polish independence, but he envisioned that once the forces of liberation were unleashed in the Congress Kingdom of Poland they would spread to all segments of Polish society thereby uniting the nation around the cause of freedom.[35] Drafts of a letter by Żeligowski to Victor Hugo describe the Polish coup as part of a universal history against tyrants on their thrones victimizing "the heart of a people" and the soldier who "fights for the nation and the liberty of the world."[36]

Another comrade, Zygmunt Sierakowski, after returning from his exile to Orenburg and Ak-Mechet, dedicated himself to ending the practice of corporal punishment—that is the use of sticks, rods, and whips—in the Russian army.[37] Because corporal punishment was considered incompatible with Enlightenment principles, it had already been abolished in much of Europe.[38] The various descriptions of beatings and whippings of exiles and prisoners in many remembrances of Dostoevsky's contemporaries attest to the shock of those witnessing the spectacle. Before focusing on this issue as part of his responsibilities at the War Ministry in St. Petersburg, Sierakowski had studied at the Academy of the General Staff, where he had organized a conspiratorial circle of Poles (who knew both Mikhailov and Chernyshevsky).[39] For this reason, when Sierakowski was sent to research penal systems in Western Europe (1860–62), he met with various proponents of Polish liberation, including Zaleski and Herzen.[40] According to Herzen, while in England, in an attempt to reduce the practice of corporal punishment, Sierakowski shared with high-level British public officials his research maintaining a direct relationship between the severity of corporal punishment and an increased frequency in crime.[41] Even though Alexander II enacted limitations on corporal punishment in April 1863, Sierakowski was not to benefit from them, since when he participated in the 1863 Polish armed struggle against the Russian army, he was wounded, captured, and hung in Vilnius by order of General Governor Mikhail Muraviev, popularly called the "Hangman of Vilnius."[42]

TRANSCENDING BARRIERS TO ADVANCE RIGHTS

Thus, although many former exiles invoke the language of rights in their poetry and prose, through their dissent and rebellion, in political tracts and memoirs of captivity, their understandings of human rights vary widely not only by nationality but also by political and social identities. Still, when they recall the hardships borne in imprisonment and exile, they can find common ground in a desire to protect others from their own sufferings and those to which they were witness by defending a universal right to life and liberty. The rebellion against the poor quality of prison food in *House of the Dead*, the failed escape attempt by Polish prisoners known as the Omsk affair (1832–33), or the Baikal Insurrection of Polish exiles (1866) reveal that already in captivity convicts and the conscripted responded to their maltreatment under extreme conditions with collective movements against the mass violation of their rights. Those who visibly displayed the physical effects of servitude or who suffered premature death as a result of it, for example, Bogusławski, Shevchenko, Durov, and Żeligowski, particularly inspired their friends as well as sympathetic readers to challenge the absolute authority of the tsar. The civil unrest stemming from the January uprising of 1863, in which many former deportees like Sierakowski and Tokarzewski participated, displays well, as the UDHR recognizes, that in the absence of basic human rights, one may "be compelled to have recourse, as a last resort, to rebellion against tyranny and oppression."[43] In a similar manner, but with a focus on liberation rather than on rebellion, the prominent civil rights leader Martin Luther King, Jr. recognized in his own famous prison letter: "Oppressed people cannot remain oppressed forever. The urge for freedom will eventually come."[44]

The way in which the Petrashevtsy communally received notice of their impending death sentences on the scaffold on Semonovsky Square differs strikingly from those narratives exploring the solitude of a man condemned to death, such as in Victor Hugo's *The Last Day of a Condemned Man* (*Le dernier jour d'un condamné*, 1829) to which Dostoevsky referred while awaiting his execution on the square (*Pss,* 28.1:162).[45] In his own account of these shared last moments in extremis, awaiting death, Dostoevsky recalls that he hugged Pleshcheev and Durov and thought of his older brother, Mikhail.[46] This sense of community may account for why, although the mature Dostoevsky objected to Pleshcheev's liberal politics, he continued to use the familiar address "ty" in their correspondence, even though he infrequently used it outside of his family circle.[47] For many of the Petrashevtsy, the subsequent sentences they served strengthened their bonds of friendship as they sought to survive the adverse living conditions in imprisonment and exile. For Pleshcheev, the desire to communicate with his new comrades even motivated him to learn Polish.

Bogusławski's remembrances suggest that non-verbal communication may suffice in the absence of a common language when victims of a diverse nature share a common abusive enemy. In such cases, intercultural cooperation may be achieved without agreement on, or even discussion of, human rights. This would suggest that when personal survival is at stake, language, political affiliation, and geographical borders do not present insurmountable barriers to intercultural collaboration on the part of those traumatized by tyranny. The way in which these former prisoners supported each other professionally and personally following exile also speaks to a camaraderie built on similar deprivation of rights in repeated and sustained life-threatening situations that defy the authors' ability to describe them using common words. Dostoevsky displays non-verbal, intercultural, and transhistorical communication when he presents the imprisoned and silent Christ kissing his tormented captor, the Grand Inquisitor, who denies him the right to speak or edit his written, recorded, and published testament (a ban on free speech that Dostoevsky and his fellow exiles understood well). A gesture's potential for intercultural communication can also be embedded in a well-worn slogan or oft-cited quotation—even if it is presented in a language incomprehensible to the speaker—especially when its historical referent situates it within a particular time of extraordinary cultural import. The otherness of the language can highlight the necessity for distinctive words to describe overwhelming, unchartered realities, whose experience may be communicated most effectively by invoking parallel situations through famous utterances like "Za naszą i waszą wolność" and "Liberté, Egalité, Fraternité!" that transcend their localized conflicts, reaching across the expanses of time and place to embolden successive generations from various cultures to take up the tricolor of human rights.

NOTES

1. For their support of the research necessary to complete this chapter, it is with gratitude that I acknowledge my share of the U.S. Department of Education Fulbright-Hays group projects abroad grant (administered through American Councils), the Mellon Grant provided by the College of Arts and Sciences at Saint Louis University, and the efforts of Timothy O'Connor and Valentina L. Gavrilova.

2. Sisil' Vess'e, *Za vashu i nashu svobodu!: Dissidentskoe dvizhenie v Rossii* (Moscow: Novoe literaturnoe obozrenie, 2015).

3. Sisil' Vess'e, *Za vashu i nashu svobodu!* 14.

4. Daniel C. Thomas argues in *The Helsinki Effect: International Norms, Human Rights, and the Demise of Communism* (Princeton, 2001) that the act undermined the dominant ideology of communism in Eastern Europe.

5. Joseph Frank, *Dostoevsky a Writer in his Time* (Princeton: Princeton University Press, 2009), 135.

6. Bolesław Prus, *The Doll*, trans. David Welsh (Central European University Press, 1996), 14.

7. Józef Bogusławski, "Wspomnienia Sybiraka: Pamiętniki Józefa Bogusławskiego," *Nowa reforma* 294 (1896): 1.

8. [Zaleski, Bronisław], *Michał Bakunin i odezwa jego do przyaciół rossyjskich i polskich* (Paris: W księgarni polskiej, 1862), 10.

9. Bogusławski concealed and brought Jan Röhr (implicated in the Poznan Uprising of 1848) to the Lithuanian border on his own horses (Rossiiskaia natsional'naia biblioteka, rukopisnyi otdel', fond 629, opis' 188, folio 45), while Tokarzewski himself fled to Galicia where he lived under an assumed name according to his testimony printed in *Rewolucyjna konspiracja w Królestwie Polskim w latach 1840–1845: Edward Dembowski* (Wrocław: Wydawnictwo Polskiej Akademii Nauk, 1981), 714–716.

10. A. I. Gertsen, *Sobranie sochinenii v tridtsati tomakh.* 30 vols (Moscow: Akademiia Nauk SSSR, 1954–65), 7: 304–305.

11. Selections from Piotrowski's *Pamiętniki z pobytu na Syberyi* (*Memoirs from a Sojourn in Siberia*, 1860–1861) appeared in *The Bell* in 1862.

12. Bronisław Zaleski, "*Wygnańcy Polscy w Orenburgu,*" *Wspomnienia z Uralu i stepów Kazachskich,* ed. Andrzej Zieliński (Wrocław: Polskie Towarzystwo Ludoznawcze, 2008), 37. Information about Zaleski's part in Röhr's conspiracy may be found in Rossiiskaia natsional'naia biblioteka, rukopisnyi otdel' (fond. 629, opis' 188, folio 45–46).

13. Zaleski, "*Wygnańcy Polscy,*" 38.

14. Joseph Frank, *Dostoevsky: The Stir of Liberation, 1860–1865* (Princeton University Press, 1986); V. Anisov and É. Sereda, *Litopys zhyttia i tvorchosti T. H. Shevchenka* (Kiev: Derzhavne Vydavnitstvo, 1959), 347.

15. A. A. Grigor'ev, "Taras Shevchenko," *Vremia* 4 (April 1861): n. pag. *Philolog.ru Biblia,* accessed January 3, 2016, http://smalt.karelia.ru/~filolog/vremja/1861/APRIL/taras.htm; Vladimir A. D'iakov, *Taras Shevchenko I ego pol'skie druz'ia* (Moscow: Izadatel'stvo Nauka, 1964), 124–125.

16. V. S. Nechaeva, *Zhurnal M. M. i F. M. Dostoevskikh "Ėpokha," 1864–1865* (Moscow: Izdatel'stvo "Nauka," 1975), 291.

17. P. D. Boborykin's memoirs are cited in: N. F. Budanova and G. M. Fridlender, eds., *Letopis' zhizni i tvorchestva F. M. Dostoevskogo v trëkh tomakh 1821–1881,* 3 vols. (St. Petersburg: Gumanitarnoe agentstvo "Akademicheskii proekt," 1995), 1: 352.

18. A. P. Miliukov, "Fedor Mikhailovich Dostoevskii," *Russkaia Starina* 31, no. 5 (May 1881): 33–34.

19. This is the second stanza of Durov's poem "Who became, beside the eternal lies" ("Kto stal, pomimo vechnykh lzhei," 1863) included in V. V. Zhdanov and V. L. Komarovich, eds. *Poėty-Petrashevtsy* (Leningrad: Sovetskii pisatel', 1957), 238.

20. P. K. Mart'ianov, "V perelome veka. (Otryvki iz staroi zapisnoi knizhki)," *Istoricheskii vestnik* 62 (November 1895): 451. His sentence read: "lishit'...vsekh prav sostoianiia [deprived of all rights of situation]" (*Pss*, 18: 189).

21. Bogusławski, "Wspomnienia Sybiraka: Pamiętniki Józefa Bogusławskiego," 1. Dostoevsky wrote three patriotic Siberian poems (1854–1856) in order to reclaim from tsarist authorities a right to publish (*Pss*, 2: 403–10; 520).

22. Szymon Tokarzewski, *Siedem lat katorgi: Pamiętniki Szymona Tokarzewskiego 1846–1857 g.*, 2nd ed. (Warsaw: Gebethner i Wolff, 1918), 167–168.

23. Bronisław Zaleski, "Zmarli na wychodztwie od 1861 roku: Żeligowski, Edward," *Rocznik towarzystwa Historyczno-Literackiego w Paryżu* (Paris: Księgarnia Luksemburska, 1867), 370.

24. Żeligowski, who helped organize the Polish language journal *Słowo* in St. Petersburg in the late 1850s, was trying to find common ground among the Polish, Ukrainian, and Russian nationalists with *Słowo*, but the journal was banned when its editor Jozafat Ohryzko published a letter by a Polish revolutionary exile, Joachim Lelewel. Turgenev petitioned Tsar Alexander II for his release.

25. M. K. Lemke, *Politicheskie protsessy: M. I. Mikhailova, D. I. Pisareva, N. G. Chernyshevskogo: Po neizdannym dokumentam* (St. Petersburg: Izdatel'stvo O. N. Popovoi, 1907), 195.

26. A. N. Pleshcheev, *Polnoe sobranie stikhotvorenii*, ed. M. Ia. Poliakov (Moscow/Leningrad: Sovetskii pisatel', 1964), 143.

27. Pleshcheev, *Polnoe sobranie*, 152.

28. Pleshcheev, *Polnoe sobranie*, 106–108; Zhdanov and Komarovich, *Poėty-Petrashevtsy,* 153.

29. [Zaleski, Bronisław], *Michał Bakunin*, 19.

30. Zaleski, *Michał Bakunin*, 20.

31. Jean-Jacques Rousseau, *On the Social Contract: Discourse on the Origin of Inequality, Discourse on Political Economy*, trans. and ed. by Donald A. Cress (Indianapolis: Hackett Publishing Company, 1983), 20; http://classiques.uqac.ca/classiques/ Rousseau_jj/contrat_social/ Contrat_social.pdf.

32. Zaleski, *Michał Bakunin*, 53; Wiesław Caban, *Z Orenburga do Paryża: Bronisław Zaleski 1820–1880* (Kielce: Wydawnictwo Akademii Świętokrzyskiej, 2006), 77.

33. Taras Shevchenko, "Kobzar'," *Osnova* (May 1862): 2.

34. G. Pisarėk, "Rol' russkikh i ukraintsev v zhizni i tvorchestve Ėdvarda Zhe-ligovskogo," in *Sviazi revoliutsionerov Rossii i Pol'shi*, eds. V. A. D'iakov, I. S. Miller, and L. A. Obushenkovaia (Moscow: Izdatel'stvo Nauka, 1968), 238.

35. Andrzej Walicki writes that Herzen connected socialism and the "rise of Slav-dom" in *Russia, Poland, and Universal Regeneration: Studies on Russian and Polish Thought of the Romantic Epoch* (University of Notre Dame Press, 1991), 40.

36. Archiwum Hotelu Lambert, MS 6976. Edward Żeligowski. Korespondencja. Listy od osób różnych. B-Ż. Biblioteka Czartoryskich w Krakowie.

37. Gertsen, *Sobranie sochinenii v tridtsati tomakh*, 218.

38. Bruce Adams, *The Politics of Punishment: Prison Reform in Russia 1863–1917* (DeKalb: Northern Illinois University Press, 1996), 13.

39. V. A. D'iakov and I. S. Miller, *Revoliutsionnoe dvizhenie v russkoi armii i vosstanie 1863 g.* (Moscow: Izdatel'stvo "Nauka," 1964), 120–125.

40. S. D. Gurvich-Lishchiner, *Letopis' zhizni i tvorchestva A. I. Gertsena 1859-iiun' 1864* (Moscow: Izdatel'stvo Nauka, 1983), 131.

41. Gertsen, *Sobranie sochinenii*, 219.

42. Adams, *The Politics of Punishment*, 13. When he emancipated the serfs, Alexander II reformed the penal system.

43. "The Universal Declaration of Human Rights," http://www.un.org/en/universal-declaration-human-rights/.

44. James Melvin Washington, ed., *A Testament of Hope: The Essential Writings of Martin Luther King, Jr.* (New York: Harper Collins Publishers, 1991), 297. This quotation is from his "Letter from Birmingham City Jail."

45. Frank, *Dostoevsky: The Stir of Liberation,* 24. Hugo here is also objecting to forms of capital punishment.

46. F. M. Dostoevskii, *Polnoe sobranie sochinenii* (Leningrad: Izdatel'stvo "Nauka," 1985), 28, no. 2: 161–162.

47. Boris N. Tikhomirov made this observation to the author.

Chapter 10

The ASEAN Declaration of Human Rights as a Case of Human Rights Translation

Marcella Ferri

The complicated relationship between the universality of human rights and the respect of cultural diversity has been greatly debated since the adoption of the Universal Declaration of Human Rights (UDHR).[1] Already during its elaboration, the genuinely "universal" nature of the Declaration has been questioned by some scholars, and especially by the supporters of cultural relativism, asserting that it was actually based upon the Western human rights notion.[2]

As noted by several scholars, the universal recognition of human rights does not imply that they have to be implemented in a uniform and homogeneous manner.[3] In particular, some authors highlight the necessity to promote "cross-cultural legitimacy" of human rights.[4] Recognizing that universal standards of human rights refer to a specific paradigm of the human being, Eva Brems points out the need to remedy the exclusion of people not included in this paradigm; she proposes the concept of "inclusive universality"[5] which allows to bridge the "gap" between the universal human rights system and non-Western cultures.

This process is not a one-way street; it needs a twofold movement. On the one hand, the flexibility of human rights and their dynamic nature make it possible to transform the universal human rights standards and adapt them to different cultural claims. On the other hand, the evolutionary and heterogeneous nature of cultures involves significant practices and traditions contrary to human rights;[6] to this end it is necessary to promote an internal debate within all societies about their cultures and fundamental values, assuring the free and effective participation of all members of societies.

Within this theoretical framework, this chapter will briefly analyze the Declaration on Human Rights adopted in 2012 by States belonging to the

Association of South-East Asian Nations (ASEAN).[7] Although ASEAN was established with the aim to strengthen the economic development and promote peace and stability among its members, since the 1990s the Association has been paying increased attention to human rights issues, starting a significant path toward the establishment of a regional system of human rights protection.[8]

The ASEAN Declaration on Human Rights (hereafter ADHR) is important, not only because it marks a critical step into the development of an ASEAN human rights system, but also because it represents the most significant document formalizing the ASEAN view on human rights. In this perspective, its analysis allows us to understand whether and to what extent the ADHR represents a good example of intercultural translation of human rights principles.

From this point of view, the ASEAN case is interesting for several reasons. One of the most significant criticisms elaborated about the UDHR came from the ASEAN Member States and, in general, Asian countries. Their disapprovals were linked with the so-called Asian values, the political ideology promoted at the end of the 1980s by the then prime minister of Singapore, Lee Kuan Yew, and supported by other Asian political leaders. This ideology proposed a set of values affirming, on the one hand, the centrality of economic development and its potential priority on human rights, and on the other hand, it rejected criticism expressed by Western countries about human rights violations carried out in some Asian countries. Instead, leaders defended the principle of national sovereignty and non-interference in the state domestic affairs, stating that universal human rights standards have a deep Western origin, which makes them not fully consistent with the values of Asian societies.[9]

Secondly, we need to recall that the ASEAN States' adhesion to the universal human rights treaties has been rather low. Indeed, the International Covenant on Civil and Political Rights and the International Covenant on Economic, Social and Cultural Rights, adopted by the United Nations in 1966, were ratified just by Cambodia, Indonesia, Laos, Philippines, Thailand, and Vietnam[10]. The only human rights treaties ratified by all ASEAN States are the Convention on the Elimination of All Forms of Discrimination against Women, the Convention on the Rights of the Child, and the International Convention on the Rights of Persons with Disabilities.[11] Moreover, several States have entered significant reservations about the human rights treaties in order to express their disagreement about certain human rights standards defined at the universal level.[12]

This chapter, by comparing UDHR and ADHR aims to show the extent to which the ADHR makes reference and accepts the human rights principles defined at the universal level, and, conversely, to what degree it expresses the cultural specificities of ASEAN. In order to retrace the ASEAN stance on human rights, it will refer to claims formalized by the ASEAN states during the early 1990s on the occasion of the United Nations World Conference on Human Rights held in Vienna in 1993.[13] In particular, it will analyze the Final Declaration of the Regional Meeting for Asia (the Bangkok Declaration), adopted by Asian countries in view of the World Conference[14] and the Kuala Lumpur Declaration on Human Rights, adopted by the ASEAN Inter-Parliamentary Organization (AIPO) a few months after the Vienna Conference.[15]

THE ASEAN VIEW ON HUMAN RIGHTS: THE BANGKOK DECLARATION AND THE KUALA LUMPUR DECLARATION ON HUMAN RIGHTS

The Bangkok Declaration provides an insight into the main claims characterizing the ASEAN human rights stance.[16] In the Declaration's Preamble, the ASEAN States reaffirm their "commitment" to the principles stated by the United Nations Charter and the UDHR, and encourage the ratification of international human rights instruments.[17] While referring to the human rights principles defined at the universal level, the Bangkok Declaration defines the specific ASEAN point of view on human rights. First, ASEAN states highlight that universality of human rights cannot go together with an undervaluation of *cultural diversity*; consequently, it is extremely important to take into account the specificities of each context where human rights are implemented[18] and explore the possibilities of ensuring some "regional arrangements" to protect human rights in Asia.[19]

A major claim concerns *national sovereignty*: the ASEAN members put emphasis on the principles of national sovereignty, territorial integrity, and non-interference in the internal affairs of States.[20] These claims are rooted in the disapproval expressed by the Western world about human rights situations in Asia, and the consequent tendency to link development programs and trade agreements with human rights standards defined by Western countries. In this context, ASEAN states express a significant criticism of international relations, underling the importance of reinforced international cooperation based on "principles of equality and mutual respect" and to move beyond the use of human rights as a condition for economic and development cooperation, as well as an instrument of political pressure.[21]

Another substantial principle affirmed by the Bangkok Declaration speaks to the importance of *economic and social rights*. Within the ASEAN view, and in particular in the Singapore School, good government, stability and order were qualified as fundamental preconditions to achieve the economic growth and, in turn, to assure human dignity.[22] While in the Bangkok Declaration the ASEAN states do not declare such a position explicitly, they refer to the principles of interdependence and indivisibility of all human rights, as well as "the need to give equal emphasis"[23] to all categories of human rights, thus highlighting the lack of attention paid to economic and social rights in the prevailing approaches.

This aspect is strictly linked to the importance accorded to *development*. In this respect, the ASEAN stance shows a kind of dualism. On the one hand, the ASEAN states make reference to an economic conception of development, remarking the fundamental role played by economic growth in achieving democracy and human rights fulfillment;[24] on the other, they invoke the Declaration on the Right to Development adopted by the United Nations in 1986[25] and refer to development as a human right.[26]

The Kuala Lumpur Declaration represents the first attempt to translate the ASEAN human rights stance into the form of a Declaration;[27] as we will see, it tries to reconcile the universal principles of human rights and the specific ASEAN approach. On this, it is an important predecessor of the ADHR.[28]

The Preamble and the first part of the Declaration (Articles 1–6) that define its founding principles reflect the human rights claims expressed in the Bangkok Declaration. We find here references to the importance of considering the "realities and value system" of contexts where human rights are implemented,[29] to the principle of national sovereignty and the necessity to not use human rights as conditions for economic cooperation,[30] to the right of people to self-determination, and the right to define their political system and carry out their economic, social, and cultural development[31].

The notion of development formalized by the Kuala Lumpur Declaration is important as it seems to embrace the person-centered notion of development that characterizes the UN Declaration on the Right to Development. The Kuala Lumpur Declaration significantly refers to the right to development as a right not only of States, but also of the "human being"[32] and identifies a close link between development and the respect for human rights, underlining that the full realization of human rights simultaneously represents a pre-condition and a goal of development.[33] In this view, states must ensure the right of everyone to an "active, free and meaningful participation"[34] in development, and this participation constitutes not only a right but also a duty and a responsibility of individuals.[35]

This relationship between duties and rights, which also has a significant presence in the UN Declaration on the Right to Development, characterizes the whole conception of human rights elaborated by the ASEAN States. Indeed, another criticism expressed by ASEAN states concerns the excessive individualism which, in their opinion, characterizes the Western notion of human rights. This individualism undervalues some fundamental aspects of ASEAN perspectives, especially Confucian, such as the importance of relationship between everyone and their community, and the consequent requirement to identify not only rights but also *duties and responsibilities* of individuals.

This aspect is not invoked by the Bangkok Declaration[36] but it emerges widely from the Kuala Lumpur Declaration which underlines the importance of "balancing" the individuals' rights and the obligations they have to the society and state.[37] In line with this communitarian approach, individual duties are defined not only in relation to specific rights, in particular to the right to development and the freedom of expression,[38] but also as regards the overall "promotion, implementation and protection of human rights."[39] Reflecting the Asian and Confucian perspectives on the state, "in which the diligent fulfilment of its duties by a state is the counterpart of the respect and obedience it receives from the citizens,"[40] the Kuala Lumpur Declaration also makes references to several duties of states.[41]

To conclude this section, it is necessary to point out that the Kuala Lumpur Declaration presents several limitations. First, while the Declaration recognizes some human rights secured at the universal level,[42] these rights are very few and do not include certain fundamental principles like the prohibition of slavery and the prohibition of torture and cruel, inhuman or degrading treatment or punishment.[43] Strangely, the Declaration refers only to civil and political rights and does not pay any attention to the economic and social rights.[44] Second, the distinction made by the Declaration between the Fundamental Human Rights (Part II) and the Basic rights and duties of citizens and states (Part III) seems to create a hierarchy giving more importance to rights recognized in the second part of the Declaration (right to life, freedom of thought and religion and right to property, liberty, and security).[45]

Another important aspect concerns the limitations on rights. The provisions concerning the right to life, the right to property, security and liberty and the right to freedom of expression provide that these rights can be limited only in accordance with the law; by not specifying the precise limiting conditions, they leave a great margin of choice to the states. Another example is found in Article 22 making reference to limitations "determined by law in respect of these right and duties to meet the requirement of morality, public order and the general well-being of society." This formulation recalls the traditional limitation clauses on human rights, with adding a reference to the "well-being of the society" which reflects the communitarian approach characterizing the ASEAN stance.

The Kuala Lumpur Declaration thus suffers several limits as regards the rights secured and the margin of discretion left to States about the rights limiting conditions. In the light of this, there is little doubt that Declaration's capacity to translate universal human rights standards into the ASEAN standpoint is extremely narrow. The only issue in relation to which it seems to harmonize with universal claims is the right to development, which—similarly to the UN Declaration—it defines as a human right, and embraces a notion of development characterized by a person-centered conception.

THE ASEAN HUMAN RIGHTS
DECLARATION: GENERAL OVERVIEW

The ASEAN Declaration of Human Rights was adopted on the occasion of the 21st Summit of ASEAN Heads of State and Governments held in Cambodia in November 2012.[46] Similar to the Bangkok Declaration and the Kuala Lumpur Declaration, in the Preamble to ADHR the ASEAN states affirm the principles formalized within the UN framework.[47] Some of the Articles of the ASEAN Declaration resemble in a significant manner the formulations of the corresponding Articles of the UDHR.[48]

The ASEAN states' wish to make reference to the universal human rights principles is evident in the two Articles opening the section on civil and political rights (Article 10) and on economic, social and cultural rights (Article 26). They state, with an identical formulation, that "ASEAN Member States affirm all the civil and political [economic, social and cultural] rights in the Universal Declaration of Human Rights. Specifically, ASEAN Member States affirm the following rights and fundamental freedoms."

These provisions need attention because at first sight one could think that the ASEAN States want to recognize human rights on identical terms with the UDHR. However the expression "Specifically" and the differences existing between the two Declarations do not allow this reading: the ADHR is not simply a reaffirmation and repetition of the UDHR. Articles 1 and 26 show that ASEAN states recognize the UDHR as a fundamental reference with regard to human rights protection but, at the same time, they want to elaborate and formalize their own, specific notion of human rights.

The Main Specificities of the ASEAN
Declaration on Human Rights

Comparing the ADHR with the UDHR, we can identify some significant differences existing between the two Declarations. In the following paragraphs we will also try to understand if they have a cultural origin, focusing on issues relevant to our analysis. In particular, we will consider the right to development, in relation to which the ADHR represents a positive example of human rights translation, and we will trace that "inclusive universality" invoked by Brems. We will also examine some of the most controversial and criticized elements of the Declaration such as the protection of cultural diversity, the limitations clause, and the reference to individual duties and responsibilities. Indeed, while several authors welcomed the adoption of the ADHR because it represents the first, if imperfect, human rights Declaration adopted within the ASEAN system, the Declaration also received several disapprovals.[49]

The Right to Development

The ADHR devotes a great deal of attention to the right to development (Articles 35–37). Its conception of the right to development presents several similarities with the notion elaborated by the Declaration on the Right to Development adopted by the United Nations.[50] In this regard it is significant that the references—present in the Bangkok Declaration—to the economic nature of development and to the close relationship between economic growth and democracy are completely absent in the ADHR which, like the UN Declaration, defines development as an inalienable right and highlights its multidimensional nature.[51]

Similar to the Kuala Lumpur Declaration, the ADHR states that development "facilitates and is necessary" in order to assure human rights, and in this way identifies it as a condition of implementing human rights.[52] However, there is a significant difference between the two Declarations as concerns the role assigned to individual persons. This is a critical aspect of the UN Declaration, as its Preamble states that "the human person is the central subject of the development process."[53] In the ADHR, this conception emerges in a more nuanced manner; while recognizing the right of every person to development, a people-oriented perspective of development seems to prevail.[54]

Unlike the Kuala Lumpur Declaration the ADHR does not refer to individuals' duties as regards development. In this respect, we should note that the principle whereby individuals are not only rights holders but also duty bearers is stated in the UN Declaration on the Right to Development.[55] This is not too surprising as the right to development, as well as the right to peace and to environment, were not included in the UDHR nor in the two International Covenants, but they have been recognized more recently at the international level (the so-called new or third generation ri). Non-Western countries have played a fundamental role in the elaboration of these rights, which are characterized by a strong collective dimension and a close link between rights and duties.[56]

Cultural Diversity

Article 7 of the ADHR states that the implementation of human rights must consider the different political, economic, legal, social, and cultural contexts.

This provision has been heavily criticized as it attempts to reopen the Asian values debate and to legitimize cultural relativism.[57]

In this regard we should note that while the importance of cultural diversity did not characterize the human rights notion articulated in the UDHR, from the 2000s the international human rights law has been paying growing attention to cultural diversity and this is no longer a stance specific to the ASEAN human rights view, and in general the non-Western views.[58] A significant milestone has been the UNESCO Universal Declaration on Cultural Diversity (2001) recognizing the value of cultural diversity and calling for its protection. In this regard, we can also point to the practice of the UN Committee on Economic, Social and Cultural Rights. This Committee elaborated the concept of "cultural adequacy" stating that the implementation of a human right has to take into account the cultural features of each context, and must be culturally adequate.[59]

While recognizing the importance to promote cultural diversity, the international law system does not ignore the fact that some cultural practices and traditions turn out to be violations of human dignity. On the contrary, the international human rights law stresses that the protection of cultural diversity does not open the way to cultural relativism, and is not in opposition to the universality of human rights; indeed, as underlined by the UNESCO Universal Declaration on Cultural Diversity and by the Committee on Economic, Social and Cultural rights, cultural diversity must be protected insofar as it does not imply a violation of human rights.[60]

Limitations Clause

ASEAN's traditional claim of national sovereignty finds several expressions in the ADHR.[61] It emerges in particular in Article 8 concerning limiting conditions for human rights.[62] This provision makes reference to the usual limitation clauses, and invokes in a significant manner Article 29 of UDHR. However, it has been heavily criticized by civil society organizations and the international community.[63] In particular it has been emphasized that since the provision is included in the section on "General principles," it can be applied to all rights secured by the Declaration as well as to non derogable rights under the international human rights law. In our opinion this possibility does not descend from the provision's location, but rather from the lack of references to the non derogable rights. We need to recognize that this kind of specification is not usually included in the Human Rights Declarations, such as the UDHR and the American Declaration of the Rights and Duties of Man (1948). However, we note that the precise identification of non derogable human rights ought to be included in an eventual future ASEAN Convention on human rights. Moreover, following the example of the other international binding acts on human rights, it would be preferable to "take a right by right approach"[64] that permits to precisely specify limitations admissible with regard to every single right.

Some civil society organizations, especially those defending women's rights,[65] have also observed that the concept of "public morality" recalled by Article 8 reflects the dominant culture, and risks the marginalization of women and vulnerable groups. While public morality is usually included in the limitations clause,[66] this concept presents some risks for several reasons.

First, as underscored by the European Court of Human Rights, the difficulty of elaborating a uniform definition of public morality makes it necessary to allow a "margin of appreciation" to states. If on the one hand, this margin permits to respect the specificities of each state, on the other hand it makes less rigorous the control taking place at the international level, and this gives to states broader discretion.

Secondly, as stated by the Human Rights Committee, the concept of public morality "derives from many social, philosophical, and religious traditions."[67] The protection of cultural practices is not absolute as it must not breach other human rights. Certainly, due to the unfeasibility of elaborating a uniform notion of morality and its links with religious and cultural practices, the possibility of limiting human rights in the name of public morality risks legitimizing some practices violating human dignity of marginalized people.

Individual Duties and Responsibilities

As a typical ASEAN human rights claim, Article 6 of the ADHR makes reference to the balance between rights and individual duties.[68] This provision was strongly criticized by the international community and civil society organizations on the grounds that the idea of balance between duties and rights is alien to international and regional human rights instruments.[69] Telling in this regard is the open letter, addressed to the ASEAN members a few days before adoption of the ADHR, by Independent Experts, holders of Special Procedures established by the Human Rights Council. They pointed out that the concept of balance does not belong to international human rights law language, and it misrepresents the real dynamic existing between rights and duties.[70] According to Independent Experts, a human rights instrument should not refer to balance because this concept gives to Governments "much greater scope" to constrain human rights in "arbitrary, disproportionate and unnecessary way."[71]

Insofar as the exercise of rights might be subjected to some restrictions, rights-bearers are at the same time duty-holders. As Brems notes, restrictions of rights may be reformulated in terms of duties—the so-called rights-restrictive duties.[72] From this angle, it is clear that rights and "rights-restrictive duties" have to be balanced, and that this issue becomes fundamental to a positive dynamic between rights and responsibilities of everyone, and to ensuring social stability.[73]

This is exactly the perspective to which several international human rights instruments make reference.[74] One is the African Charter on Human and Peoples' Rights (1981) statement that "the enjoyment of rights and freedoms also *implies* the performance of duties on the part of everyone."[75] Similarly, the Preamble of the American Declaration of the Rights and Duties of Man (1948) affirms "the fulfilment of duty by each individual is a *prerequisite* to the rights of all. Rights and duties are *interrelated* in every social and political activity of man."[76] Also Article 29 of UDHR includes a reference to individual duties;[77] although the Declaration does not qualify the relationship between duties and rights, during the *Travaux Préparatoires* the drafters had repeatedly pointed out the interdependence existing between them.[78]

In all of these instruments the fulfillment of individuals' duties represents an essential element ("*a prerequisite*") ensuring the enjoyment of the rights of all. In other words, the exercise of rights cannot be absolute, but it is limited by the necessity to respect certain duties. This balance of rights and duties creates a dynamic equilibrium for social life.

With regard to the necessity, stressed by the Independent Experts, to regulate limitations on human rights decided by national states, such a goal needs a specific provision—such as that of Article 8 of ADHR—regulating in a strict manner the conditions for such constraints. Specific and precise limitation clauses can restrain the power of government and offer an additional guarantee to individual rights. In such cases calls for balancing duties and rights are less relevant, and do not imply an extension of state power.

Finally, it is important to point out that, unlike the American Declaration of the Rights and Duties of Man and the African Charter on Human and Peoples' Rights, the ADHR does not identify the specific duties of individuals. While the ADHR is not a binding instrument, the absence of such a list is a significant blank space, especially compared to the American Declaration. The precise identification of individual responsibilities and duties, even in a non-binding instrument, is of utmost importance for providing specific limits on the power of national states.

Conclusion

The above comparison between the UDHR and the ADHR reveals that the ASEAN Declaration, while making meaningful references to the universal human rights standards, embodies several specificities that take a critical view of the universal human rights standards defined by the UN. However, despite these differences and the significant resistance of some ASEAN states to the ratification of the human rights treaties, the ADHR represents an important outcome. Especially if we take into account the Kuala Lumpur Declaration, the ADHR represents a positive achievement.

The ADHR certainly does not represent a perfect result; on the contrary, arguably, the Declaration includes some provisions which could be ambiguous and potentially dangerous. Two such aspects have been highlighted. The provisions concerning individuals duties (Article 6) and the limitations clause (Article 8) need some specifying. The concept of "balance" is not problematic in itself, but it calls for further elaboration in terms of concrete duties and responsibilities of individuals. Likewise, the limitations clause should better identify fundamental human rights which, according to the international human rights principles, cannot be derogated; moreover it should define, right by right, the specific limitations applicable to them.

If the Declaration could not specify these issues, they should be included in a binding Convention on human rights that could reinforce the ASEAN human rights system. Such a Convention could specify the content of specific human rights and reinforce their implementation by creating a regional, supranational monitoring body.

A second area of concern is the reference to "public morality" included in Article 8 which could legitimize some traditional practices contrary to human rights. Similarly, with reference to Article 7, ASEAN human rights system must ensure—in line with the international human rights law–that cultural diversity cannot be invoked to violate the human rights of vulnerable groups. There is an apparent necessity to foster an "internal human rights debate" able to change certain cultural traditions that conflict with broad human rights principles.[79] As an inspiring example, one can point to Article 5 of the Convention on the Elimination of All Forms of Discrimination against Women stating that the "States Parties shall take all appropriate measures: To modify the social and cultural patterns of conduct of men and women, with a view to achieving the elimination of prejudices and customary and all other practices which are based on the idea of the inferiority or the superiority of either of the sexes or on stereotyped roles for men and women." Similarly the Convention on the Rights of the Child affirms the state obligations to adopt necessary measures aiming to abolish the "traditional practices prejudicial to the health of children" (Article 24.3).

These provisions have been understood to be responding to certain harmful practices having cultural or religious origins. Considering that these provisions are binding for all ASEAN members states, they can potentially represent an instrument for generating an international debate aiming at transforming these harmful traditional practices, and ensuring "the active participation of all relevant stakeholders, particularly women and girls."[80] Within the framework of such a debate, public morality and cultural traditions could be sustained insofar as they are made compatible with fundamental human rights. Some of the issues we have identified, such as cultural diversity and the right to development, make clear that the ASEAN perspective on human rights does not imply an insurmountable conflict with the UDHR principles. On the contrary, it offers an alternative view of human rights that can largely be reconciled with the universal standards. In this sense the ADHR represents a positive example of human rights translation, a case of that "inclusive universality" invoked by Brems. It proposes a human rights view that welcomes universal standards and represents a constructive approach to dialogue. At the same time, the interpretations being currently debated in terms of a universal perspective are clearly moving toward a human rights notion capable of embracing cultural outlooks that are different from the Western one, revealing a genuine intercultural opening.

NOTES

1. This study was made possible thanks to a grant awarded by the Catholic University of the Sacred Heart of Milan, Italy (Supervisor: Professor Francesco Bestagno), within the Project "Going East"—Fondazione Cariplo.

2. See inter alia Jack Donnelly, *Universal Human Rights in Theory and Practice* (Ithaca: Cornell University Press, 2013), 93–118; Eva Brems, *Human Rights: Universality and Diversity* (The Hague: Martinus Nijhoff Publishers, 2001), 4–25; Wiktor Osiatynski, *Human Rights and Their Limits* (Cambridge: Cambridge University Press, 2009), 144–186; Susan Marks and Andrew Clapham, *International Human Rights Lexicon* (Oxford: Oxford University Press, 2005), 385–398.

3. Mary Ann Glendon, "The Rule of Law in the Universal Declaration of Human Rights," *Northwestern University Journal of International Human Rights* 2, no. 1 (2004): 15; Jack Donnelly, "The Relative Universality of Human Rights," *Human Rights Quarterly* 29, no. 2 (2007): 283; Pieter van Dijk, "Common Standard of Achievement-About Universal Validity and Uniform Interpretation of International Human Rights Norms," *Netherlands Quarterly of Human Rights* 13, no. 2 (1995): 106–121.

4. Abdullahi An-Na'im, "Towards a Cross-cultural Approach to Defining International Standards of Human Rights: The Meaning of Cruel, Inhuman or Degrading Treatment or Punishment," in *Human Rights in Cross-Cultural Perspectives. A Quest for Consensus*, ed. Abdullahi An-Na'im (Philadelphia: University of Pennsylvania Press, 1991), 4.

5. Brems, *Human Rights*, 308; Eva Brems, "Reconciling Universality and Diversity in International Human Rights: A Theoretical and Methodological Framework and its Application in the Context of Islam," *Human Rights Review* 5, no. 3 (2004): 5.

6. In this regard see also An-Na'im, "Towards a Cross-Cultural Approach to Defining International Standards of Human Rights," 20–29; the author underlines that

the "cross-cultural legitimacy" of universal human rights standards can be reinforced by promoting the internal debate within societies ("internal discourse") and encouraging the interaction between cultures and a "cross-cultural" dialogue."

7. ASEAN Member States are Brunei Darussalam, Cambodia, Indonesia, Lao People's Democratic Republic, Malaysia, Myanmar, Philippines, Singapore, Thailand, and Vietnam.

8. It is significant to recall that in 2009 the 42nd annual meeting of ASEAN Foreign Ministers approved the Terms of Reference ruling the ASEAN Intergovernmental Commission on Human Rights which, while having several limitations, is an intergovernmental body aiming to promote and protect human rights. For a detailed analysis about the human rights protection within the ASEAN system see, inter alia, Attilio Pisanò, "Human Rights and Sovereignty in the ASEAN Path towards a Human Rights Declaration," *Human Rights Reviews* 15, no. 4 (2014): 391–403; Theoben Jerdan C. Orosa, "ASEAN Integration in Human Rights: Problems and Prospects for Legalization and Institutionalization," *Asian Regional Integration Review* 4 (2012): 66–88; Gerard Clarke, "The Evolving ASEAN Human Rights System: The ASEAN Human Rights Declaration of 2012," *Northwestern Journal of International Human Rights* 11, no. 1 (2012): 10–15; Wu Xiaodan, "The Current Situation and Prospects for Regional System(s) of Human Rights in Asia," *Diritti umani e diritto internazionale* 6, no. 1 (2012): 45–77; Shaun Narine, "Human Rights Norms and the Evolution of ASEAN: Moving without Moving in a Changing Regional Environment," *Contemporary Southeast Asia: A Journal of International and Strategic Affairs* 34, no. 3 (2012): 365–388; Yuyun Wahyuningrum, *The ASEAN Intergovernmental Commission on Human Rights: Origins, Evolution and the Way Forward* (Strömsborg: International IDEA, 2014), 13–26, https://www.idea.int/sites/default/files/publications/the-asean-intergovernmental-commission-on-human-rights-origins-evolution-and-the-way-forward.pdf.

9. For a detailed analysis of reasons giving rise to Asian States claims see inter alia Brems, *Human Rights*, 80–81; Michael Freeman, "Human Rights: Asia and the West," in *Human Rights and International Relations in the Asia-Pacific Region*, ed. James Tuck-Hong Tang (London, New York: Painter, 1995), 13–24; Yash Ghai, "Asian Perspective on Human Rights," in *Human Rights and International Relations in the Asia-Pacific Region*, ed. James Tuck-Hong Tang (London, New York: Painter, 1995), 54–67.

10. Brunei, Malaysia and Singapore neither signed nor ratified either Treaty; Myanmar has only ratified the International Covenant on Economic, Social and Cultural Rights.

11. With regard to other human rights Treaties, the Convention on the Elimination of All Forms of Racial Discrimination was not ratified by Brunei, Malaysia, Myanmar; the Convention against Torture and Other Cruel, Inhuman or Degrading Treatment was not ratified by Brunei, Malaysia, Myanmar and Singapore; the International Convention on the Protection of the Rights of All Migrant Workers and Members of Their Families was ratified solely by Indonesia and Philippines and signed by Cambodia; the International Convention for the Protection of All Persons from Enforced Disappearance was ratified by Cambodia and signed by Indonesia, Laos and Thailand. In

order to look into the status of ratification of International human rights Treaties, see http://indicators.ohchr.org.

12. See William J. Jones, "Human Rights Treaty Ratification Behavior: The ASEAN Way of Creating Standards," in *Proceedings of International Academic Conferences*, eds. Jiri Rotschedl and Klara Čermáková (Vienna: International Institute of Social and Economic Sciences, 2014), 321–336. See also Matthew Davies, "States of Compliance? Global Human Rights Treaties and ASEAN Member States," *Journal of Human Rights* 13, no. 4 (2014): 414–433. As regards the role played by Treaties' reservations to express cultural diversity, see inter alia Eric Neumayer, "Qualified Ratification: Explaining Reservations to International Human Rights Treaties," *Journal of Legal Studies* 36, no. 2 (2007): 397–398; Yvonne Donders, "Cultural Pluralism in International Human Rights Law: The Role of Reservations," in *The Cultural Dimension of Human Rights*, ed. Ana Vrdoljak (Oxford: Oxford University Press, 2013), 205–239.

13. The Conference had among others the objectives to assess the progress made in the field of human rights and examine the issue of universality of human rights and cultural diversity; in this regard UN Doc. A/RES/45/155 and A/RES/45/155, 1.

14. Final Declaration of the Regional Meeting for Asia of the World Conference on Human Rights, Report of the Regional Meeting for Asia of the World Conference on Human Rights (Bangkok, March 29–April 2, 1993), UN Doc. A/Conf.1 57/ASRM/8 - A/Conf.157/PC/59 (1993), 3. The preparatory process of the World Conference included three regional meetings (Bangkok, Tunis and San José); every meeting ended with the adoption of a Final Declaration underlining the specific perspective of each region about human rights.

15. The AIPO is an organization created in 1977 to reinforce the cooperation between the parliaments of ASEAN States; in 2007 the AIPO's Statute was amended and the organization transformed in the ASEAN Inter-Parliamentary Assembly (AIPA).

16. It is necessary to recall that the Regional meeting for Asia was attended not only by some ASEAN members (namely Brunei Darussalam, Indonesia, Malaysia, Myanmar, Philippines, Lao People's Democratic Republic, Singapore, Thailand, and Vietnam), but also by many other Asian countries. At the same time we have to specify that, while our examination will focus on the ASEAN Countries, their claims were largely shared by all (South-East) Asian States; for an analysis of the (South-East) Asian human rights claims and some specific references to "Asian Values", see inter alia Brems, *Human Rights*, 33–54; Jack Donnelly, "Human Rights and Asian Values: A Defence of "Western" Universalism," in *The East Asian Challenge for Human Rights*, eds. Joanne R. Bauer and Daniel A. Bell (Cambridge: Cambridge University Press, 1999), 60–87; Diane K. Mauzy, "The Human Rights and "Asian Values" debate in Southeast Asia: Trying to Clarify the Key Issues," *The Pacific Review* 10, no. 2 (1997): 210–236; Xiaorang Li, "Asian Values" and the Universality of Human Rights," *Business and Society Review* 102–103 (1999): 81–87; Freeman, "Human Rights: Asia and the West," 13–24; Michael Freeman, "Human Rights, Democracy and 'Asian Values,'" *The Pacific Review* 9, no. 3 (1996): 352–366; Joseph Chan, "The Asian Challenge to Universal Human Rights: A Philosophical

Appraisal," in *Human Rights and International Relations in the Asia-Pacific Region*, ed. James Tuck-Hong Tang (London, New York: Painter, 1995), 25–38; Ghai, "Asian Perspective on Human Rights," 54–67.

17. Bangkok Declaration, Preamble, 4th and 7th recitals and 1.

18. Bangkok Declaration, Preamble, 2nd recital and 8 stating "Recognize that while human rights are universal in nature, they must be considered in the context of a dynamic and evolving process of international norm-setting, bearing in mind the significance of national and regional particularities and various historical, cultural and religious backgrounds."

19. Bangkok Declaration, 26.

20. Bangkok Declaration, Preamble, 8th recital and 5.

21. Bangkok Declaration, Preamble, 10th recital and 3-4-5.

22. In this regard see the statements made at the Vienna Conference by Ministers of Foreign Affairs of some Asian States, and in particular the Ministers of Foreign Affairs of Singapore, Malaysia and Myanmar; in this regard, see James Tuck-Hong Tang, ed., *Human Rights and International Relations in the Asia-Pacific Region* (London, New York: Painter, 1995), 222–247. In order to study how this aspect was approached by the Singapore School, see among others Bilahari Kausikan, "An Asian Approach to Human Rights," *American Society of International Law. Proceedings of the Annual Meeting* 89 (1995): 147–150; Kishore Mahbubani, "The West and the Rest," *The National Interest* 28 (1992): 3–13.

23. Bangkok Declaration, 10; Preamble, 11th recital.

24. Bangkok Declaration, Preamble, 14th recital and 9.

25. General Assembly, Declaration on the Right to Development, December, 4, 1986, UN doc. A/RES/41/128.

26. Bangkok Declaration, Preamble, 12th recital, 17–18.

27. For a comment on the Declaration see Brems, *Human Rights*, 75.

28. Similarly to the Bangkok Declaration, in the Kuala Lumpur Declaration, ASEAN States reaffirm their will to observer the UDHR and the Vienna Declaration (Preamble, 7th recital) and underline the necessity to establish a regional human rights system (Art. 21).

29. Kuala Lumpur Declaration, Preamble, 5th recital.

30. Kuala Lumpur Declaration, Art. 5.

31. Kuala Lumpur Declaration, Preamble, 3rd recital and Arts. 3–4.

32. Kuala Lumpur Declaration, Preamble, 6th recital and Art. 2 stating that "All human beings [. . .] have the right to live in dignity and to enjoy the fruits of development and should, on their part, contribute to and participate in it"; it recalls in a significant way the UN Declaration of the Right to development and in particular Art. 1.1. ("The right to development is an inalienable human right by virtue of which every human person and all peoples are entitled to participate in, contribute to, and enjoy economic, social, cultural and political development, in which all human rights and fundamental freedoms can be fully realized") and Art. 2.2 ("All human beings have a responsibility for development, individually and collectively, taking into account the need for full respect for their human rights and fundamental freedoms as well as their duties to the community, which alone can ensure the free and complete fulfilment of

the human being, and they should therefore promote and protect an appropriate political, social and economic order for development").

33. Kuala Lumpur Declaration, Art. 16; see also Arts. 6 and 19.

34. Kuala Lumpur Declaration, Arts. 1, 2, 16, 19.

35. Kuala Lumpur Declaration, Arts. 1 and 2.

36. However, this claim emerges from statements made by Ministers of Foreign Affairs of some ASEAN States at the Vienna Conference; see Tang, *Human Rights and International Relations in the Asia-Pacific Region*, 228–234. In this regard we can recall also the Joint Communiqué, adopted by the 26th ASEAN Ministerial Meeting in July 1993, after the conclusion of the Vienna Conference stating that "freedom, progress and national stability are promoted by a balance between the rights of the individual and those of the community, through which many individual rights are realized, as provided for in the Universal Declaration of Human Rights" (17); it is really interesting that, referring to individuals role into the community, the Joint Communiqué recalls the UDHR.

37. Kuala Lumpur Declaration, 4th recital stating "the peoples of ASEAN recognize that human rights have two mutually balancing aspects; those with respect to rights and freedom of the individual, and those which stipulation obligations of the individual to society and state." This balance assures that individuals can live "responsibly and humanely toward one another" (Preamble, 2nd recital), and it is a guarantee for the "freedom, progress and national stability" (Art. 1).

38. Kuala Lumpur Declaration, Art. 12.

39. Kuala Lumpur Declaration, Art. 20.

40. Brems, *Human Rights*, 77.

41. In this regard it is really significant that the Third Part of the Declaration concerns explicitly the "Basic rights and duties of citizens and States"; as underlined by Brems the Kuala Lumpur Declaration identifies more duties on States than on individuals (Brems, *Human Rights*, 77); see in particular the duties concerning the development (Art. 16), the participation of citizens and the realization of human rights (Art. 19), the promotion, implementation and protection of human rights (Art. 20), the establishment of a regional mechanism of human rights protection (Art. 21).

42. The Declaration refers to the right to life (Art. 7), the freedom of thought, opinion, conscience and religion (Art. 8), the right to property, liberty and security (Art. 9), the right to equality before the law (Art. 11), the right to freedom of expression (Art. 12), the right to freedom of association (Art. 13), the right to be presumed innocent until proven otherwise (Art. 14) and the right to participate in conduct of public affairs (Art. 15).

43. In particular the Declaration does not include any references to the prohibition of slavery, arbitrary arrest, torture and cruel, inhuman or degrading treatment or punishment, the right of recognition as a person before the law, the right to a fair trial, the right to freedom of movement and residence, the right to seek and receive asylum, the right to a nationality, the right to marry and to found a family.

44. The only reference is included in Art. 17 but it seems to be really limited: it is formulated in terms of state duty to assure equality of opportunity to access to "basic

resources, education, health services, food, housing, employment, public services and the faire distribution of income" and it makes reference only to citizens.

45. This thesis finds a confirmation in Art. 10 stating that "Any violation of these fundamental human rights should be redressed in accordance with law"; as this is the final provision of the first part of the Declaration, it seems to limit the principle of violations' redress only to "fundamental" rights.

46. For some comments concerning the ADHR see inter alia Clarke, "The Evolving ASEAN Human Rights System," 15–27; Pisanò, "Human Rights and Sovereignty in the ASEAN Path towards a Human Rights Declaration," 403–409; Catherine Shanahan Renshaw, "The ASEAN Human Rights Declaration 2012," *Human Rights Law Reviews* 13, no. 3 (2013): 557–579; Catherine Shanahan Renshaw, "The ASEAN Human Rights Declaration – Cause for Celebration?" *Regarding Rights. Academic and Activist Perspectives on Human Rights*, January 25, 2013, http://asiapacific. anu.edu.au/regarding-rights/2013/01/25/the-asean-human-rights-declaration-cause-f or-celebration/; American Bar Association, *Experts' Note on the ASEAN Human Rights Declaration* (Washington, DC: Rule of Law Initiative, 2012), http://www .americanbar.org/content/dam/aba/directories/roli/asean/asia_aba_roli_expert_note_ asean_human_rights_declaration_05121.authcheckdam.pdf; Joel Ng, "The ASEAN Human Rights Declaration: Establishing a Common Framework," RSIS Commentary. 114 (July 3, 2012), https://www.rsis.edu.sg/wp-content/uploads/2014/07/CO12 114.pdf; Joel Ng, "ASEAN Human Rights Declaration: A Pragmatic Compromise," *RSIS Commentary* 211 (November 21, 2012), https://dr.ntu.edu.sg/bitstream/han dle/10220/11694/RSIS2112012.pdf?sequence=1; William J. Jones, "Universalizing Human Rights The ASEAN Way," *International Journal of Social Sciences* 3, no. 3 (2014): 72–89.

47. ADHR, Preamble, 2nd recital: the ASEAN States declare to reaffirm "our commitment to the Universal Declaration on Human Rights, the Charter of the United Nations, the Vienna Declaration and Programme of Action, and other international human rights instruments to which ASEAN Member States are parties." For a critical comment about these "rhetorical statements", see Jones, "Universalizing Human Rights The ASEAN Way," 83.

48. See in particular the norms concerning the principle of freedom and equality of all people (Art. 1), the principle of non-discrimination (Art. 2), the right to be recognized as a person before the law, the right to equality before the law, the right to equal protection of the law (Art. 3) and the right to an effective and enforceable remedy in the case of violation of rights (Art. 5).

49. Renshaw, "The ASEAN Human Rights Declaration"; American Bar Association, *Experts' Note on the ASEAN Human Rights Declaration*; Clarke, "The Evolving ASEAN Human Rights System," 15–16.

50. The ADHR defines the right to development as "an inalienable human right by virtue of which every human person and the peoples of ASEAN are entitled to participate in, contribute to, enjoy and benefit equitably and sustainably from economic, social, cultural and political development"; this formulation corresponds to the first part of the definition of the UN Declaration on the right to development (Art. 1).

51. ADHR, Art. 37 includes a general reference to "the multidimensional aspects of the right to development" (Art. 7); UN Declaration on the right to development, Preamble, 2nd and 9th recitals, Art. 6.

52. As regards the relationship between human rights and right to development, the ADHR and the UN Declarations have some differences; the specification, included in the UN Declaration, according to which development is a process "in which all human rights and fundamental freedoms can be fully realized" (Art. 1) is absent in the ADHR; this is an important specification because it permits to define the right to development as the right assuring the effectiveness of principles of interdependency and indivisibility of human rights; see Arjun Sengupta, "On the Theory and Practice of the Right to Development," *Human Rights Quarterly* 24, no. 4 (2002): 837–889; Raajeev Malhotra, "Towards Implementing the Right to Development: A Framework for Indicators and Monitoring Methods," in *Development as a Human Right. Legal, Political and Economic Dimensions*, eds. Bård A. Andreassen and Stephen P. Marks (Antwerp, Oxford, Portland: Intersentia, 2010), 259.

53. UN Declaration on the right to development, Preamble, 12th recital, Art. 2.1.

54. In this regard see in particular Art. 36 stating "ASEAN Member States should adopt meaningful people-oriented and gender responsive development programmes."

55. See in particular UN Declaration on the right to development, Art. 2.2 stating "All human beings have a responsibility for development, individually and collectively, taking into account the need for full respect for their human rights and fundamental freedoms as well as their duties to the community, which alone can ensure the free and complete fulfilment of the human being, and they should therefore promote and protect an appropriate political, social and economic order for development."

56. As specific regards the right to development see, inter alia, Sengupta, "On the Theory and Practice of the Right to Development," 837–889; Bård A. Andreassen and Stephen P. Marks, eds., *Development as a Human Right. Legal, Political and Economic Dimensions* (Antwerp, Oxford, Portland: Intersentia, 2010); Freedman Rosa, "Third Generation' Rights: Is there Room for Hybrid Constructs within International Human Rights Law?" *Cambridge Journal of International and Comparative Law* 2, no. 4 (2013): 935–959.

57. Asian Forum for Human Rights and Development, *Open letter to Foreign Ministers at Informal ASEAN Foreign Ministers Meeting on the ASEAN Human Rights Declaration*, September 26, 2012. www.forum-asia.org/?p=15461.

58. See in particular African Charter on Human and Peoples' Rights, Art. 29.7: "The individual shall also have the duty: To preserve and strengthen positive African cultural values in his relations with other members of the society."

59. Committee on Economic, Social and Cultural rights, *General Comment 21 (2009) "Right of Everyone to Take Part in Cultural Life"* (Geneva: United Nations, UN Doc. E/C.12/GC/21, 2009), 16 (e): "Appropriateness refers to the realization of a specific human right in a way that is pertinent and suitable to a given cultural modality or context, that is, respectful of the culture and cultural rights of individuals and communities." Within this perspective for some years, the Committee has started referring to a right to cultural identity as the right of everyone to choose and express their cultural identity.

60. UNESCO Universal Declaration on Cultural Diversity (2001), Art. 4; Committee on Economic, Social and Cultural rights 2009, 19.

61. In this regard it is extremely relevant the Art. 9 which, recalling the wording of the Bangkok Declaration, states the necessity to avoid double standards and politicization in the human rights implementation and aims to limit the use of human rights as an instrument of political pressure.

62. Art. 8 ADHR: "The exercise of human rights and fundamental freedoms shall be subject only to such limitations as are determined by law solely for the purpose of securing due recognition for the human rights and fundamental freedoms of others, and to meet the just requirements of national security, public order, public health, public safety, public morality, as well as the general welfare of the peoples in a democratic society."

63. See in particular International Commission of Jurists, *ICJ Condemns Fatally Flawed ASEAN Human Rights Declaration*, November 19, 2012, http://www.icj.org/icj-condemns-fatally-flawed-asean-human-rights-declaration/.

64. American Bar Association, *Experts' Note on the ASEAN Human Rights Declaration*, 7.

65. See in particular ASEAN Lesbian, Gay, Bisexual, Transgender, Intersex and Queer People's Caucus Statement, *Inclusion of SOGI issues and Rights in the ACSC/APF and in the ASEAN Human Rights Declaration*, March 29, 2012, https://www.outrightinternational.org/content/inclusion-sogi-issues-and-rights-acscapf-and-asean-human-rights-declaration.

66. See for example the European Convention on Human Rights, Art. 8 (Right to respect for private and family life), Art. 9 (Freedom of thought, conscience and religion), Art. 10 (Freedom of expression), and Art. 11 (Freedom of assembly and association).

67. Human Rights Committee, *General Comment 22 (1993) on Freedom of Thought, Conscience and Religion* (Geneva: United Nations, UN Doc. CCPR/C/21/Rev.1/Add.4, 1993).

68. Art. 6 ADHR: "The enjoyment of human rights and fundamental freedoms must be balanced with the performance of corresponding duties as every person has responsibilities to all other individuals, the community and the society where one lives."

69. See in particular International Commission of Jurists, "ICJ condemns fatally flawed ASEAN Human Rights Declaration"; Tayler, secretary general of the ICJ, stressed that "The idea of balancing the enjoyment of rights vis-à-vis duties and responsibilities of an individual turns on its head the entire raison d'être of human rights."

70. Office of the High Commissioner for Human Rights, *Asean Human Rights Declaration Should Maintain International Standards. An Open Letter from the Coordination Committee of the Special Procedures of the Human Rights Council on the draft ASEAN Human Rights Declaration* (Geneva: United Nations, 2012), http://www.ohchr.org/Documents/HRBodies/SP/LetterASEAN_Nov2012.doc.

71. Office of the High Commissioner for Human Rights, *Asean Human Rights Declaration Should Maintain International Standards*.

72. Brems, *Human Rights*, 424.

73. This dynamic was otherwise recalled during the *Travaux Préparatoires* when most drafters agreed to include a provision about duties in order to avoid that the freedoms' exercise could lead to anarchy; see Erica-Irene A. Daes, *Freedom of the Individual under Law. A Study on the Individual's Duties to the Community and the Limitations in Human Rights and Freedoms under Article 29 of the Universal Declaration of Human Rights* (New York: United Nations, 1990), 19; International Council on Human Rights, *Taking Duties Seriously: Individual Duties in International Human Rights Law. A Commentary* (Versoix: International Council on Human Rights Policy, 1999), 19; Brems, *Human Rights*, 426.

74. In this regard see Ralph Beddard, "Duties of Individuals under International and Regional Human Rights Instruments," *The International Journal of Human Rights* 3, no. 4 (1999): 30–48.

75. African Charter on Human and Peoples' Rights, Preamble, 7th recital (underlining added); see also Arts. 27-28-29.

76. American Declaration of the Rights and Duties of Man, Preamble, 2nd recital (underlining added); see in particular the second chapter (Arts. 29-38) of the Declaration including a list of individual duties.

77. UDHR, Art. 29: "Everyone has duties to the community in which alone the free and full development of his personality is possible." A reference to individuals duties is included also in the Preamble of the International Covenant on Civil and Political Rights (5th recital).

78. See in particular the amendment proposed by the Cuban delegate stating that "In all human activity, [. . .] rights and duties are indissolubly linked with one another"; see General Assembly, Third Committee, *Draft International Declaration of Human Rights. Amendment to Art. 23 to 27 of the draft Declaration: Cuba* (New York: United Nations, UN Doc. A/C.3/261, 1948), p. 2. See Daes, *Freedom of the Individual under Law*, 19; the Author highlights: "The most important task, [. . .], in promoting human progress was to find the proper *balance between the interests of the individual and the interests of society and between individual and collective rights*" (emphases added).

79. In this regard see Brems, "Reconciling Universality and Diversity in International Human Rights," 15.

80. For our analysis it is sufficient to recall Committee on the Elimination of Discrimination against Women, Committee on the Rights of the Child, *Joint General Recommendation/General Comment No. 31 of the Committee on the Elimination of Discrimination against Women and No. 18 of the Committee on the Rights of the Child on Harmful Practices* (Geneva: United Nations, UN Doc. CEDAW/C/GC/31-CRC/C/GC/18, 2014). On this occasion the Committees underlined that the prevention of harmful practices can be achieved "through a rights-based approach to changing social and cultural norms"; this approach must include "the active participation of all relevant stakeholders, especially women and girls" (59–60).

Chapter 11

The Color Curtain

Richard Wright on Race, Rights, and Western Values

Anders Walker

Few American authors railed more bitterly against the United States[1] than Richard Wright, an African American writer born on a plantation in Mississippi in 1908 who published several novels, short stories, and memoirs focusing on the violence and racism that beset the American South, and also the American North, in the twentieth century. Wright's best known work, a 1940 novel named *Native Son,* described the descent of a young black male into a labyrinth of racism in Chicago, a city that Wright had escaped to in 1927. By 1947, Wright had grown so tired of discrimination in America that he left the United States for good and resettled in France, only to encounter the legacies of European colonialism—a sobering experience that led him to reevaluate the core principles upon which his own native country was founded. Though unapologetic in his indictment of America's treatment of blacks, Wright nevertheless came to appreciate the central role that rights played in American legal culture, recognizing that rights-based systems relied on the primacy of the individual over the group and on reason over what he termed "religion"; both traits that he found lacking in the developing world.

Wright's faith in Western values provides an intriguing intercultural counterpoint to his indictments of the United States, particularly at a moment in American history when racism became a sensitive issue in foreign relations, and a new focal point of federal policy. The same year that Wright moved to Europe, President Harry Truman endorsed a report declaring that the "protection" of civil rights was a "national problem" and that a "broad and immediate program" was warranted to address the plight of African Americans. Such was not the case prior to World War II, when the United States tolerated racial segregation in the American South and also in the federal government. The rise of Nazi Germany, however, coupled with the expansion of global communism pressed Truman to reconsider formal policies of racial discrimination in the United States, a pivot that emerged in his report "To Secure These Rights," which lamented that "Communist propagandists" had "tried to prove our democracy an empty fraud, and our nation a consistent oppressor of underprivileged people." To counter this narrative, Truman endorsed a robust agenda of reform that included a federal anti-lynching law, an end to poll taxes, desegregation of the military, a federal law preventing discrimination in private employment, and an end to restrictive covenants in housing.[2]

Building on the Truman report, this chapter will take a brief look at Wright's intervention in the global debate over race and rights, demonstrating that even as he remained eternally critical of the United States, so too did he express a surprising degree of faith in core American values. This became apparent in 1955, when Wright attended a conference of developing nations at Bandung, Indonesia. To understand Wright's reflections on Bandung, it is helpful to look briefly at his personal history, then to discuss how that history shaped his thoughts on the postcolonial world. By the end of his life, he came to see hope in African independence provided that emerging nations like Ghana could bridge traditional African modes with Western values and approaches to individual rights.

BACKGROUND

Much of Wright's childhood was spent in the Deep South, an experience that haunted him well into his adult years. Early memories included white children attacking him with broken bottles in Arkansas, sadistic employers in Mississippi, and a maze of prohibitions and restrictions so Byzantine that Wright had trouble doing things as simple and mundane as borrowing books from the Memphis local library. By the time he turned nineteen, he decided to leave the South for good and relocate to Chicago, thereby joining one of the largest demographic shifts in American history, what historians came to call the "Great Migration" of African Americans out of Dixie.[3]

Wright spent ten years in Chicago, working odd jobs, joining the Communist Party and writing. In 1937, he moved to New York, joined the editorial staff of the *Daily Worker* and published his first collection of short stories under the title *Uncle Tom's Children* to widespread acclaim. While working on *Children,* Wright befriended Ralph Ellison—then a 24-year-old aspirant—helping him publish some of his first pieces in left leaning journals like *New Challenge* and *New Masses,* meanwhile securing him a job with the New York Writer's Project, a subsidiary of the Works Progress

Administration. Ellison looked up to Wright, drew inspiration from his political views, and even served as best man at his wedding in 1939, to a ballet dancer named Dhima Rose Meadman.[4]

However, the two disagreed on the legacy that segregation had for African Americans, in particular the system's impact on the cultural lives of southern blacks: a rift that came to a head over a study of race relations in the United States by a Swedish sociologist named Gunnar Myrdal styled *An American Dilemma*. Ellison found the study dismissive of black culture and uncritical in its endorsement of mainstream white ideals, a point that became clear in a chapter on African American institutions. According to Myrdal, black institutions forged in the Jim Crow South not only were inferior to white institutions, but were themselves so warped by white racism that they had become pathological, ultimately exacting a negative toll on black life. Better, argued Myrdal, to abandon black institutions, whether churches, fraternal organizations, or schools for assimilation into mainstream white society. Ellison found this preposterous, complaining that black institutions provided support to the black community, while white institutions were so riven with racism and violence that they themselves had become pathological.[5]

Wright, on the other hand, hailed the project. As he saw it, Myrdal had captured the harsh nature of white racism in the South, showing how it created perverse incentives that in turn forced African Americans to debase themselves simply to survive. He told this story himself in 1945, a year after *American Dilemma* came out, in a memoir called *Black Boy* that presented a battery of grim vignettes about Jim Crow, all drawn from Wright's own experience. In one, a black elevator operator let a white patron kick him for a quarter. In another, Wright himself agreed to fight a black acquaintance before a crowd of leering whites in the hopes of earning $5. Anyone who refused to grovel before whites suffered recriminations, usually violent, and anyone who aspired to any kind of professional achievement, education, or self-fulfillment met white opposition. "This was the culture from which I sprang," he concluded before recounting his exodus to Chicago, "this was the terror from which I fled."[6]

Wright's indictment of southern culture was not new. In 1938, he panned a novel written by an African American writer and folklorist from Florida named Zora Neale Hurston who relied heavily on black vernacular speech. Titled *Their Eyes Were Watching God,* Hurston's book told the story of an African American woman named Janie who endured two failed marriages before meeting an attractive drifter named Tea Cake and establishing a fulfilling relationship, only to confront tragedy when Tea Cake suffered a rabid dog bite, forcing Jeanie to shoot him. Though later celebrated for its nuanced depiction of black life in Florida, *Their Eyes were Watching God* struck Wright as a caricature, its prose "cloaked in that facile sensuality that has dogged Negro expression since the days of Phyllis Wheatley," an African American poet who lived in the eighteenth century and extolled American ideals, even though she was a slave.[7]

Hurston, incidentally, returned fire critiquing Wright's work for being overly violent and deliberately dismissive of black achievement. Others joined, including Alain Locke—one of the key figures in the Harlem Renaissance—who expressed private reservations about *Black Boy,* and Ben Burns, who derided Wright's memoir in the prominent black newspaper the Chicago *Defender,* criticizing it for exaggerating "the hopelessness of the Negro's lot."[8]

Wright dismissed such complaints. For him, African Americans occupied an important place in American society not simply as exponents of a special culture—*a la* Hurston—but also as critics and reformers. This was particularly true, he believed, of African American writers, a point he made in 1937—a year before panning Hurston's novel—about the relationship between black culture and social change. According to Wright, "two separate cultures" had emerged in Black America, "one for the Negro masses, unwritten and unrecognized," and one for the "rising Negro bourgeoisie, parasitic and mannered." Wright respected authors like Hurston to the extent that they focused on the culture of "the masses" by focusing on folklore, an aspect of black culture that was important precisely because it contained "the collective sense of Negro life in America," and also because it held "memories and hopes" of the African American "struggle for freedom." However, Wright felt that writers active in the Harlem Renaissance, like Hurston, had focused too heavily on catering to white patrons and not enough on elevating "the consciousness of the Negro people," which was one of the black writer's primary functions. This explained Wright's critique of *Their Eyes Were Watching God,* a novel that included little mention of racial injustice and therefore struck him as more of a "minstrel" show than a bid to raise black consciousness. Of course, Hurston disagreed, seeing her work not simply as a form of plantation entertainment but rather a tribute to the creative genius of the black folk, a literary and artistic contribution that elevated the profile of African America, for black and white alike.[9]

To the extent that Wright believed black writers should write for white audiences, he leaned toward rubbing their noses in the excrement of their own racism, not celebrating black culture. He excoriated the South for its mistreatment of African Americans in books like *Black Boy* and *Uncle Tom's Children,* and indicted the North as well, a point he made vividly in 1940 by publishing a novel about a black protagonist named Bigger Thomas who worked for a wealthy white family in Chicago, "the Daltons," only to find himself committing two brutal murders. Thomas's first victim, Mary, was the Daltons's daughter: a budding communist who invited Thomas out with some friends only to become severely drunk, leaving Bigger to help her home and into bed. Once in her room, however, Thomas feared being discovered by Mary's mother, prompting him to silence her with a pillow, accidentally killing her. To evade detection, Thomas burned Mary's body in the family furnace, killed his girlfriend Bessie after she suspected he was responsible, and ended up on a death row.[10]

Though Wright prepared himself for white backlash, critics hailed it. The *Atlantic Monthly* declared it a "performance of great talent," while the *New York Times* found it "enormously stirring," an "American tragedy" evocative of Theodore Dreiser. Most understood *Native Son* to be a tale not of innate criminality, but the perverse incentives engendered by northern racism. For example, Mr. Dalton, a real estate broker, made his fortune by renting apartments to African Americans in overcrowded, segregated ghettos. Thomas lived in one such apartment and found himself with few opportunities to support his family other than menial jobs or crime, an ironic dilemma given that he chose a menial job but then felt it necessary to commit violence after Mary Dalton's mother—who was blind—walked in on him and her daughter. As Wright saw it, Bigger's actions were completely rational given the racist norms of the day. He did not kill Mary Dalton because he was innately violent, but because he was responding to irrational American taboos against interracial sex. Similarly, Bigger killed his black girlfriend not out of primal rage, but a desperate bid to escape the electric chair by preventing her from serving as a witness against him.[11]

Even as *Native Son* became a bestseller, Wright found himself hounded by many of the same problems that had stalked Bigger Thomas, including discrimination in housing. He first encountered this while trying to purchase a house in New York's quaint Greenwich Village neighborhood in 1945, only to meet a snarl of restrictions against black buyers that forced him to hide his identity. When white neighbors finally learned his race, they moved to outbid him, a desperate gambit that failed but outraged the black author. Wright and his wife then moved to purchase a country house in Vermont only to make a deposit and then suffer rejection once again when the seller learned that he was black. Wright later identified this final humiliation as a pivotal moment in his Sisyphean struggle against American racism, an event that convinced him to leave the United States for good.[12]

Wright relocated his family to France in 1947, a move that inspired him to take his critique of the United States and apply it to the West generally. From Europe, Wright saw that many of the same evils he had witnessed in America were also inherent in European colonialism. By colonizing Africa and Asia, observed Wright, European nations like England, Holland, and France had spread racism around the globe, threatening a violent backlash by colonial peoples. To avoid such a cataclysm, Wright came to believe that Western powers needed to aid in the creation of postcolonial states, but not along lines that replicated Western imperialism. Instead, the West should aid in the creation of independent nations where Asians and Africans could exercise independence free from white violence and control.

Though Wright derided Hurston's depictions of black life in Florida, he shared her view that vibrant black communities were normatively more attractive than integrated communities, in part because integrated communities tended to be dominated by condescending, racist whites. He did not oppose desegregation in theory, but remained convinced that white racism was so pervasive in America that even integrated institutions would prove oppressive to blacks. France, on the other hand, struck him as an alternative, an integrated land that lacked America's history of slavery and segregation, and therefore was more conducive to black liberation. This proved true, to some extent, though Wright soon soured on French colonialism, a project that included its own forms of virulent racism, a sentiment that led him to focus his attention on Africa.

Wright visited Africa in 1953, sailing by ship from Liverpool, England to Sierra Leone and then to the Gold Coast, a sub-Saharan British colony that was in the midst of a rousing movement for independence, led by a former educator named Kwame Nkrumah. Nkrumah had studied in the United States and England, met W. E. B. Du Bois, and had come to the conclusion that Africa needed to gain independence from white rule in order to advance, meanwhile developing a new culture along African lines, free from economic exploitation, respectful of African traditions, and devoid of condescending white rulers. By the time Wright arrived, in 1953, Nkrumah had risen to the position of prime minister, and seemed on the verge of breaking from Britain.

Wright puzzled at many aspects of African society, its "disorder," "polygamy," and "strange burial customs," but grew to respect Nkrumah, for overcoming "tribal differences" and building "a bridge between tribalism and twentieth-century forms of political mass organization." Nkrumah seemed to Wright an inspirational figure who had restored African confidence after the British "smashed" it with an obnoxious insistence on Anglo Saxon cultural supremacy. "All that the African personality seemed to have gotten from the West," observed Wright, "was a numbed defensiveness, a chronic lack of self-confidence." Nkrumah's vision of an independent state defied this, holding out hope for a new, decidedly African future.[13]

THE BANDUNG CONFERENCE

Even as Wright took heart in the Gold Coast, he also saw a looming danger in the prospect of independence, a possibility that Africans might simply adopt a version of the same racism that their white overlords had embraced, mixing it with superstition and religion—two forces that threatened progress. Wright crystallized these ideas in April 1955, two years after his Africa trip, when he traveled to the former Dutch Colony of Indonesia to report on a conference held by postcolonial nations at Bandung. No whites were allowed, and Wright proved to be one of the few Americans to attend. He was struck by two things. First, he recoiled at the heavy-handed legacy of Dutch colonial rule, its absolute insistence on treating people of color as servants and inferiors— much like the British had done in the Gold Coast. Second, Wright became intrigued by the surging racial and religious fervor exhibited by many of the participants at the conference, all from former European colonies.

Wright conveyed his views of the Bandung conference in a book about the meeting entitled *The Color Curtain,* published in 1956. "It was strange," he recalled, "how the moment I left the dry, impersonal, abstract world of the West, I encountered at once: religion . . . . And it was a passionate, unyielding religion, feeding on itself, sufficient unto itself." Wright had suffered negative experiences with religion as a child in the South, mainly from his Seventh Day Adventist grandparents, and found the developing world's religiosity frightening, "irrationalism meeting irrationalism," as he put it. To Wright, the developing world's adherence to religion made it "static," a condition that needed to be addressed before poverty, illiteracy, and other problems could be ameliorated. While some blamed Western imperialism for this, Wright found indigenous causes as well, in particular a tendency by Africans and Asians to view society not from the standpoint of individuals, but rather through "collectivist visions," that lent themselves "toward hierarchy," and "social collectivities of an organic nature."[14]

Collectivist thinking struck Wright as rooted, again, in religion—a sense that social organization stemmed from a communalist, almost sacred, view of the world. "It was no accident," he observed, "that most of the delegates were deeply religious men representing governments and vast populations steeped in mystical visions of life." Third world mysticism struck Wright as fertile ground for racism, particularly anti-white racism stoked by centuries of colonial rule. "Racial feeling manifested itself at Bandung in a thousand subtle forms," he observed, noting that one of the few things uniting the diverse participants was their hatred for Europeans. "The feeling of inferiority that the white man has instilled in these people corrodes their very souls," he noted, opening the door to hostile, anti-Western alliances.[15]

Though critical of colonial attitudes toward indigenous people, Wright also understood that certain aspects of the "dry, impersonal, abstract world of the West" were positive. He praised the West's "secular, rational base of thought and feeling," and explained that it was in many ways superior to the "traditional and customary" worldviews that had "stagnated" developing countries "for centuries." This included the West's adherence to science, which had debunked racial stereotypes, and also America's commitment to rights, which Wright found rooted in a larger concept of the individual as the primary unit of society. Rights had no place, he surmised, in a truly communal world. Nor did rights have any place in a truly religious state.[16]

However, the West's commitment to rights and science were undermined by its irrational commitment to white supremacy, a problem that had actually stirred anti-colonial sentiment across the globe, threatening a violent, reactionary backlash. As Wright saw it, Europe's racist actions engendered equal and opposite reactions—much like American racism engendered Bigger Thomas—jeopardizing that which was most positive about European and American civilization. "It is not difficult to imagine Moslems, Hindus, Buddhists, and Shintoists," warned Wright, "launching vast crusades, armed with modern weapons, to make the world safe for their mystical notions." The entire conference at Bandung seemed to simmer with resentment and thoughts of revenge against Europeans, threatening new global alliances hostile to Western interests. Because these alliances were forged on religious and racial ground, believed Wright, military solutions were futile. "To wage war against racial and religious emotion," cautioned Wright, "is ultimately meaningless and impossible; atom and hydrogen bombs would only inflame racial and religious passions."[17]

Like Max Weber, Wright saw the world through the lens of culture—with efficient, scientific, secular nations rising above what he perceived to be inefficient, superstitious, "pagan" nations. Even some European nations struck Wright as pagan, including Spain, a country "as sacred and irrational as the sacred state of Akan in the African jungle." Wright's thoughts on Spain, which he toured in 1954, led him to believe that certain isolated segments of the West were themselves rooted in superstition and irrational thought—like the American South. "I grew up in the Methodist and Seventh Day Adventist churches," noted Wright, "and I saw and observed religion in my childhood; and these people are religious."[18]

The South's religiosity, to Wright's mind, was not unconnected to its unflinching adherence to racism. Both were rigid ideologies that stifled individuality and trampled creative self-expression. They were similar, he believed, to communism, also a rigid ideology that demanded conformity and discouraged diversity, whether artistic or political. Though originally enthusiastic about communism, Wright became increasingly disenchanted with its authoritarian leanings, both in the Soviet Union and the United States, ultimately abandoning the Party in 1944. While listening to the Chinese delegates at Bandung, Wright came to fear that communists might exploit Third World religiosity and racial solidarity for their own ends, merging the communalism of traditional societies with the communalism endorsed by Marxist theory. China was an obvious candidate for such an operation, since it had itself melded Marxist thought onto thousands of years of Chinese culture, a process that it could conceivably replicate throughout the developing world, essentially "rip[ping]" postcolonial countries "out of the traditional and customary soil in which they have stagnated for centuries."[19]

However, communism exacted an even steeper price than American racism. Joseph Stalin's policies of collectivization and political consolidation in Russia and Ukraine alone had led to millions of deaths, both through political persecution and famine, leading Wright to warn of communism's appetite for "limitless murder and terror, its wholesale sacrifices of human freedom and human life." This was arguably even worse than Jim Crow, which for all its violence had never even come close to the number that Stalin killed in the name of egalitarian, proletarian ideals. Yet, if the West did not reach out to the developing world, precisely such promises of equality might drive that world into communist hands. "I think that the very intensity of their racial and religious conditioning would," argued Wright, "lead these masses to accept such a desperate path," for their traditional communalist cultures had "prepared them to re-enact on a global scale ceremonies of collective crucifixion and rituals of mass rebirth." Faced with this imminent threat of "horror and blood," Wright concluded by wondering whether there was "no stand-in for these sacrifices, no substitute for these sufferings?"[20]

The answer, he concluded, was Western intervention. Not imperial intervention aimed at extracting resources from undeveloped nations, to be sure, but an active effort aimed at helping postcolonial states develop into independent, secular powers, in part by educating "static" peoples in secular, Western values but also by aiding in the construction of functioning economies that did not hinge on sending raw materials to Europe only to then demand that colonials buy them back once they had been made into finished goods. It would be "far preferable," reasoned Wright, for the West to assist African economic development, even if it meant a "radical adjustment of the West's own systems of society and economics," than to face militant hordes buoyed and sustained by racial and religious passions."[21]

Wright elaborated on these ideas back in Europe, first at his home in Ailly, France, then on a speaking tour of Scandinavia. Swedish publishing house Bonniers invited him to Stockholm in November 1956, culminating in a series of lectures in a string of cities that built on some of the same ideas that he had developed in the Gold Coast and Bandung, all of which Wright published in a 1957 book entitled *White Man Listen!* Standing before auditoriums full of blue eyed Nordics, Wright talked of the Gold Coast, describing how black revolutionaries like Kwame Nkrumah had drawn from European ideas and merged them with indigenous traditions to forge a new national identity, calling for universal male suffrage and a representative—rather than imperial—government, meanwhile bringing back the "ancient national dress of the Gold Coast, togas draped about the body in Roman style."[22] The result was not an emulation of Europe so much as a reinvention of Africa with the help of specific Western ideas, a sudden jump "into the twentieth century, with its present tribal structure and all."[23] For Wright, the role of Europeans as overlords was over, and the way forward was for Europeans to check their privilege and engage Africa "in the spirit of civil servants rather than civil masters."[24] Meanwhile, there was also an important role for Europeans to play in Europe, building on the critique of Western imperialism that leaders like Nkrumah had pioneered in Africa. "In my opinion," declared Wright, "the greatest aid that any white Westerner can give Africa is by becoming a missionary right in the heart of the Western world, explaining to his own people what they have done to Africa."[25] It was a role that Wright himself had played, and was playing again, on a global scale.

Behind Wright's campaign lurked a basic faith in core Western values like reason, science, the individual, and rights. Though Europeans and Americans had been wrong to embrace racism, believed Wright, the notion that society should move away from collectivist approaches to government was one that Wright associated with Western thought: a basic belief that led him to adopt a remarkably American approach to African reform. Indeed, the South's racism struck Wright as itself un-American, part of a fundamentalist, superstitious worldview that had placed the region behind even in the United States. Recovering Wright's views on this matter, based on the idea that the American South was itself a type of developing nation, helps explain both Wright's critique of American racism, and also his endorsement of core American ideals.

NOTES

1. This chapter was previously published in Anders Walker, *The Burning House: Jim Crow and the Making of Modern America* (Yale University Press, 2018).

2. "To Secure These Rights: The Report of the President's Committee on Civil Rights" (1947) available at www.trumanlibrary.org/civilrights/srights1.htm#contents.

3. Richard Wright, *Uncle Tom's Children* (1938) reprinted in Richard Wright, *Early Works* (New York: Library of America, 1991), 225–237.

4. Lawrence P. Jackson, "The Birth of the Critic: The Literary Friendship of Ralph Ellison and Richard Wright," *American Literature* 72 (June 2000), 324–335.

5. Ralph Ellison, "An American Dilemma: A Review," in *Shadow and Act* (New York: Random House, 1964), 303–317.

6. Richard Wright, *Black Boy* (1945), reprinted in Wright, *Early Works*, 246. For Wright on Myrdal, see Michel Fabre, *The Unfinished Quest of Richard Wright* (Urbana: University of Illinois Press, 1993), 270.

7. Richard Wright, "Review of Their Eyes Were Watching God," *New Masses,* October 5, 1937, 22–23. For Wright's views on Wheatley, see Richard Wright, *White Man Listen!* (1957, New York: Anchor, 1964), 76.

8. Fabre, *The Unfinished Quest of Richard Wright*, 281.

9. Richard Wright, "Blueprint for Negro Writing," (1937) reprinted in *Within the Circle: An Anthology of African American Literary Criticism from the Harlem Renaissance to the Present,* ed. Angelyn Mitchell (Durham: Duke University Press, 1994), 99–101.

10. Richard Wright, *Native Son* (New York: Harper, 1940). For Wright's critique of American culture, see Fabre, *The Unfinished Quest of Richard Wright,* 258.

11. Charles Poore, "Books of the Times," *New York Times,* March 1, 1940, 25.

12. Fabre, *Wright,* 275–276, 297.

13. Richard Wright, *Black Power* (London: Dennis Dobson, 1954), 55, 60, 104.

14. Richard Wright, *The Color Curtain* (1956, Jackson: University Press of Mississippi, 1994), 73, 78.

15. Wright, *The Color Curtain*, 140, 175, 187.

16. Ibid., 219, 220.

17. Ibid., 217, 218.

18. Richard Wright, *Pagan Spain* (1957, New York: HarperCollins, 1995), 229; Wright, *The Color Curtain*, 15.

19. Wright, *The Color Curtain*, 220.

20. Ibid., 220–21.

21. Ibid., 217.

22. Richard Wright, *White Man Listen!* (1958, New York: Harper Perennial, 2008), 133.

23. Wright, *White Man Listen,* 139.

24. Ibid., 140.

25. Ibid., 135.

Bibliography

Abebe, Semahagn G. "The Relevance of African Culture in Building Modern Institutions and the Quest for Legal Pluralism." *Saint Louis University Law Journal* 57, no. 2 (2013): 429–46.

Ackerly, Brooke A. *Universal Human Rights in a World of Difference.* Cambridge: Cambridge University Press, 2008.

Adams, Bruce. *The Politics of Punishment: Prison Reform in Russia 1863–1917.* DeKalb: Northern Illinois University Press, 1996.

Afanasieva, Dasha. "Turkey will not Give Syrian Refugees Right to Work – Labour Minister." *Reuters*, August 7, 2015. Accessed October 26, 2015. http://uk.reute rs.com/article/uk-turkey-syria-refugees-workers-idUKKCN0QC1UH20150807.

"After Paris, Drawbridges Up?" *The Economist*, November 21, 2015. Accessed February 6, 2016. http://www.economist.com/news/europe/21678832-schengen-syste m-open-borders-was-already-under-pressure-latest-terrorist-attacks-may.

Aleinikoff, Alexander T. "From Dependence to Self-Reliance: Changing the Paradigm in Protracted Refugee Situations." Transatlantic Council on Migration. Accessed July 15, 2016. http://www.migrationpolicy.org/research/dependence-self -reliance-changing-paradigm-protracted-refugee-situations.

Ali, Ameer. *Mahommedan Law, Vol. II.* Calcutta: Thacker, Spink, and Co., 1908.

Allport, Gordon W. *The Nature of Prejudice.* Reading, MA: Addison-Wesley, 1954.

AL-MARGHINANI, Burhan al-Din al-Farghani. *The Hedaya, or Guide; A Commentary on the Mussalman Laws,* vol. II. Translated by Charles Hamilton. London: T. Bensley, 1791.

American Bar Association. *Experts' Note on the ASEAN Human Rights Declaration.* Washington, DC: Rule of Law Initiative, 2012. http://www.americanbar.org/ content/dam/aba/directories/roli/asean/asia_aba_roli_expert_note_asean_human_r ights_declaration_05121.authcheckdam.pdf.

Amos, Deborah. "Gulf Countries Face Criticism for Refusing to Resettle Syrian Refugees." *NPR*, October 6, 2015. Accessed October 21, 2015. http://www.npr. org/2015/09/22/442582465/gulf-countries-face-criticism-for-refusing-to-resettle- syrian-refugees.

Anderson, Kristen. "Lessons in Whiteness: German Immigrants and Racial Ideology in Nineteenth-Century America." In *Cross-Cultural History and the Domestication of Otherness*, edited by Michal Jan Rozbicki and George O. Ndege, 173–91. New York: Palgrave Macmillan, 2012.

Anderson, Mark. "Norway Minister Threatens to Deport Eritrean Migrants." *The Guardian*, June 27, 2014. Accessed October 21, 2015. http://www.theguardian.co m/global-development/2014/jun/27/norway-deport-eritrean-migrants-asylum-see kers-immigration.

Anderson, Michael. "Islamic Law and Colonial Encounter in British India." In *Institutions and their Ideologies: A SOAS South Asia Reader*, edited by David Arnold and Peter Robb, 165–85. Richmond, Surrey: Curzon Press, 1993.

András Sajó, ed. *Human Rights with Modesty: The Problem of Universalism.* Leiden: Martinus Nijhoff Publishers, 2004.

Anisov V. and É. Sereda. *Litopys zhyttia i tvorchosti T. H. Shevchenka.* Kiev: Derzhavne Vydavnitstvo, 1959.

An-Na'im, Abdullahi Ahmed. "Banning Sharia Is a 'Red Herring': The Way Forward for All Americans." *Saint Louis University Law Journal* 57, no. 2 (Winter 2013): 287–96.

An-Na'im, Abdullahi. "Towards a Cross-cultural Approach to Defining International Standards of Human Rights: The Meaning of Cruel, Inhuman or Degrading Treatment or Punishment." In *Human Rights in Cross-Cultural Perspectives. A Quest for Consensus*, edited by Abdullahi An-Na'im. Philadelphia: University of Pennsylvania Press, 1991.

An-Na'im, Abdullahi Ahmed. *Towards an Islamic Reformation: Civil Liberties, Human Rights, and International Law.* Syracuse, NY: Syracuse University Press, 1990.

Anthony, Augustine. "Hard-Line Pakistani Students Release Chinese Women." *Reuters*, June 23, 2007. http://www.reuters.com/article/us-pakistan-mosque-idUSS P14126820070623.

"Anti-Muslim Sentiments Fairly Commonplace." Gallup. Accessed February 17, 2016. http://www.gallup.com/poll/24073/antimuslim-sentiments-fairly-commonpl ace.aspx.

Appadurai, Arjun. "Number in the Colonial Imagination." In *Orientalism and the Postcolonial Predicament: Perspectives on South Asia*, edited by Carol Breckenridge and Peter van der Veer, 314–39. Philadelphia: University of Pennsylvania Press, 1993.

Arendt, Hannah. *The Origins of Totalitarianism.* London: Allen & Unwin, 1961.

Asad, Talal, et al. *Is Critique Secular? Blasphemy, Injury and Free Speech.* Berkeley: University of California Press, 2009.

Asad, Talal. "The Concept of Cultural Translation in British Social Anthropology." In *Writing Culture: The Poetics and Politics of Ethnography*, edited by James Clifford and George E. Marcus, 141–64. Berkeley: University of California Press, 1986.

ASEAN Lesbian, Gay, Bisexual, Transgender, Intersex and Queer People's Caucus Statement. *Inclusion of SOGI Issues and Rights in the ACSC/APF and in the ASEAN Human Rights Declaration.* March 29, 2012. https://www.outrightinter

national.org/content/inclusion-sogi-issues-and-rights-acscapf-and-asean-human-ri
ghts-declaration.

Ashton, Glenn. "Helping Africa to Help Itself: The Ideology of Food." The South
African Civil Society Information Service. Accessed October 20, 2015. http://
sacsis.org.za/site/article/1744.

Asian Forum for Human Rights and Development. *Open letter to Foreign Ministers
at Informal ASEAN Foreign Ministers Meeting on the ASEAN Human Rights Declaration.* September 26, 2012. www.forum-asia.org/?p=15461.

"Asylum in the UK." UNHCR. Accessed July 17, 2016. http://www.unhcr.org/en-u
s/asylum-in-the-uk.html.

Ayalon, David. *Eunuchs, Caliphs and Sultans: A Study in Power Relationships.*
Jerusalem: Magnes Press, Hebrew University, 1999.

Bachelard, Gaston. *Le Rationalisme Appliqué.* Paris: PUF, 1969.

Bahaduri, Amit. "On the Formation of Usurious Interest Rates in Backward Agriculture." *Cambridge Journal of Economics* 1, no. 4 (1977): 341–52.

Baillie, N. B. E. *The Digest of Moohummudan Law.* London: Smith, Elder, &
Co., 1875.

Barnett, Don. "The Progress of Refugees: How Are We Doing?" Center for Immigration Studies. Accessed November 6, 2013. http://www.cis.org/Barnett/Refugees-
Self-Sufficient.

Barrett, Ted. "Senate Democrats Block Syrian Refugee Bill." *CNN*, January 20, 2016.
Accessed February 6, 2016. http://www.cnn.com/2016/01/20/politics/syrian-refu
gees-senate-vote-2016/.

Barrier, Gerald. *The Punjab Alienation of Land Bill of 1900. Monograph and
Occasional Paper Series Number Two.* Durham: Duke University Program in
Comparative Studies on Southern Asia, 1966.

Bashir, Shahzad. "Islamic Tradition and Celibacy." In *Celibacy and Religious Traditions*, edited by Carl Olson, 133–50. New York: Oxford University Press, 2007.

Basu, Kaushik. "Implicit Interest Rates, Usury and Isolation in Backward Agriculture." *Cambridge Journal of Economics* 8, no. 2 (1984): 145–59.

Bauman, Zygmunt and Citlali Rovirosa-Madrazo. *Living on Borrowed Time: Conversations with Citlali Rovirosa-Madrazo.* Cambridge: Polity Press, 2007.

Baumgartner, Michael. "Paul Klee: From Structural Analysis and Morphogenesis
to Art." In *The Philosophical Vision of Paul Klee*, edited by John Sallis. Leiden:
Brill, 2014.

Baxi, Upendra. *The Future of Human Rights.* Oxford: Oxford University Press, 2002.

Bayly, Susan. *Caste, Society and Politics in India.* Cambridge: Cambridge University
Press, 1999.

Beddard, Ralph. "Duties of Individuals under International and Regional Human
Rights Instruments." *The International Journal of Human Rights* 3, no. 4 (1999):
30–48.

Benedict, Ruth. *Patterns of Culture.* Boston: Houghton Mifflin Co., 1934.

Benner, Marie T., Aree Muangsookjarouen, Egbert Sondorp, and Joy Townsend.
"Neglect of Refugee Participation." *Forced Migration Review* 30 (2008). Accessed
October 22, 2015. http://www.fmreview.org/FMRpdfs/FMR30/25.pdf.

Bershidsky, Leonid. "Why Germany Welcomes Refugees." *Bloomberg View*, September 9, 2015. Accessed October 22, 2015. http://www.bloombergview.com/articles/2015-09-09/why-germany-welcomes-refugees.

Bhaba, Jacqueline, "Internationalist Gatekeepers?: The Tension Between Asylum Advocacy and Human Rights." *Harvard Human Rights Journal* 15 (2002): 155–82.

Bhambhra, Gurminder K. *Rethinking Modernity: Postcolonialism and the Sociological Imagination*. New York: Palgrave Macmillan, 2007.

Bhambra, Gurminder K. *Rethinking Modernity: Postcolonialism and the Sociological Imagination*. Basingstoke: Palgrave Macmillan, 2009.

Bielfeldt, Heiner. "Muslim Voices in the Human Rights Debate." *Human Rights Quarterly* 17, no. 4 (1995): 587–617.

Biernat, Monica, Theresa K. Vescio, Shelley A. Theno, and Christian S. Crandall. "Values and Prejudice: Toward Understanding the Impact of American Values on Outgroup Attitudes." In *The Psychology of Values: The Ontario Symposium on Personality and Social Psychology*, edited by Clive Seligman et al., 153–90. Mahwah, NJ: L. Erlbaum Associates, 1996.

Boehm, Gottfried. "Genesis: Paul Klee's Temporalization of Form." In *The Philosophical Vision of Paul Klee*, edited by John Sallis. Leiden: Brill, 2014.

Bogusławski, Józef. "Wspomnienia Sybiraka: Pamiętniki Józefa Bogusławskiego." *Nowa reforma* 286 (1896).

Boland, Barbara. "Why the Islamic Gulf States Aren't Taking Syrian Refugees." *Washington Examiner,* September 4, 2015. Accessed July 17, 2016. http://www.washingtonexaminer.com/why-the-islamic-gulf-states-arent-taking-syrian-refugees/article/2571469.

Bouchard, Gérard. "What is Interculturalism?" *McGill Law Journal - Revue de droit de McGill* 56, no. 2 (2011): 461.

Bourdieu, Pierre. *Distinction: A Social Critique of the Judgement of Taste*. London: Routledge, 1979.

Brems, Eva. "Reconciling Universality and Diversity in International Human Rights: A Theoretical and Methodological Framework and its Application in the Context of Islam." *Human Rights Review* 5, no. 3 (2004): 5–21.

Brems, Eva. *Human Rights: Universality and Diversity*. The Hague: Martinus Nijhoff Publishers, 2001.

Brenner, Yermi. "Sweden's Refugee Policy sets High Standard." *Al Jazeera*, November 24, 2013. Accessed October 21, 2015. http://www.aljazeera.com/indepth/features/2013/11/sweden-refugee-policy-sets-high-standard-2013112485613526863.html.

Brewer, Marilynn B. and Samuel L. Gaertner. "Toward Reduction of Prejudice: Intergroup Contact and Social Categorization." In *Blackwell Handbook of Social Psychology: Intergroup Processes*, edited by Rupert Brown and Samuel L. Gaertner. Malden, MA: Blackwell, 2002.

Brown, Richard D. *Modernization: The Transformation of American Life, 1600–1865*. New York: Hill and Wang, 1976.

Brown, Rupert, James Vivian, and Miles Hewstone. "Changing Attitudes through Intergroup Contact: The Effects of Group Membership Salience." *European Journal of Social Psychology 29,* no. 5–6 (1999): 741–764.

Budanova, N. F. and G. M. Fridlender, eds. *Letopis' zhizni i tvorchestva F. M. Dostoevskogo v trekh tomakh 1821–1881,* 3 vols. St. Petersburg: Gumanitarnoe agentstvo "Akademicheskii proekt," 1995.

Burke, Peter. *Cultural Hybridity.* Cambridge: Polity Press, 2009.

Butler, Daren and Ece Toksabay. "Troubling Image of Drowned Boy Captivates, Horrifies." *Reuters,* September 2, 2015. Accessed February 5, 2016. http://www.reuters.com/article/us-europe-migrants-turkey-idUSKCN0R20IJ20150902.

Caban, Wiesław. *Z Orenburga do Paryża: Bronisław Zaleski 1820–1880.* Kielce: Wydawnictwo Akademii Świętokrzyskiej, 2006.

Calhoun, Craig, ed. *Rethinking Secularism.* New York: Oxford University Press, 2011.

Çali, Başak and Saladin Meckled-García. "Introduction: Human Rights Legalized: Defining, Interpreting, and Implementing an Ideal." In *The Legalization of Human Rights: Multidisciplinary Perspectives on Human Rights and Human Rights Law,* edited by Başak Çali and Saladin Meckled-García. Abingdon: Routledge, 2006.

Campbell, Tom, Keith D. Ewing, and Adam Tomkins, eds. *Sceptical Essays on Human Rights.* Oxford: Oxford University Press, 2003.

Cappelletti, Paolo. *L'inafferrabile visione. Pittura e scrittura in Paul Klee.* Milano: Jaca Book, 2003.

Casanova, José. "The Secular, Secularizations, Secularisms." In *Rethinking Secularism,* edited by Craig Calhoun, Mark Juergensmeyer, and Jonathan VanAntwerpen. New York: Oxford University Press, 2011.

Casanova, José. "Rethinking Secularization: A Global Comparative Perspective." *The Hedgehog Review* (Spring/Summer 2006): 6.

Chabal, Patrick and Jean Pascal Daloz. *Culture Troubles: Politics and the Interpretation of Meaning.* Chicago: The University of Chicago Press, 2006.

Chan, Joseph. "The Asian Challenge to Universal Human Rights: A Philosophical Appraisal." In *Human Rights and International Relations in the Asia-Pacific Region,* edited by James Tuck-Hong Tang, 25–38. London, New York: Painter, 1995.

Charlton, Corey. "Turkey Warns it Now Expects up to One Million Syrians to Arrive at its Borders." *Daily Mail,* February 9, 2016. Accessed February 15, 2016. http://www.dailymail.co.uk/news/article-3438558/Turkey-warns-expects-600-000-Syrians-arrive-borders-warns-goal-host-refugees-OUTSIDE-Turkey.html.

Chryssochoou, Xenia. *Cultural Diversity: Its Social Psychology.* Malden, MA: Blackwell, 2004.

Clarke, Gerard. "The Evolving ASEAN Human Rights System: The ASEAN Human Rights Declaration of 2012." *Northwestern Journal of International Human Rights* 11, no. 1 (2012): 10–15.

Cohen, Roberta. "China's Forced Repatriation of North Korean Refugees Incurs United Nations Censure." Brookings, July 7, 2014. Accessed July 20, 2016. https://www.brookings.edu/opinions/chinas-forced-repatriation-of-north-korean-refugees-incurs-united-nations-censure/.

Cohn, Bernard S. "The Census, Social Structure and Objectification in South Asia." In *An Anthropologist Among the Historians and Other Essays,* edited by Bernard S. Cohn, 224–54. Delhi: Oxford University Press, 1987.

Colic-Peisker, Val. "At Least You're the Right Colour: Identity and Social Inclusion of Bosnian Refugees in Australia." *Journal of Ethnic and Migration Studies* 31 (2005): 615–38.

Committee on Economic, Social and Cultural Rights. *General Comment 21 (2009) "Right of Everyone to take part in Cultural Life."* Geneva: United Nations, UN Doc. E/C.12/GC/21, 2009), 16 (e).

Committee on the Elimination of Discrimination against Women, Committee on the Rights of the Child. *Joint General Recommendation/General Comment No. 31 of the Committee on the Elimination of Discrimination against Women and No. 18 of the Committee on the Rights of the Child on Harmful Practices.* Geneva: United Nations, UN Doc. CEDAW/C/GC/31-CRC/C/GC/18, 2014.

Conley, John M. and William M. O'Barr. *Rules Versus Relationships: The Ethnography of Legal Discourse.* Chicago: University of Chicago Press, 1990.

"Convention Relating to the Status of Refuges." United Nations Audiovisual Library of International Law. Accessed February 1, 2016. http://legal.un.org/avl/ha/prsr/prsr.html.

Cowan, Jane K, et al., eds. *Culture and Rights: Anthropological Perspectives.* Cambridge, UK: Cambridge University Press, 2001.

Cowan, Jane K., Marie-Bénédicte Dembour, and Richard A. Wilson, eds. *Culture and Rights: Anthropological Perspectives.* Cambridge: Cambridge University Press, 2001.

Cowan, Jane K., Marie-Benedict Dembour, and Richard Wilson, eds. *Culture and Rights.* Cambridge: Cambridge University Press, 2001.

Crandall, Christian S. and Amy Eshleman. "A Justification-Suppression Model of the Expression and Experience of Prejudice." *Psychological Bulletin* 129 (2003): 414–46. Accessed February 16, 2016. http://dx.doi.org/10.1037/0033-2909.129.3.414.

D'iakov, Vladimir A. *Taras Shevchenko I ego pol'skie druz'ia.* Moscow: Izadatel'stvo Nauka, 1964.

Daes, Erica-Irene A. *Freedom of the Individual under Law. A Study on the Individual's Duties to the Community and the Limitations in Human Rights and Freedoms under Article 29 of the Universal Declaration of Human Rights.* New York: United Nations, 1983.

Damasio, Antonio R. *Decartes' Error: Emotion, Reason and the Human Brain.* New York: Avon Books, 1994.

Daniel C. Thomas argues in *The Helsinki Effect: International Norms, Human Rights, and the Demise of Communism* (Princeton 2001) that the act undermined the dominant ideology of communism in Eastern Europe.

Dathan, Matt. "Germany Says it Can Take in 500,000 Syrian Refugees Every Year – As David Cameron Insists on Accepting no more than 20,000 in 5 Years." *The Independent*, September 8, 2015. Accessed February 5, 2016. http://www.independent.co.uk/news/uk/politics/germany-says-it-can-take-in-500000-syrian-refugees-every-year-as-david-cameron-insists-on-accepting-10491080.html.

Davie, Grace. "Believing Without Belonging: Just How Secular is Europe?" Transcript, Pew Research Center Bi-Annual Faith Angle Conference, December 5, 2005.

Davies, Matthew. "States of Compliance? Global Human Rights Treaties and ASEAN Member States." *Journal of Human Rights* 13, no. 4 (2014): 414–33.

Davy, Richard. "Helsinki Myths: Setting the Record Straight on the Final Act of the CSCE, 1975." *Cold War History* 9, no. 1 (2009): 1–22.

De, Rohit. "Mumtaz Bibi's Broken Heart: The Many Lives of the Dissolution of Muslim Marriages Act." *Indian Economic and Social History Review* 46, no. 1 (2009): 105–30.

De, Rohit. "The Two Husbands of Vera Tiscenko: Apostasy, Conversion, and Divorce in Late Colonial India." *Law and History Review* 28, no. 4 (2010): 1011–41.

Dembour, Marie-Bénédicte. "What are Human Rights? Four Schools of Thought." *Human Rights Quarterly* 32, no. 1 (2010): 1–20.

Dembour, Marie-Bénédicte. *Who Believes in Human Rights? Reflections on the European Convention.* New York: Cambridge University Press, 2006.

Derrett, Duncan. *Religion, Law and the State in India.* London: Faber and Faber, 1968.

Dervin, Fred. "Researching Identity and Interculturality: Moving Away from Methodological Nationalism for Good?" In *Intersecting Identities and Interculturality: Discourse and Practice*, edited by Regis Machart et al. Newcastle upon Tyne: Cambridge Scholars Publishing, 2013.

Devji, Faisal. *Muslim Zion: Pakistan as a Political Idea.* Cambridge, MA: Harvard University Press, 2013.

Dewey, John. "The Historic Background of Corporate Legal Personality." *Yale Law Journal* 35 (1926): 655–73.

D'iakov, V. A. and I. S. Miller. *Revoliutsionnoe dvizhenie v russkoi armii i vosstanie 1863 g.* Moscow: Izdatel'stvo Nauka, 1964.

Dijk, Pieter van. "Common Standard of Achievement-About Universal Validity and Uniform Interpretation of International Human Rights Norms." *Netherlands Quarterly of Human Rights* 13, no. 2 (1995): 106–21.

Donders, Yvonne. "Cultural Pluralism in International Human Rights Law: The Role of Reservations." In *The Cultural Dimension of Human Rights*, edited by Ana Vrdoljak, 205–39. Oxford: Oxford University Press, 2013.

Donnelly, Jack. "Human Rights and Human Dignity: An Analytic Critique of Non-Western Conceptions of Human Rights." *The Political Science Review* 76, no. 2 (June 1982): 303–16.

Donnelly, Jack. "The Relative Universality of Human Rights." *Human Rights Quarterly* 29, no. 2 (2007): 281–306.

Donnelly, Jack. *Realism and International Relations.* New York: Cambridge University Press, 2000.

Donnelly, Jack. *Universal Human Rights in Theory and Practice.* Ithaca: Cornell University Press, 2013.

Dostoevskii, F. M. *Polnoe Sobranie Sochinenii.* Leningrad: Izdatel'stvo Nauka, 1985.

Douzinas, Costas. *The End of Human Rights: Critical Legal Thought and the Turn of the Century.* Oxford: Hart Publishing, 2000.

"Drawing Closer to a Final Peace Deal--Colombia and FARC." *The Economist*, September 23, 2015.

Dunn, Elizabeth Cullen. "The Failure of Refugee Camps." *Boston Review*, September 28, 2015. Accessed July 16, 2016. https://bostonreview.net/editors-picks-world/elizabeth-dunn-failure-refugee-camps.

Ellison, Ralph. *"An American Dilemma*: A Review." *In Shadow and Act,* 303–17. New York: Random House, 1964.

Elzas, Sarah. "Syrian Refugees Agree to Stay in France, Despite Negative Reputation." *RFI*, September 21, 2015. Accessed February 5, 2016. http://en.rfi.fr/eur ope/20150921-syrian-refugees-agree-stay-france-despite-negative-reputation.

Eppinger, Monica E. "The Health Exception." *Georgetown Journal of Gender & the Law* 17 (2016): 665–744.

"EU Migrant Crisis: UK Will Accept More Syrian Refugees." *BBC*, September 4, 2015. Accessed February 5, 2016. http://www.bbc.co.uk/newsround/34152641.

Fabbri, Paolo. "Transcritture in Alberto Savinio: il dicibile e il visibile." In *il Verri*, no. 33 (2007). Also available at: www.paolofabbri.it/saggi/savinio.html.

Fabre, Michel. *The Unfinished Quest of Richard Wright*. Urbana: University of Illinois Press, 1993.

Fabre, Michel. *The Unfinished Quest of Richard Wright*. Urbana: University of Illinois Press, 1993.

Farmer, Paul. "An Anthropology of Structural Violence." *Current Anthropology* 45, no. 3 (2004): 305–25.

Fassin, Didier. *Humanitarian Reason. A Moral History of the Present*. Berkeley and Los Angeles: University of California Press, 2012.

Feller, Erika. "The Evolution of the International Refugee Protection Regime." *Journal of Law & Policy* 5, no. 129 (2001). Accessed October 20, 2015. http://openscho larship.wustl.edu/law_journal_law_policy/vol5/iss1/11.

Ferri, Marcella. "The Recognition of the Right to Cultural Identity under (and beyond) Human Rights International Law." *Journal of Law, Social Justice and Global Development*, forthcoming 2018.

"Figures at a Glance." UNHCR (United Nations High Commissioner for Refugees). Accessed July 28, 2016. http://www.unhcr.org/en-us/figures-at-a-glance.html.

Final Declaration of the Regional Meeting for Asia of the World Conference on Human Rights, Report of the Regional Meeting for Asia of the World Conference on Human Rights. Bangkok, 29 March - 2 April 1993. UN Doc. A/Conf.1 57/ASRM/8 - A/Conf.157/PC/59 (1993), 3.

Fish, Stanley. *Is There A Text in This Class?* Cambridge: Harvard University Press, 1980.

Fitzpatrick, Peter. "The Revolutionary Past: Decolonizing Law and Human Rights." *Metodo. International Studies in Phenomenology and Philosophy* 2, no. 1 (2014): 117–33.

Fitzpatrick, Peter. "Legal Theology: Law, Modernity and the Sacred." 32 SEATTLE U. L. REV. 321 (2008).

Flynn, Jeffrey. *Reframing the Intercultural Dialogue on Human Rights: A Philosophical Approach*. New York: Routledge, 2014.

Foucault, Michel. *The History of Sexuality, Volume 1: An Introduction*, translated by Robert Hurley. New York: Pantheon Books, 1978.

Frank, Joseph. *Dostoevsky: The Stir of Liberation, 1860–1865.* Princeton University Press, 1986.

Freeman, Michael. "Human Rights, Democracy and 'Asian Values'." *The Pacific Review* 9, no. 3 (1996): 352–66.

Freeman, Michael. "Human Rights: Asia and the West." In *Human Rights and International Relations in the Asia-Pacific Region,* edited by James Tuck-Hong Tang, 13–24. London, New York: Painter, 1995.

Gall, Carlotta. "Musharraf Resigns as Army Chief." *New York Times,* November 28, 2007. http://www.nytimes.com/2007/11/28/world/asia/28iht-28pakistan-resigned. 8509070.html?_r=0.

Gall, Carlotta. "Siege of Red Mosque Highlights Pakistan's Malaise." *New York Times,* July 8, 2007. http://www.nytimes.com/2007/07/08/world/asia/08iht-isla mabad.1.6547663.html?_r=0.

Galtung, Johan. "Violence, Peace, and Peace Research." *Journal of Peace Research* 6 (1969): 167–91.

Garcia Ponce de Leon, Paz. *Juan Gris: La Pasión por el Cubismo.* Madrid: Libsa, 2008.

General Assembly, Third Committee. *Draft International Declaration of Human Rights. Amendment to Art. 23 to 27 of the draft Declaration: Cuba.* New York: United Nations, UN Doc. A/C.3/261 (1948).

"Germany Sees Rise in Crimes Against Refugees." *Al Jazeera,* December 7, 2015. Accessed July 16, 2016. http://america.aljazeera.com/articles/2015/12/7/germany-sees-rise-in-crimes-against-refugees.html.

Gertsen, A. I. *Sobranie sochinenii v tridtsati tomakh.* 30 vols. Moscow: Akademiia Nauk SSSR, 1954–65.

Gertsen, A. I. *Sobranie sochinenii v tridtsati tomakh.* 30 vols. Moscow: Akademiia Nauk SSSR, 1954–65.

Ghai, Yash. "Asian Perspective on Human Rights." In *Human Rights and International Relations in the Asia-Pacific Region,* edited by James Tuck-Hong Tang, 54–67. London, New York: Painter, 1995.

Ghose, Jogendra Chandar. *Principles of Hindu Law,* 2nd ed. Calcutta: S. C. Ruddy & Co., 1906.

Giddens, Anthony. *New Rules for Sociological Method.* London: Hutchinson, 1976.

Gilbert, Liette and Mustafa Dikeç. "Right to the City." In *Space, Difference, Everyday Life: Reading Henri Lefebvre,* edited by Kanishka Goonewardena, Stefan Kipfen, Richard Milgrom, and Christian Schmid. Abingdon: Routledge, 2008.

Glaser, Daniel. "Dynamics of Ethnic Identification." *American Sociological Review* 23, no. 1 (1958): 31–40. Accessed July 5, 2016. http://www.jstor.org/stable/2088621.

Glendon, Mary Ann. *A World Made New, Eleanor Roosevelt and the Universal Declaration of Human Rights.* New York: Random House, 2001.

Glendon, Mary Ann. "The Rule of Law in the Universal Declaration of Human Rights." *Northwestern University Journal of International Human Rights* 2, no. 1 (2004): 1–19.

Gökariksel, Banu and Ann Secor. "Post-Secular Geographies and the Problem of Pluralism: Religion and Everyday Life in Istanbul, Turkey." *Political Geography* 46 (2015): 26.

Good, Anthony. *Anthropology and Expertise in the Asylum Courts*. London: Routledge, 2007.

Goodale, Mark and Sally Engle Merry, eds. *The Practice of Human Rights: Tracking Law between the Global and the Local*, 418–35. Cambridge: Cambridge University Press, 2007.

Goodale, Mark. "Human Rights and Moral Agency." In *Human Rights: The Hard Questions*, edited by Cindy Holder and David Reidy. Cambridge: Cambridge University Press, 2013.

Goodwin-Gil, Guy. "Convention Relating to the Status of Refuges." United Nations Audiovisual Library of International Law. Accessed February 1, 2016. http://legal.un.org/avl/ha/prsr/prsr.html.

Greenberg, Stanley B. *Race and State in Capitalist Development*. London: Yale University Press, 1980.

Gribaldo, Alessandra. "The Paradoxical Victim: Intimate Violence Narratives on Trial in Italy." *American Ethnologist* 41, no. 4 (2014): 743–56.

Grigor'ev, A. A. "Taras Shevchenko." *Vremia* 4 (April 1861): n. pag. *Philolog.ru Biblia*. Accessed January 3, 2016. http://smalt.karelia.ru/~filolog/vremja/1861/APRIL/taras.htm.

Gris, Juan. *Posibilidades de la pintura*. 1946. Madrid: Casimiro, 2013.

Guha, Ranajit. *The Rule of Property in Bengal*. Mouton: Paris, 1963.

Guignon, Charles B. *Heidegger and the Problem of Knowledge*. Indianapolis: Hackett, 1983.

Gurvich-Lishchiner, S. D. *Letopis' zhizni i tvorchestva A. I. Gertsena 1859-iiun' 1864*. Moscow: Izdatel'stvo Nauka, 1983.

Hagelund, Anniken and Hanne Kavli. "If Work is Out of Sight. Activation and Citizenship for New Refugees." Accessed October 26, 2015. http://fafo.no/~fafo/media/com_netsukii/Hagelund_Kavli.pdf.

Hakovirta, Harto. "The Global Refugee Problem: A Model and Its Application." *International Political Science Review* 14, no. 1 (1993). Accessed October 20, 2015. http://www.jstor.org/stable/1601374.

Hamann, Greta. *DW (Deutsche Welle)*, January 10, 2015. Accessed October 24, 2015. http://www.dw.com/en/when-refugees-want-to-work-in-germany/a-18737104.

Hardy, Peter. "Modern European and Muslim Explanations of Conversion to Islam in South Asia: A Preliminary Survey of the Literature." *Journal of the Royal Asiatic Society of Great Britain and Ireland* 2 (1977): 178–79.

Harris, Gardiner, David E. Sanger, and David M. Herszenhorn. "Obama Increases Number of Syrian Refugees for U.S. Resettlement to 10,000." *The New York Times*, September 10, 2015. Accessed February 5, 2016. http://www.nytimes.com/2015/09/11/world/middleeast/obama-directs-administration-to-accept-10000-syrian-refugees.html?_r=0.

Hasan, Syed Shoaib. "Profile: Islamabad's Red Mosque." *BBC News*, July 27, 2007. http://news.bbc.co.uk/2/hi/6503477.stm.

Hayden, Robert M. "Turn-Taking, Overlap, and the Task at Hand: Ordering Speaking Turns in Legal Settings." *American Ethnologist* 14, no. 2 (1987): 251–70.

Henare, Amiria, Martin Holbraad, and Sari Wastell, eds. *Thinking Through Things: Theorising Artefacts Ethnographically*. London: Routledge, 2007.

Herskovits, Melville J. *Cultural Relativism, Perspectives in Cultural Pluralism*, edited by Frances Herskovits. New York: Random House, 1972.

Hewstone, Miles and Rupert Brown. "Contact is not Enough: An Intergroup Perspective on the 'Contact Hypothesis.'" In *Contact and Conflict in Intergroup Encounters Social Psychology and Society*, edited by Miles Hewstone and Rupert Brown. New York: Blackwell, 1986.

Holden, Livia S., ed. *Cultural Expertise and Litigation: Patterns, Conflicts, Narratives*. London: Routledge, 2011.

Hollande, François. Speech by the President of the Republic before a joint session of Parliament (Versailles, November 16, 2015). Available at: http://www.diplomati e.gouv.fr/en/french-foreign-policy/defence-security/parisattacks-paris-terror-at tacks-november-2015/article/speech-by-the-president-of-the-republic-before-a-joi nt-session-of-parliament.

Hooker, B. *An Introduction to Colonial and Neo-colonial Laws*. Oxford: Clarendon Press, 1975.

Hopgood, Stephen. *The Endtimes of Human Rights*. Ithaca: Cornell University Press, 2013.

Human Rights Committee. *General Comment 22 on Freedom of Thought, Conscience and Religion.* 1993. Geneva: United Nations, UN Doc. CCPR/C/21/Rev.1/Add.4, 1993.

Human Rights Watch. "France: Abuses Under State of Emergency, Halt Warrantless Search and House Arrest." Published February 3, 2016; available at: https://www. hrw.org/news/2016/02/03/france-abuses-under-state-emergency.

Hunt, Lynn. *Inventing Human Rights: A History.* New York: Norton, 2007.

Hussain, Murtaza. "Hate Crimes Rise Along with Donald Trump's Anti-Muslim Rhetoric." *The Intercept,* May 5, 2016. Accessed July 16, 2016. https://theintercept.com/ 2016/05/05/hate-crimes-rise-along-with-donald-trumps-anti-muslim-rhetoric/.

Ife, Jim. "Cultural Relativism and Community Activism in *Challenges.*" In *Human Rights: A Social Work Perspective*, edited by Elizabeth Reickert. New York: Columbia University Press, 2007.

Indaimo, Joseph A. *The Self, Ethics and Human Rights: Lacan, Levinas & Alterity.* Abingdon: Routledge, 2015.

International Commission of Jurists. *ICJ Condemns Fatally Flawed ASEAN Human Rights Declaration.* November 19, 2012. http://www.icj.org/icj-condemns-fatally-flawed-asean-human-rights-declaration/.

International Council on Human Rights. *Taking Duties Seriously: Individual Duties in International Human Rights Law. A Commentary.* Versoix: International Council on Human Rights Policy, 1999.

Iser, Wolfgang. "Coda to the Discussion." In *The Translatability of Cultures: Figurations of the Space Between*, edited by Sanford Budick and Wolfgang Iser. Stanford: Stanford University Press, 1996.

Jackson, Lawrence P. "The Birth of the Critic: The Literary Friendship of Ralph Ellison and Richard Wright." *American Literature* 72 (June 2000): 324–35.

Jackson, Michael. "Introduction: Phenomenology, Radical Empiricism, and Anthropological Critique." In *Things as They Are: New Directions in Phenomenological Anthropology*, edited by Michael Jackson. Bloomington, IN: Indiana University Press, 1996.

Jacob, Christian. *Qu'est-ce qu'un lieu de savoir?* Marseille: Open Edition Press, 2014. Accessed November 5, 2014. http://books.openedition.org/oep/423>.IS BN:9782821834583. DOI:10.4000/books.oep.423.

Jacobsen, Michael Hviid, ed. *Encountering the Everyday: An Introduction to the Sociologies of the Unnoticed.* New York: Palgrave MacMillan, 2009.

Jahangir, Asma and Hina Jilani. *The Hudood Ordinances: A Divine Sanction?* Lahore: Rhotas Books, 1990.

Jalal, Ayesha and Anil Seal. "Alternative to Partition: Muslim Politics between the Wars." *Modern Asian Studies* 15, no. 3 (1981): 415–54.

Jay, Martin. *The Virtues of Mendacity: On Lying in Politics.* Charlottesville and London: University of Virginia Press, 2010.

"JEN Recognizes the Needs in the Fields and Builds and Maintains Self-Reliance." JEN (Japan Emergency NGO). Accessed October 22, 2015. http://www.jen-npo.o rg/en/project/project_jordan.php.

Jewell, Keala J. *The Art of Enigma: The De Chirico Brothers and the Politics of Modernism.* University Park, PA: Pennsylvania University Press, 2004.

Johnson, Mark. *The Meaning of the Body: Aesthetics of Human Understanding.* Chicago: University of Chicago Press, 2007.

Jones, William J. "Human Rights Treaty Ratification Behavior: The ASEAN Way of Creating Standards." In *Proceedings of International Academic Conferences*, edited by Jiri Rotschedl and Klara Čermáková, 321–36. Vienna: International Institute of Social and Economic Sciences, 2014.

Jones, William J. "Universalizing Human Rights The ASEAN Way." *International Journal of Social Sciences* 3, no. 3 (2014): 72–89.

Joseph, Frank. *Dostoevsky a Writer in his Time.* Princeton: Princeton University Press, 2009, 135.

Józef, Bogusławski. "Wspomnienia Sybiraka: Pamiętniki Józefa Bogusławskiego." *Nowa reforma* 294 (1896): 1.

Judgment of New Jersey Supreme Court Justice David Bauman, February 4, 2015. Available at: http://www.becketfund.org/wp-content/uploads/2015/02/America n-Humanist-v-Matawan-Aberdeen-Regional-School-District.pdf.

Katz, Irwin and Glen Hass. "Racial Ambivalence and American Value Conflict: Correlational and Priming Studies of Dual Cognitive Structures." *Journal of Personality & Social Psychology* 55 (1988): 893–905. Accessed February 17, 2016. doi: 10.1037/0022-3514.55.6.893.

Katz, Irwin, Joyce Wackenhut, and Glen Hass. "Racial Ambivalence, Value Duality, and Behavior." In *Prejudice, Discrimination, and Racism*, edited by J. F. Dovidio and S. L. Gaertner. Toronto: Academic Press, 1986.

Kausikan, Bilahari. "An Asian Approach to Human Rights." *American Society of International Law. Proceedings of the Annual Meeting* 89 (1995): 147–50.

Kaviraj, Sudipta. "Religion and Identity in India." *Ethnic and Racial Studies* 20, no. 2 (1997): 325–44.

Kazmi, Muhammad. 'Extract from the Legislative Assembly Debate', vol. V, no. 1, 26 August 1938, at 1–3, Public and Judicial Department Records, IOR L/ PJ/7/1065.

Khan, Azam. "Transgender Rights: SC Tells NADRA to Amend Gender Verification Process." *Express Tribune*, April 26, 2011. http://tribune.com.pk/story/156256/sc-directs-nadra-to-include-eunuchs-in-gender-column/.

Khan, Shahnaz. "What is in a Name? *Khwaja Sara, Hijra*, and Eunuchs in Pakistan." *Indian Journal of Gender Studies* 23, no. 2 (2016): 218–42.

Khan, Shahnaz. *Zina, Transnational Feminism and the Moral Regulation of Pakistani Women*. Vancouver: UBC Press, 2006.

Knight, Kyle. "How Nepal's Constitution Got Queered." *Los Angeles Review of Books*, October 14, 2015. https://lareviewofbooks.org/article/how-nepals-constitution-got-queered.

Konyndyk, Jeremy. "Towards a New Model for Post-Emergency Refugee Assistance." *Humanitarian Exchange Magazine* 31 (2005). Accessed November 1, 2013. http://www.odihpn.org/humanitarian-exchange-magazine/issue-31/towards-a-new-model-for-post-emergency-refugee-assistance.

Kozlowski, Gregory C. *Muslim Endowments and Society in British India*. Cambridge: Cambridge University Press, 1985.

Krohn, Jonathan. "Amid Ethnic Tension in Turkey, Some Syrian Refugees Return to a War Zone." *The Atlantic*, May 17, 2013. Accessed 30 October 2013. http://www.theatlantic.com/international/archive/2013/05/amid-ethnic-tension-in-turkey-some-syrian-refugees-return-to-a-war-zone/275966/.

Kugle, Alan. "Framed, Blamed, and Renamed: The Recasting of Islamic Jurisprudence in Colonial South Asia." *Modern Asian Studies* 35, no. 2 (2001): 257–314.

Lakoff, George. *Women, Fire and Dangerous Things: What Categories Reveal About the Mind*. Chicago: The University of Chicago Press, 1987.

Lal, K. S. *Muslim Slave System in Medieval India*. New Delhi: South Asia Books, 1994.

Latour, Bruno. *We Have Never Been Modern*. Cambridge: Harvard University Press, 1991.

Lau, Martin. "The Legal Mechanism of Islamization: The New Islamic Criminal Law of Pakistan." *Journal of Law and Society* 11 (1992): 43–58.

Lefebvre, Henri. *Critique of Everyday Life*, vol. 2, trans. John Moore. London: Verso, 1961/2002.

Lefort, Claude. *The Political Forms of Modern Society: Bureaucracy, Democracy, Totalitarianism*. Cambridge: The MIT Press, 1986.

Lemke, M. K. *Politicheskie protsessy: M. I. Mikhailova, D. I. Pisareva, N. G. Chernyshevskogo: Po neizdannym dokumentam*. St. Petersburg: Izdatel'stvo O. N. Popovoi, 1907.

Lenzerini, Federico. *The Culturalization of Human Rights Law*. Oxford: Oxford University Press, 2014.

Li, Xiaorang. "Asian Values" and the Universality of Human Rights." *Business and Society Review* 102–103 (1999): 81–7.

Loescher, Gil. *Beyond Charity: International Cooperation and the Global Refugee Crisis*. New York: Oxford University Press, 1993.

Luckmann, Thomas. *The Invisible Religion: The Problem of Religion in Modern Society*. Boston: MacMillan, 1967.

Macdonald, Roderick A. "Pluralistic Human Rights? Universal Human Wrongs?" In *Dialogues on Human Rights and Legal Pluralism*, edited by René Provost and Colleen Sheppard. Dordrecht: Springer, 2013.

Mahbubani, Kishore. "The West and the Rest." *The National Interest* 28 (1992): 3–13.

Maio, Gregory R., D. W. Bell, and Victoria M. Esses. "Ambivalence in Persuasion: The Processing of Messages about Immigrant Groups." *Journal of Experimental Social Psychology* 32 (1996): 513–36. Accessed February 17, 2016. doi: 10.1006/jesp.1996.0023.

Malhotra, Raajeev. "Towards Implementing the Right to Development: A Framework for Indicators and Monitoring Methods." In *Development as a Human Right. Legal, Political and Economic Dimensions*, edited by Bård A. Andreassen and Stephen P. Marks. Antwerp, Oxford, Portland: Intersentia, 2010.

Malik, Hasnaat. "Lal Masjid Cleric Moves SC on Imposition of Sharia Law." *Express Tribune*, December 10, 2015. http://tribune.com.pk/story/1007500/lal-masjid-cleric-moves-sc-on-imposition-of-sharia-law/.

Marks, Stephen P., ed. *Development as a Human Right. Legal, Political and Economic Dimensions*. Antwerp, Oxford, Portland: Intersentia, 2010.

Marks, Susan and Andrew Clapham. *International Human Rights Lexicon*. Oxford: Oxford University Press, 2005.

Marmon, Shaun. *Eunuchs and Sacred Boundaries in Islamic Society*. New York: Oxford University Press, 1995.

Mart'ianov, P. K. "V perelome veka. (Otryvki iz staroi zapisnoi knizhki)." *Istoricheskii vestnik* 62 (November 1895): 451.

Mastny, Vojtech. "The Soviet Union's Partnership with India." *Journal of Cold War Studies* 12, no. 3 (2010): 50–90.

Matsuo, Hisako, Kathryn Kuhn, Emmanuel Uwalaka, Cynthia Wessel, Thu Do, Wala Almostadi, and Candace M. Ruocco. "Refugee Resettlement in St. Louis, Missouri: Race, Religion, and Identity." *Journal of Humanities and Social Sciences* 4, no. 11 (2014): 207–16. Accessed August 20, 2016. http://www.ijhssnet.com/journals/Vol_4_No_11_1_September_2014/22.pdf.

Matsuo, Hisako, Lisa Willoughby, Kevin McIntyre, and Emmanuel Uwalaka. "Attitude toward Immigrants: Test of Protestant Work Ethic, Egalitarianism, Social Contact, and Ethnic Origin." *IAFOR Journal of the Social Sciences* 1, no. 1 (2013): 11–21. Accessed August 20, 2016. https://issuu.com/iafor/docs/social-science-journal-vol1-issue1.

Matsuo, Hisako. "Bosnian Refugee Resettlement in St. Louis, Missouri." In *Homeland Wanted: Interdisciplinary Perspective on Refugee Resettlement in the West*, edited by P. Waxman and V. Colic-Peisker. New York: Nova Science Publishers, Inc., 2005.

Matsuo, Hisako. "Identificational Assimilation of Japanese Americans: A Reassessment of Primordialism and Circumstantialism." *Sociological Perspectives* 35 (1992): 505–23. Accessed February 18, 2016. doi: 10.2307/1389332.

Mauzy, Diane K. "The Human Rights and "Asian Values" Debate in Southeast Asia: Trying to Clarify the Key Issues." *The Pacific Review* 10, no. 2 (1997): 210–36.

Mayer, Ann L. *Islam and Human Rights: Tradition and Politics*. Boulder, Colorado: Westview Press, 2012.

McAnear, Sharon. "What it Means to be a Good Samaritan." *U.S. News & World Report*, December 9, 2015. Accessed February 6, 2016. http://www.usnews.com/opinion/blogs/faith-matters/2015/12/09/calls-to-ban-muslims-and-only-accept-christian-refugees-arent-christian.

McNeill, J. R. and William H. McNeill. *The Human Web: A Bird's Eye View of World History.* New York and London: W.W. Norton, 2013.

Merry, Sally E. "Transnational Human Rights and Local Activism: Mapping the Middle." *American Anthropologist* 108, no. 1 (2006): 38–51.

Merry, Sally Engle. "Translational Human Rights and Local Activism: Mapping the Middle." In *Dialogues on Human Rights and Legal Pluralism,* edited by René Provost and Colleen Sheppard. Dordrecht: Springer, 2013.

Merry, Sally Engle. *Human Rights and Gender Violence: Translating International Law into Local Justice.* Chicago: Chicago University Press, 2006.

Messina, Mariagrazia. *Paul Gauguin: un esotismo controverso.* Firenze: Firenze University Press, 2006.

Miliukov, A. P. "Fedor Mikhailovich Dostoevskii." *Russkaia Starina* 31, no. 5 (May 1881): 33–4.

Mohdin, Aamna. "When Refugees Camps Last Three Generations, We Must Accept they're not Going Anywhere." *Quartz*, November 30, 2015. Accessed July 15, 2016. http://qz.com/560768/when-refugees-camps-last-three-generations-we-must-accept-theyre-not-going-anywhere/.

Morales, Maria Cristina. "Ethnic-Controlled Economy or Segregation? Exploring Inequality in Latina/o Co-Ethnic Jobsites." *Sociological Forum* 24 (2009): 589–610. Accessed February 17, 2016. doi: 10.1111/j.1573-7861.2009.01121.x.

Morsink, Johannes. *The Universal Declaration of Human Rights: Origins, Draftings, and Intent.* Philadelphia: The University of Pennsylvania Press, 1999.

Munir, Muhammad. *Punjab Disturbances of 1953: Report of the Court of Inquiry.* Lahore: Government Printing, 1954.

Najmabadi, Afsaneh. *Professing Selves: Transsexuality and Same-Sex Desire in Contemporary Iran.* Durham, NC: Duke University Press, 2014.

Nand, Bhai Parma. 'Extract from Legislative Assembly Debate', Vol. V, no. 1, 26 August 1938, at 9, Public and Judicial Department Records, IOR L/PJ/7/1065.

Narine, Shaun. "Human Rights Norms and the Evolution of ASEAN: Moving without Moving in a Changing Regional Environment." *Contemporary Southeast Asia: A Journal of International and Strategic Affairs* 34, no. 3 (2012): 365–88.

Nechaeva, V. S. *Zhurnal M. M. i F. M. Dostoevskikh "Épokha," 1864–1865.* Moscow: Izdatel'stvo Nauka, 1975.

Neuman, Gerald L. "Human Rights and Constitutional Rights: Harmony and Dissonance." *Stanford Law Review*, 55, no. 5 (May 2003): 1863–900.

Neumayer, Eric. "Qualified Ratification: Explaining Reservations to International Human Rights Treaties." *Journal of Legal Studies* 36, no. 2 (2007): 397–8.

Ng, Joel. "The ASEAN Human Rights Declaration: Establishing a Common Framework." RSIS Commentary 114 (July 3, 2012). https://www.rsis.edu.sg/wp-content/uploads/2014/07/CO12114.pdf.

Ng, Joel. "The ASEAN Human Rights Declaration: A Pragmatic Compromise." *RSIS Commentary* 211 (November 21, 2012). https://dr.ntu.edu.sg/bitstream/handle/1 0220/11694/RSIS2112012.pdf?sequence=1.

Noonan, John, Jr. "The Tensions and the Ideals." In *Religious Human Rights in Global Perspective: Legal Perspectives.* The Hague: Kluwer Law International, 1996.

"Norway." European Resettlement Network. Accessed October 21, 2015. http://www .resettlement.eu/country/norway.

"Norway to Limit Social Security Benefits for Refugees." The Nordic Page. Accessed August 3, 2016. http://www.tnp.no/norway/politics/5330-norway-to-limit-socia l-security-benefits-for-refugees.

Obordo, Rachel. "Teaching Refugees Languages: 'No Specific Skills Required, Just a Desire to Help and a Friendly Smile." *The Guardian,* September 11, 2015. Accessed July 17, 2016. https://www.theguardian.com/world/2015/sep/11/teac hing-refugees-languages-no-specific-skills-required-just-a-desire-to-help-and-a-friendly-smile.

Office of the High Commissioner for Human Rights. *Asean Human Rights Declaration Should Maintain International Standards. An Open Letter from the Coordination Committee of the Special Procedures of the Human Rights Council on the Draft ASEAN Human Rights Declaration.* Geneva: United Nations, 2012. http:// www.ohchr.org/Documents/HRBodies/SP/LetterASEAN_Nov2012.doc.

Onuf, Peter. "American Exceptionalism and National Identity." *American Political Thought: A Journal of Ideas, Institutions, and Culture* 1 (2012): 77–99.

Opsahl, Torkel and Vojin Dimitrijevic. "Articles 29 and 30." In *The Universal Declaration of Human Rights: A Common Standard of Achievement,* edited by Gurdmundur S. Alfredsson and Asbjørn Eide. The Hague: Martinus Hijhoff, 1999.

Orosa, Theoben Jerdan C. "ASEAN Integration in Human Rights: Problems and Prospects for Legalization and Institutionalization." *Asian Regional Integration Review* 4 (2012): 66–88.

Osiatynski, Wiktor. *Human Rights and Their Limits.* Cambridge: Cambridge University Press, 2009.

Pamment, Claire. "Hijraism: Jostling for a Third Space in Pakistani Politics." *TDR: The Drama Review* 54, no. 2 (2010): 29–50.

Parkinson, Joe and David George-Cosh. "Image of Drowned Syrian Boy Echoes Around the World." *The Wall Street Journal,* September 3, 2015. Accessed February 5, 2016. http://www.wsj.com/articles/image-of-syrian-boy-washed-up-on-beach-hits-hard-1441282847.

Perugini, Nicola and Neve Gordon. *The Human Right to Dominate.* Oxford: Oxford University Press, 2015.

Pettigrew, Thomas F. "Intergroup Contact Theory." *Annual Review of Psychology* 49 (1998): 65–85. Accessed February 16, 2016. doi: 10.1146/annurev.psych.49.1.65.

Pettigrew, Thomas F. "Generalized Intergroup Contact Effects on Prejudice." *Personality & Social Psychology Bulletin* 23 (1997): 173–85. Accessed February 16, 2016.

Pisanò, Attilio. "Human Rights and Sovereignty in the ASEAN Path towards a Human Rights Declaration." *Human Rights Reviews* 15, no. 4 (2014): 391–403.

Pisarėk, G. "Rol' russkikh i ukraintsev v zhizni i tvorchestve Ėdvarda Zheligovsk-ogo." *Sviazi revoliutsionerov Rossii i Pol'shi*, edited by V. A. D'iakov, I. S. Miller, and L. A. Obushenkovaia. Moscow: Izdatel'stvo Nauka, 1968.

Pleshcheev, A. N. *Polnoe sobranie stikhotvorenii*, edited by M. Ia. Poliakov. Moscow/Leningrad: Sovetskii pisatel', 1964.

Poore, Charles. "Books of the Times." *New York Times*, March 1, 1940, 25.

Preston, Laurence W. "A Right to Exist: Eunuchs and the State in Nineteenth-Century India." *Modern Asian Studies* 21, no. 2 (1987): 371–87.

Provost, René and Colleen Shepherd, eds. *Dialogues on Human Rights and Legal Pluralism*. Dordrecht: Springer, 2013.

Prus, Bolesław. *The Doll*, trans. David Welsh. Central European University Press, 1996, 14.

Puar, Jasbir K. *Terrorist Assemblages: Homonationalism in Queer Times*. Durham, NC: Duke University Press, 2007.

Rashid, Ahmed. "The Pakistan Paradox: U.S. Support for Musharraf Undermines War on Terror." *New York Times*, November 28, 2003. http://www.nytimes.com/2003/11/28/opinion/the-pakistan-paradox-us-support-for-musharraf-undermines-war-on.html.

Rattigan, William. "The Scientific Study of the Muhammadan Law." *The Law Quarterly Review* (October 1901): 401–14.

Redding, Jeffrey A. "From 'She-males' to 'Unix': Transgender Rights and the Productive Paradoxes of Pakistani Policing." In *Regimes of Legality: Ethnography of Criminal Cases in South Asia*, edited by Daniela Berti and Devika Bordia, 258–89. New Delhi, India: Oxford University Press, 2015.

Redding, Jeffrey A. "Querying Edith Windsor, Querying Equality." *Villanova Law Review* (Tolle Lege) 59 (2013): 9–16.

Reddy, Gayatri. *With Respect to Sex: Negotiating Hijra Identity in South India*. Chicago: University of Chicago Press, 2005.

"Refugees." UNHCR. Accessed February 1, 2016. http://www.unhcr.org/pages/49c3646c125.html.

"Refugees." USCIS (U.S. Citizenship and Immigration Services). Accessed July 17, 2016. http://www.uscis.gov/humanitarian/refugees-asylum/refugees.

Renshaw, Catherine Shanahan. "The ASEAN Human Rights Declaration 2012." *Human Rights Law Reviews* 13, no. 3 (2013): 557–79.

Renshaw, Catherine Shanahan. "The ASEAN Human Rights Declaration – Cause for Celebration?" Regarding Rights. Academic and Activist Perspectives on Human Rights, January 25, 2013. http://asiapacific.anu.edu.au/regarding-rights/2013/01/25/the-asean-human-rights-declaration-cause-for-celebration/.

"Resettlement Year at a Glance." International Institute of St. Louis. Accessed February 5, 2016. http://www.iistl.org/newsbriefjanuary16.html.

"Resources for Speakers on Global Issues." United Nations. Accessed February 1, 2016. http://www.un.org/en/globalissues/briefingpapers/refugees/aboutUNHCR.html.

Rewolucyjna konspiracja w Królestwie Polskim w latach 1840–1845: Edward Dembowski, edited by W. A. Djakow, S. Kieniewicz, and W. Śliwowska. Wrocław: Zakład Narodowy im. Ossolińskich, 1981.

Ricca, Mario. "Errant Law: Spaces and Subjects." Acessed June 30, 2016. https://ssrn.com/abstract=2802528 or http://dx.doi.org/10.2139/ssrn.2802528.

Ricca, Mario. "Intercultural Law, Interdisciplinary Outlines: Lawyering and Anthropological Expertise in Migration Cases Before the Courts." *Rivista dell'Associazione italiana di Studi semiotici.* Accessed March 3, 2014. www.ec-aiss.it.

Ricca, Mario. *Oltre Babele. Codici per una democrazia interculturale.* Bari: Dedalo, 2008.

Ricca, Mario. *The Intercultural Use of Human Rights and Legal Chorology.* Accessed July 9, 2016. http://ssrn.com/abstract=2807424.

Ringrose, Kathryn M. *The Perfect Servant: Eunuchs and the Social Construction of Gender in Byzantium.* Chicago: University of Chicago Press, 2003.

Robertson, Kristina and Lydia Breiseth. "How to Support Refugee Students in the ELL Classroom." *Colorín Colorado.* Accessed July 17, 2016. http://www.colorincolorado.org/article/how-support-refugee-students-ell-classroom.

Rokeach, Milton. *The Open and Closed Mind: Investigation into the Nature of Belief Systems and Personality Systems.* New York: Basic Books, 1960.

Rosa, Freedman. "Third generation' Rights: Is There Room for Hybrid Constructs within International Human Rights Law?" *Cambridge Journal of International and Comparative Law* 2, no. 4 (2013): 935–59.

Rousseau, Jean-Jacques. *On the Social Contract: Discourse on the Origin of Inequality, Discourse on Political Economy*, trans. and edited by Donald A. Cress. Indianapolis: Hackett Publishing Company, 1983. http://classiques.uqac.ca/classiques/Rousseau_jj/contrat_social/ Contrat_social.pdf.

Rozbicki, Michal Jan. "Cross-Cultural History: Toward an Interdisciplinary Theory." In *Cross-Cultural History and the Domestication of Otherness*, edited by Michal Jan Rozbicki and George Ndege. New York: Palgrave-Macmillan, 2015.

Rozbicki, Michal Jan. *Culture and Liberty in the Age of the American Revolution.* Charlottesville and London: University of Virginia Press, 2013.

Santos, Bonaventura de Sousa. "Toward a Multicultural Conception of Human Rights." In *Moral Imperialism: A Critical Anthology,* edited by Berta Hernández-Truyol. New York: New York University Press, 2002.

Sauerbrey, Anna. "Paris and Europe's Anti-Refugee Backlash." *The New York Times,* November 16, 2015. Accessed February 6, 2016. http://www.nytimes.com/2015/11/17/opinion/paris-and-europes-anti-refugee-backlash.html.

Saunders, Doug."Germany: Where the Refugee Flood is a Solution, not a Problem." *The Globe and Mail*, May 23, 2015. Accessed October 21, 2015. http://www.theglobeandmail.com/globe-debate/germany-where-the-refugee-flood-is-a-solution-not-a-problem/article24565583/.

Savinio, Alberto. *Alberto Savinio: Paintings and Drawings, 1925–1952.* Milano: Electa, 1992.

Sbriccoli, Tommaso and Mario Ricca. "Shylock del Bengala. Debiti migratori, vite in ostaggio e diritto d'asilo. (Un approccio corologico alle implicazioni anti-umanitarie del patto commissorio)." *Calumet, Intercultural Law and Humanities Review* 2 (2016).

Sbriccoli Tommaso and Stefano Jacoviello. "The Case of S.: Elaborating the 'Right' Narrative to Fit Normative/Political Expectations in Asylum Procedure in Italy." In

Cultural Expertise and Litigation: Patterns, Conflicts, Narratives, edited by Livia S. Holden, 172–94. London: Routledge, 1990.

Sbriccoli, Tommaso and Stefano Jacoviello. "The Voice in C. The Creole Attitude of a Bangladeshi Refugee in Italy." In *Shifting Borders. European Perspectives on Creolisation*, edited by Tommaso Sbriccoli and Stefano Jacoviello, 83–109. Newcastle upon Tyne: Cambridge Scholars Publishing, 2012.

Schmitt, Carl. *Political Theology: Four Chapters on the Concept of Sovereignty*, trans. George Schwab. Chicago: University of Chicago Press, 1932/1985.

Schriefer, Paula. "Remarks by Paula Schriefer." *Proceedings of the Annual Meeting (American Society of International Law)* 106 (2012): 352.

Schuback, Marcia Sá Cavalcante. "In-between Painting and Music—or, Thinking with Paul Klee and Anton Webern." In *The Philosophical Vision of Paul Klee,* edited by John Sallis. Leiden: Brill, 2014.

Schutz, Alfred. *The Phenomenology of the Social World*. Evanston: Northwestern University Press, 1932/1972.

Sen, Amartya. "Development as Capability Expansion." *Journal of Development Planning* 19 (1989). Accessed October 20, 2015. http://morgana.unimore.it/Picc hio_Antonella/Sviluppo%20umano/svilupp%20umano/Sen%20development.pdf.

Sen, Amartya. *The Idea of Justice*. Cambridge: Harvard University Press, 2009.

Sengupta, Arjun. "On the Theory and Practice of the Right to Development." *Human Rights Quarterly* 24, no. 4 (2002): 837–89.

Sherlock, Ruth. and Harriet Alexander. "US Politicians Vote to Ban Entry to the Country for Syrian Refugees." *The Telegraph*, November 19, 2015. Accessed February 6, 2016. http://www.telegraph.co.uk/news/worldnews/northamerica/usa/1 2006741/US-politicians-vote-to-ban-entry-to-the-country-for-Syrian-refugees.html.

Singer, Audrey and H. Jill. *From 'There' to 'Here':Refugee Resettlement in Metropolitan America*. Washington, DC: Metropolitan Policy Program, Brookings Institution, 2006.

Sisil' Vess'e. *Za vashu i nashu svobodu!: Dissidentskoe dvizhenie v Rossii*. Moscow: Novoe literaturnoe obozrenie, 2015.

Smith, Adam. *An Inquiry into the Nature and Causes of the Wealth of Nations*. London: Electric Book Co., 2001.

Soergel, Andrew. "Refugees: Economic Boon or Burden?" *U.S. News*, September 15, 2015. Accessed October 21, 2015. http://www.usnews.com/news/blogs/data-mi ne/2015/09/15/would-syrian-refugees-be-an-economic-boon-or-burden.

Starr, Paul D. and Alden E. Roberts. "Attitudes Toward New Americans: Perceptions of Indo-Chinese in Nine Cities." *Research in Race & Ethnic Relations* 3 (1982): 165–86. Accessed February 17, 2016. http://psycnet.apa.org/psycinfo/1983-25519-001.

Steinmetz, Katy. "Why LGBT Advocates Say Bathroom 'Predators' Argument Is a Red Herring." *Time*, May 2, 2016. http://time.com/4314896/transgender-bath room-bill-male-predators-argument/.

Stephan, Walter G., Oscar Ybarra, and Guy Bachman. "Prejudice Toward Immigrants." *Journal of Applied Social Psychology* 29 (1999): 2221–37. Accessed February 17, 2016. doi: 10.1111/j.1559-1816.1999.tb00107.x.

Stephen H. Watson, ed. *Crescent Moon over the Rational: Philosophical Interpretations of Paul Klee*. Stanford: Stanford University Press, 2009.

Stephenes, Michael. "Migrant Crisis: Why the Gulf States are Not Letting Syrians In." *BBC*, September 7, 2015. Accessed October 21, 2015. http://www.bbc.com/n ews/world-middle-east-34173139.

Stone, Jon. "Germany's Economy Will Grow Faster because of the Million Refugees it is Helping, Study Finds." *The Independent*, October 5, 2015. Accessed October 21, 2015. http://www.independent.co.uk/news/uk/politics/germanys-economy-will-gr ow-faster-because-of-the-million-refugees-it-is-helping-study-finds-10505647.html.

Stout, David. "Mrs. Bush Cites Women's Plight Under Taliban." *New York Times*, November 18, 2001. http://www.nytimes.com/2001/11/18/us/a-nation-challenge d-the-first-lady-mrs-bush-cites-women-s-plight-under-taliban.html.

Strenger, Carol. "Brexit Reflects EU's Failure to Create a European Identity – Isreal Should Take Heed." Haaretz, June 24, 2016. Accessed August 22, 2016. http:// www.haaretz.com/world-news/europe/.premium-1.726906.

Stuart, Tessa. "17 Anti-Trans Bills That Could Become Law Next." *Rolling Stone*, March 28, 2016. http://www.rollingstone.com/politics/news/17-anti-trans-bills-tha t-could-become-law-next-20160328.

Talbot, Ian. *Punjab and the Raj, 1849–1947.* New Delhi: Manohar, 1988.

Tang, James Tuck-Hong, ed. *Human Rights and International Relations in the Asia-Pacific Region.* London, New York: Painter, 1995.

"Thailand: Forced Repatriation of Hmong Refugees to Laos Denounced." Doctors Without Borders, May 20, 2009. Accessed October 22, 2015. http://www.doct orswithoutborders.org/news-stories/press-release/thailand-forced-repatriation-hm ong-refugees-laos-denounced.

Thinking Through Things: Theorising Artefacts Ethnographically. Edited by Amiria Henare, Martin Holbraad, and Sari Wastell. New York: Routledge, 2007.

Thirsk, Joan. "The European Debate on Customs of Inheritance, 1500–1700." In Joan Thisk, and E. P. Thompson, *Family and Inheritance: Rural Society in Western Europe, 1200–1800,* edited by Jack Goody, 177–91. Cambridge: Cambridge University Press, 1976.

Tibi, Bassan. "Islamic Law/Shari'a, Human Rights, Universal Morality ad International Law." *Human Rights Quarterly* 16, no. 2 (1994): 277–99.

Tierney, Brian. *The Idea of Natural Rights: Studies on Natural Rights, Natural Law, and Church Law 1550–1625.* Grand Rapids, MI: Eerdmans, 1997.

"To Secure These Rights: The Report of the President's Committee on Civil Rights" (1947). Available at: www.trumanlibrary.org/civilrights/srights1.htm#contents.

Todorov, Tzvetan. *Fear of the Barbarians: Beyond the Clash of Civilizations*, trans. Andrew Brown. Cambridge: Polity Press, 2010.

Tokarzewski, Szymon. *Siedem lat katorgi: Pamiętniki Szymona Tokarzewskiego 1846–1857,* 2nd ed. Warsaw: Gebethner i Wolff, 1918.

Troyan, Mary. "After Attacks in Paris, Governors Refuse to Accept Syrian Refugees." *USA Today*, November 16, 2015. Accessed February 6, 2016. http://www.usat oday.com/story/news/politics/2015/11/16/alabama-refuses-syrian-refugees-paris-terror-attack/75857924/.

Trump, Donald J. Republican National Convention speech, July 21, 2016. Accessed August 22, 2016. http://www.politico.com/story/2016/07/full-transcript-donald-trump-nomination-acceptance-speech-at-rnc-225974#ixzz4FiNnOL3l.

Tyabji, Faiz Badruddin. *Principles of Muhammadan Law,* 2nd ed. Calcutta: Butter-worth & Co., 1919.

"Understand Permanent Resident Status." Government of Canada. Accessed July 15, 2016. http://www.cic.gc.ca/english/newcomers/about-pr.asp.

UN General Assembly. "Protocol Relating to the Status of Refugees." *United Nations, Treaty Series,* no. 606: 268–76. Accessed October 21, 2015. https://treaties.un.org/pages/ViewDetails.aspx?src=TREATY&mtdsg_no=V-&chapter=5&lang=en.

"UNHCR Dismayed at Forced Repatriation of Iraqis; Reports Increase in Flight of Iraqi Christians." UNHCR, December 17, 2010. Accessed October 22, 2015. http://www.unhcr.org/4d0b45476.html.

"United Republic of Tanzania." UNHCR. Accessed July 16, 2016. http://www.unhcr.org/50a9f81f16.pdf.

"The Universal Declaration of Human Rights." United Nations. Accessed June 15, 2016. http://www.un.org/en/universal-declaration-human-rights/.

Valcavi, Giovanni. "Intorno al divieto di patto commissorio, alla vendita simulata a scopo di garanzia ed al negozio fiduciario." *Il Foro,* (1990). [An English translation, "On the Prohibition of the Agreement of Forfeiture, the Simulated Sale for the Purpose of Guarantee and the Trust Agreement," is available at the following link: http://www.fondazionegiovannivalcavi.it/english/writings-on-civil-law/14_On-the-prohibition-of-the-agreement-of-forfeiture.pdf.

Valentine, David. *Imagining Transgender: An Ethnography of a Category.* Durham, NC: Duke University Press, 2007.

Venuti, Lawrence. *Translation Changes Everything: Theory and Practice.* Abingdon, UK: Routledge, 2013.

Voci, Alberto and Miles Hewstone, "Intergroup Contact and Prejudice Toward Immigrants in Italy: The Mediational Role of Anxiety and the Moderational Role of Group Salience." *Group Processes & Intergroup Relations* 6 (2003): 37–54. Accessed February 17, 2016. doi: 10.1177/1368430203006001011.

"Volunteering Project." North of England Refugee Service. Accessed July 17, 2016. http://www.refugee.org.uk/volunteering.

Wahyuningrum, Yuyun. *The ASEAN Intergovernmental Commission on Human Rights: Origins, Evolution and the Way Forward.* Strömsborg: International IDEA, 2014, 13–26. https://www.idea.int/sites/default/files/publications/the-asean-intergovernmental-commission-on-human-rights-origins-evolution-and-the-way-forward.pdf.

Walicki, Andrzej. *Russia, Poland, and Universal Regeneration: Studies on Russian and Polish Thought of the Romantic Epoch.* University of Notre Dame Press, 1991.

Walsh, Declan. "Harassed, Intimidated, Abused: But Now Pakistan's Hijra Transgender Minority Finds its Voice." *Guardian,* January 30, 2010. http://www.theguardian.com/world/2010/jan/29/hijra-pakistan-transgender-rights.

Waltz, Eileen. "Universal Human Rights: The Contribution of Muslim States." *Human Rights Quarterly* 26, no. 4 (2004): 799–844.

Warner, Robert. *Secularization and Its Discontents.* London: Continuum International Publishing, 2010.

Washbrook, David. "Law, State, and Agrarian Society in Colonial India." *Modern Asian Studies* 15, no. 3 (1981): 649–721.

Washington, James Melvin, ed. *A Testament of Hope: The Essential Writings of Martin Luther King, Jr.* New York: Harper Collins, 1991.

Wells, Thomas. "Sen's Capability Approach." Internet Encyclopedia of Philosophy. Accessed February 2, 2016. http://www.iep.utm.edu/sen-cap/#SH3a.

West, Raymond and Johann Georg Buhler. *A Digest of the Hindu Law of Inheritance, Partition, and Adoption,* vol. 1, 3rd ed. Bombay: Education Society's Press, 1884.

West, Raymond. "Modern Developments of Mohammedan Law." *Journal of the Society of Comparative Legislation* 2, no. 2 (1900): 271–75.

West, Raymond. "Mohammedan Law in India: Its Origins and Growth." *Journal of the Society of Comparative Legislation* 2, no. 1 (1900): 40.

White, Philip L. "Globalization and the Mythology of the 'Nation State.'" In *Globalization in World History*, edited by A. G. Hopkins. London: Pimlico, 2002.

Whiteley, Paul and Harold D. Clarke. "Why Did Older Voters Choose Brexit? It's a Matter of Identity." *The Conversation*, June 25, 2016. Accessed August 22, 2016. http://theconversation.com/why-did-older-voters-choose-brexit-its-a-matter-of-id entity-61636.

Wiesel, Elie. "A Tribute to Human Rights." In *The Universal Declaration of Human Rights: Fifty Years and Beyond*, edited by Yael Danieli, Elsa Stamatopoulou, and Clarence J. Dias. Amityville, NY: Baywood, 1999.

Witte, John, Jr. *Law and Protestantism: The Legal Teachings of the Lutheran Reformation.* Cambridge: Cambridge University Press, 2002.

Wright, Richard. "Blueprint for Negro Writing," 1937. Reprinted in *Within the Circle: An Anthology of African American Literary Criticism from the Harlem Renaissance to the Present.* Edited by Angelyn Mitchell. Durham: Duke University Press, 1994.

Wright, Richard. "Review of *Their Eyes Were Watching God.*" *New Masses* (October 5, 1937): 22–23.

Wright, Richard. *Black Boy. 1945.* Reprinted in Richard Wright, *Early Works.* New York: Library of America 1991.

Wright, Richard. *Pagan Spain.* 1957. Reprint, New York: HarperCollins, 1995.

Wright, Richard. *White Man Listen!* 1957. Reprint, New York: Anchor, 1964.

Wright, Richard. *The Color Curtain.* 1956. Reprint, Jackson: University Press of Mississippi, 1994.

Wright, Richard. *Black Power.* London: Dennis Dobson, 1954.

Wright, Richard. *Native Son.* New York: Harper, 1940.

Wright, Richard. *Uncle Tom's Children.* 1938. Reprinted in Richard Wright, *Early Works.* New York: Library of America, 1991, 225–37.

Xiaodan, Wu. "The Current Situation and Prospects for Regional System(s) of Human Rights in Asia." *Diritti umani e diritto internazionale* 6, no. 1 (2012): 45–77.

Zafrullah, Khan. "Extract from Legislative Assembly Debates." Vol. V, no. 11, 9 September 1938, at 13–22, Public and Judicial Department Records, IOR L/PJ/7/1065.

Zakharia, Leila and Sonya Knox. "The International Aid Community and Local Actors: Experiences and Testimonies from the Ground." Civil Society Knowledge Center. Accessed October 22, 2015. http://cskc.daleel-madani.org/paper/internati onal-aid-community-and-local-actors.

Zaleski, Bronisław. *"Wygnańcy Polscy w Orenburgu,"* Wspomnienia z Uralu i stepów Kazachskich, edited by Andrzej Zieliński. Wroclaw: Polskie Towarzystwo Ludoznawcze, 2008.

Zaleski, Bronislaw. "Zmarli na wychodźtwie od 1861 roku: Żeligowski, Edward." *Rocznik towarzystwa Historyczno-Literackiego w Paryżu.* Paris: Księgarnia Luksemburska, 1867.

Zaleski, Bronisław. *Michał Bakunin i odezwa jego do przyaciół rossyjskich i polskich.* Paris: W księgarni polskiej, 1862.

Zhdanov, V. V. and V. L. Komarovich, eds. *Poèty-Petrashevtsy.* Leningrad: Sovetskii pisatel', 1957.

Zong, Jie and Jeanne Batalova. "Refugees and Asylees in the United States." Migration Information Source. Accessed February 5, 2015. http://www.migration information.org/feature/display.cfm?ID=907.

UNAUTHORED JOURNALISM & WEBPAGES

"A Chronology of Lal Masjid Saga." *Dawn,* July 11, 2007. http://www.dawn.com/news/255802/a-chronology-of-lal-masjid-saga.

"Dream Come True: Transgender Community Celebrates CNICs, Voter Registration." *Express Tribune,* January 25, 2012. http://tribune.com.pk/story/326911/dream-come-true-transgender-community-celebrates-cnics-voter-registration/.

"Eunuch Protest Leads to 3 Cops' Suspension." *Daily Times,* January 28, 2009.

"Fatwa Allows Transgender Marriage." *Dawn,* June 27, 2016. http://www.dawn.com/news/1267491.

"India's Transgender Talk Show Host." *BBC News,* March 5, 2008. http://news.bbc .co.uk/2/hi/south_asia/7265463.stm.

"International Work: Campaigning for Global LGBT Equality." *Stonewall.* Accessed March 4, 2018. http://www.stonewall.org.uk/our-work/international-work-1.

"Islamic Students Abduct Alleged Brothel Owner." *Associated Press,* March 28, 2007. http://www.nbcnews.com/id/11497286/ns/world_news-south_and_centra l_asia/t/islamic-students-abduct-alleged-brothel-owner/#.VzTxQPkrLIU.

"Mosque Leader in Burka Escape Bid." *BBC News,* July 4, 2007. http://news.bbc. co.uk/2/hi/6270626.stm.

"National Identity Card (NIC)." *National Database and Registration Authority.* Accessed March 13, 2018. https://www.nadra.gov.pk/identity/identity-cnic/.

"Pakistan 'Brothel Woman' Released." *BBC News,* March 29, 2007. http://news.bbc .co.uk/2/hi/south_asia/6507205.stm.

"Q&A: Pakistan's Swat Offensive." *BBC News,* May 20, 2009. http://news.bbc.co.u k/2/hi/south_asia/8044604.stm.

"Watched by Foreign Journalists, Troops Seized the State TV Station," digital image, *BBC News,* August 23, 2007. Accessed March 3, 2018. http://news.bbc.co.uk/2/h i/south_asia/6960670.stm.

"Way Opens For Eunuchs' Right to Inheritance." *Dawn,* October 13, 2011. http:// www.dawn.com/news/665914/way-opens-for-eunuchs-right-to-inheritance.

LEGAL DECISIONS AND MISCELLANEOUS
LEGAL DOCUMENTS

Constitution Petition No. 43 of 2009, 20.11.2009 Order.

Constitutional Petition No. 43 of 2009, 23.12.2009 Order.

Defense of Marriage Act, Pub. L. No. 104–199, § 3, 110 Stat. 2419, 2419 (1996) (codified at 1 U.S.C. § 7 (2012)).

"Government of the Punjab, Social Welfare, Women Development and Bait ul Maal Department, Memo to the Registrar, Supreme Court of Pakistan on Human Right Case No. 63/2009" (August 13, 2009).

Human Rights Const. P. No. 63 of 2009, 16.06.2009 Order.

"Memorandum from the Government of NWFP Social Welfare & Women Dev: Department to the Registrar, Supreme Court of Pakistan & the Advocate General, NWFP, Peshawar on Petition under article 184(3) of the Constitution of the Islamic Republic Pakistan 1973" (August 15, 2009).

National Legal Services Authority v. Union of India, (2014) 5 S.C.C. 438.

Obergefell v. Hodges, 135 S. Ct. 2584 (2015).

Price Waterhouse v. Hopkins, 490 U.S. 228 (1989).

"Report prepared by the Regional Police Officer, Rawalpindi for the Inspector General of Police" (Punjab, Lahore, 2009).

United States v. Windsor, 133 S. Ct. 2675 (2013).

Waqar Ali v. Federation of Pakistan, etc., W.P. No. 37499/2016, Lahore High Court (Lahore), 09.01.2017 Order.

Index

About the Contributors

Shazia Ahmad is Adjunct Professor of Asian history in Webster University, St. Louis. Previously she taught at the University of London. She holds a PhD in History from the University of London, School of Asian Studies (2015). Dissertation: "A New Dispensation in Islam: the Ahmadiyya and the Law in Colonial India, 1872–1930." Research field: history of colonial law in India.

Elizabeth Blake is Assistant Professor of Russian at Saint Louis University. She holds a PhD in Slavic Literatures and Linguistics from the Ohio State University, 2001. She is author of the monograph, *Dostoevsky and the Catholic Underground* (Northwestern University Press, 2014), and various articles on gender, spirituality, and ethnicity related to Russian and Polish literature. Her collection of translated Siberian remembrances, *Travel from Dostoevsky's Siberia*, is forthcoming.

Marcella Ferri holds a PhD in Science of International Cooperation (2013), University of Bergamo, Italy. She is Adjunct Professor of International Human Rights Law at the Graduate School of Economics and International Relations (ASERI), Catholic University of the Sacred Heart (Milan), and Adjunct Professor of Institutions of Comparative and European Law at the University of Bergamo. Her main research interests are the international protection of human rights, with a specific focus on cultural rights, freedom of religion, and state positive obligations under human rights treaties.

Hisako Matsuo is Professor in the Department of Sociology and Anthropology, Saint Louis University. PhD from the University of California, Riverside (1994). Her areas of specialization are race relations, organizations, and statistics. She is also the author of numerous publications, and a recipient of extensive research grants for research on the immigrant experience in American society.

Jeffrey A. Redding University of Melbourne, Australia, India Institute and Law School, Melbourne, Australia. J.D. University of Chicago Law School. Author of numerous publications in law journals. Visiting Fellowships from L'École des Hautes Études en Sciences Sociales Paris, France; Centre National de la Recherche Scientifique, Paris; Yale Law School, New Haven; Columbia Law School's Center for the Study of Law and Culture, New York; Harvard Law School's Islamic Legal Studies Program; and Sustainable Development Policy Institute, Islamabad, Pakistan.

Mario Ricca is Professor of Intercultural Law, History of Religions, and Ecclesiastical Law at the University of Parma, Italy. His research areas include Human Rights, Constitutional Law, Law and Religion, Semiotics, Law and Anthropology, Legal Geography, Legal Theory and Philosophy. His most recent books include *Oltre Babele. Codici per una democrazia interculturale* (Dedalo 2008) [Beyond Babel: *Codes for an Intercultural Democracy*]; *Pantheon*; *Agenda della laicità interculturale* (Torri del Vento 2012) [Pantheon: Agenda of Intercultural Secularism]; and *Culture interdette. Modernità, migrazioni, diritto interculturale* (Bollati Boringhieri, 2013) [Cultures Interdicted: Modernity, Migrations, Intercultural Law].

Michal Jan Rozbicki is Professor of History at Saint Louis University. He is the author or editor of twelve books, including the award-winning *Culture and Liberty in the Age of the American Revolution* (University of Virginia Press, 2011). He has held fellowships from the Rockefeller Foundation, American Council of Learned Societies, Oxford University, and the Kennedy Institute for North American Studies in Berlin. He had served as Chair of the History Department, and is the founding Director of the Center for Intercultural Studies.

Rachel Santon is a doctoral candidate in Public and Social Policy with International Development concentration, and Graduate Research Assistant, Saint Louis University. She received Master's degree in Political Science from Saint Louis University in 2013. Her dissertation examines international refugee policy.

Tommaso Sbriccoli is a political and legal anthropologist. He holds a PhD from the University of Siena (2009). He has been doing research in North India since 2003 on topics related to traditional legal systems, kinship, social change, and political violence. In Italy, his research is in South Asian asylum seekers. He has published articles both on his Indian work, and on refugees in Italy, in Italian and international journals and books. He is coeditor of *Shifting Borders. European Perspectives on Creolisation* (Cambridge Scholars Publishing, 2012).

Melisa Vazquez is a doctoral candidate in Religion and Law at the Sapienza University of Rome, Rome, Italy. Her research focuses on secularism and religion in modern European states, with an emphasis on Sweden as an under-researched locus of modern dilemmas within the field of secularism, and on issues involved in the relationship between religion and human rights.

Anders E. Walker is Lillie Myers Professor of Law, Center for International and Comparative Law, Saint Louis University School of Law. He holds a JD/MA from the Duke University School of Law, 1998 (MA in History), PhD Yale University (2003). His research areas include intersections between constitutional law, criminal law, and legal history. He is the Winner of 2010 Law & Society Association Article Prize. He is the author of the book, *The Ghost of Jim Crow: How Southern Moderates Used Brown v. Board of Education to Stall Civil Rights* (Oxford University Press, 2009).

Lightning Source UK Ltd.
Milton Keynes UK
UKHW010603251118
332909UK00008B/564/P